John Andrews

Letters to a young gentleman, on his setting out for France: containing a survey of Paris, and a review of French literature

John Andrews

Letters to a young gentleman, on his setting out for France: containing a survey of Paris, and a review of French literature

ISBN/EAN: 9783742886255

Manufactured in Europe, USA, Canada, Australia, Japa

Cover: Foto ©ninafisch / pixelio.de

Manufactured and distributed by brebook publishing software (www.brebook.com)

John Andrews

Letters to a young gentleman, on his setting out for France: containing a survey of Paris, and a review of French literature

CONTENTS.

LETTER I.   P. 1.

Proper age and motives for travelling. France particularly deserving an Englishman's attention.

LETTER II.   P. 6.

The same subject continued.

LETTER III.   P. 11.

General appearance of France and of Paris. Caution against too much admiration and fondness for pictures and statues, and other objects of mere amusement and curiosity.

LETTER IV.   P. 16.

Method of travelling profitably.

CONTENTS.

LETTER V. P. 24.

The same subject continued.

LETTER VI. P. 27.

Languages necessary to a gentleman.

LETTER VII. P. 41.

Coffee-houses at Paris. Utility of conversing with people of understanding of all degrees. A travelling companion preferable to a travelling tutor.

LETTER VIII. P. 54.

Company of officers and abbés. Anecdotes of two gentlemen. Necessity of a good intelligence between the opulent and the ingenious.

LETTER IX. P. 65.

Jesuits. Acquaintance with monastics not to be neglected.

CONTENTS.

LETTER X. P. 72.

Study of the present legislation, circumstances, and politics of France. French fond of anecdotes and history. Good translators. Compared with the English in these respects.

LETTER XI. P. 82.

French of late years much addicted to philosophical speculations. Consequences of this turn of mind. Descartes. Buffon. Encyclopedia. Literature on a more agreeable footing in France than in England.

LETTER XII. P. 94.

Review and examination of French literature. Tragic writers. Corneille. Racine. Crebillon. Voltaire. Comic writers. Moliere. Regnard. Destouches. Lachauffée. Boiffy. Marivaux. French opera.

LETTER XIII. P. 104.

Other poets. Boileau. Rouffeau. La Fontaine. Henriade. Philofophe de Sans Soucy.

CONTENTS.

LETTER XIV. P. 112.

French novelists. Marmontel. Prevot. Hamilton. Le Sage. Telemachus. Travels of Cyrus.

LETTER XV. P. 118.

French historians. Bossuet. Fleury. Daniel. Rollin. Rapin Thoiras. Orleans. Vertot. Dubos. Perefixe. Henaut. St. Real. Tillemont. Raynal. Montesquieu. Voltaire. Duclos. Coyer. Lableterie. Great utility of historical knowledge. Ancients far superior to the moderns in this branch. Causes of that superiority.

LETTER XVI. P. 131.

Reflections upon oratory. French and English compared. Daguesseau. Lamoignon. Patru. Pelisson. Bourdaloue. Massillon. Bossuet. Flechier.

LETTER XVII. P. 144.

French philosophical writers. Art de Penser. Charon. Montaigne. Labruiere. Rochefoucault.

CONTENTS.

foucault. Alembert. Diderot. Maupertuis. Bayle. Fontenelle. Rousseau of Geneva. Helvetius. Malbranche. Croufas.

LETTER XVIII. P. 152.

French writers on miscellaneous subjects. Rollin's Belles Lettres. Montesquieu's Lettres Persannes. His Esprit des Loix. Sully's Memoirs. Mably's Droit publique de l'Europe. Dubos on Poetry, Painting and Music. Madam de Sevigné's Letters. St. Evremont. Bossu. Bouhours. Rapin. Cardinal de Retz. Gourville. La Condamine. Le Blanc. Marquis Dargens. Muralt. Deshoulieres. La Fayette. Lambert. Grassigny. Restaut. Girard.

LETTER XIX. P. 162.

French periodical publications. Utility resulting from their perusal.

LETTER XX. P. 169.

The same subject continued.

LETTER

CONTENTS.

LETTER XXI. P. 177.

Institutions in France in favour of learning and literature. Charlemagne. Lewis the Ninth. Francis the First. Henry the Fourth. Cardinal Richelieu. Changes and improvements in the French language. Account of the French academy.

LETTER XXII. P. 193.

Academy of Inscriptions and Belles Lettres. Academy of Sciences.

LETTER XXIII. P. 199.

Academy of Surgery. Academy of Architecture. Academy of Painting, Sculpture, and Engraving. Partiality of the French to their artists. Fresnoy's poem on painting. Drouessin's on sculpture.

LETTER XXIV. P. 206.

Public libraries at Paris. Royal library. Its antient and present state. Usefulness.

CONTENTS.

LETTER XXV. P. 215.

Library of the abbey of St. Germain. Library of St. Victor. Santeuil. Library of St. Genevieve. Late Duke of Orleans. Boffu. Other libraries. Their intent and use. Directions in the pursuit of studies.

LETTER XXVI. P. 234.

Largeness and magnificence of the churches at Paris. Reflections on the monastic and collegial foundations during the Gothic ages. On connoisseurship. On architecture; Greek, Roman, Gothic. Anecdote of a French preacher.

LETTER XXVII. P. 260.

Cathedral of Notre Dame. Utility of the examination of churches. On tombs and public monuments.

LETTER XXVIII. P. 269.

Church of St. Eustatius. Colbert. Chevert. Church of St. Sulpice. Character of its late

CONTENTS.

late rector. Church of the Carmes. Anecdote. Church of the Jesuits. Prince of Condé. Church of St. Andrew. Dethou. Church of the Abbey of St. Genevieve. Devotion of the Parisians for this saint. Church of St. Stephen. Cell of the late Duke of Orleans. Church of the Carthusians. Church of the Augustines. Order of the Holy Ghost. Church of St. Gervais. Le Tellier. Church of St. Paul. Church of the Capuchine Nuns. Louvois. Church of St. Roch. Anecdote. Church of St. Honoré. Cardinal Dubois. Church of St. Thomas du Louvre. Cardinal Fleury. Church of Sorbonne. Cardinal Richelieu. Church of the abbey of St. Germain. Church of the Celestines. Church of the Dominicans. Church of the Cordeliers. Church of the abbey of Val de Grace. Ann of Austria. Church of the Carmelites. Duchess of La Valiere. Observations on these churches. On Epitaphs.

LETTER

CONTENTS.

LETTER XXIX. P. 306.

Hymns ancient and modern. Religious abſurdities of old. Romiſh ſaints. Their prodigious number. On Canonization. On the Pariſian preachers. Funeral ſolemnities.

LETTER XXX. P. 328.

Strictures on religious opinions and controverſies.

LETTER XXXI. P. 338.

Obſervations and anecdotes relating to the public buildings of note in Paris. Louvre. Palais Royal. Luxemburg. Invalids. Military ſchool. Obſervatory. Place Royale. Place Vendome. Place Victoires. Place Louis Quinze. Statue of Henry the Fourth. Hotel de Ville. College Mazarin. Univerſity. School of Surgery. School of Civil Law. Foundling Hoſpital.

LETTER

CONTENTS.

LETTER XXXII. P. 372.

General hospital for women. Bicetre. Story of an astrologer. French formerly much addicted to astrology.

LETTER XXXIII. P. 390.

Regulating disposition of the French government. Horse-market. Farriery-School. Tapestry of the Gobelins. Carpets of Chaillot. Manufactory of glass. Manufactory of china. Observations on the preceding articles.

LETTER XXXIV. P. 402.

Montmartre. Constable of Montmorency. Mont-Valerien. Hermitage there. A remarkable character. Curious chapels on this mountain. Strictures on some religious practices.

LETTER XXXV. P. 436.

History of the Countess of Chateau Brian.

CONTENTS.

LETTER XXXVI. P. 471.

Palace of Conflans. Anecdote of a Polish gentleman.

LETTER XXXVII. P. 481.

Abbey of St. Denis. Palace of St. Germain. Anecdote of Lewis the Fourteenth and James the Second.

LETTER XXXVIII. P. 490.

Strictures on Versailles and other buildings of Lewis the Fourteenth. Plan of a history of that monarch.

LETTER XXXIX. P. 500.

Observations on the public walks and gardens in Paris. Boulevards. Cours la Reine. Champs Elisées. Old officer.

LETTER XL. P. 513.

Jardin du Roi. Garden of the Arsenal. Garden of the Luxemburg. A singular character

CONTENTS.

ter. Garden of the Palais Royal. Anecdote of Cardinal Richelieu.

LETTER XLI.   P. 525.

Garden of the Tuillieres. Garden of Prince Soubife. Utility refulting from the gardens in Paris.

LETTER XLII.   P. 534.

Shews and fights at Paris. Fête Dieu. Foire St. Germain. Longchamp. St. Cloud. Palais Marchand.

LETTER XLIII.   P. 544.

Change at Paris. Lotteries. Bathing-places. Amufements. Concert fpirituel. Combats of wild beafts. Vauxhall. Colifée.

LETTER XLIV.   P. 554.

Recapitulation. Concluding advice.

LETTERS

LETTERS

TO A

YOUNG GENTLEMAN

ON

His setting out for FRANCE.

LETTER I.

YOU are now arrived at the proper age for travelling. Until we are five-and-twenty, little or no benefit results to the far greater part of those who make what is called the grand tour. Nature has given to few men such talents as will enable them to travel at an earlier period. A Bacon, a Wotton, and a few others, are exceptions which will not justify the sending abroad mere youths, unacquainted with their own country, and totally unfit therefore to draw those comparisons between it and others, which are the very intent of travelling.

France is doubtless the country which, next to their own, it behoves Englishmen to be best acquainted with. This knowledge is now become more indispensible than ever. The immense alterations that have taken place in the circumstances of the British nation, render it a duty of the first magnitude for every English gentleman, whose line of life intitles him to visit foreign parts.

It is much to be regretted, that the majority of our travellers run over to France from no other motives than those which lead them to Bath, Tunbridge, or Scarborough. Amusement and dissipation are their principal, and often their only views.

Happily you are not of that number. Instruction and laudable curiosity, are the incentives that influence your wishes to see France.

France. In such a light you are highly commendable; the more indeed, as you did not embrace this determination, until you had duly seasoned your mind for such an undertaking, by studying the language of that country, and by obtaining a previous insight of as many things relating to it, as reading and conversation could procure.

The want of such a necessary preparation is too common among our young gentlemen; and is the real cause why most of them return from their travels, so remarkably unimproved in what is principally worth attaining, the science of the government, political circumstances, history, and literature of the nations they have visited.

How many persons not deficient in understanding, after spending two or three years abroad, bring little else home with them, than the remembrance of the gaieties in which their rank and fortune have enabled them to participate, and the names of those from whom they have received notice and civilities?

The mere frequentation of what is called the *beau monde*, will never repay the expences which the system of travelling established in England, entails on such a number of genteel families. There is no need to go out of our own country to learn politeness and engaging manners. Many judicious foreigners prefer ours to the French, as more manly and becoming. The reason why I have mentioned the French, is that most of our travellers make them a particular object of imitation.

The chief end of travelling is to improve one self in the knowledge of what cannot be learned otherwise. Such as the actual ideas, manners, morals, and state of countries, and nations. The information we receive concern-

concerning these matters, from books and the company of intelligent individuals, is highly to be valued; but we shall certainly be far better able to judge of them from ocular inspection and personal experience.

Segnius irritant animos demissa per aures,
Quam quæ sunt oculis Subjecta fidelibus, et quæ
Ipse sibi tradit Spectator.

For this reason, such as possess the means of gratifying their curiosity, and are at the same time destined or liable from their birth to arrive at eminent stations, should not fail to dedicate a reasonable portion of their time to the visitation of foreign parts.

I have united the probability of acting in a public sphere to the possession of fortune, from a conviction that the latter alone confers no right to ramble over the world, unless it is in quest of health, or from the necessity of business. Pleasure is a motive which ought to be discarded; enough may be found at home; and it is shameful to hear men assign it as a reason for squandering so much money, and losing so much time beyond sea, both which they might employ to so much better purposes, without stirring out of their own country.

LETTER II.

HAVING from various causes had frequent occasion to reside among the French, I will endeavour to make you share my acquaintance with them. This I propose doing in a summary, compendious manner; such as may, without loading your memory with unnecessary details, be sufficiently copious to remind you of what is worth knowing and retaining concerning that country and people.

The historical and geographical descriptions of France, do not make any part of the

the subject here intended to be laid before you. You are well acquainted with both. It is the now existing and acting principles, manners, and genius of that nation, with which you are to become acquainted.

The termination of the fatal quarrel with America, will in all probability open a new scene to the English who visit France.

Before the loss of our colonies, the French looked upon us as dangerous neighbours. They viewed us with an hostile and suspicious eye: their friendliness and esteem, for we always met with both, were accompanied with the idea of the many future mischiefs they expected from us.

Though to some this may appear groundless refinement, yet I will venture to appeal to those who have been conversant with the serious and thinking among them, for the truth of the observation.

But now that the danger is so much lessened, and that their apprehensions are of course so much removed, it is not improbable, that entertaining no immediate dread of our power, they will feel the less repugnance to bestow their good-will and amity upon the natives of this country.

One of the first rules I would have you diligently observe, is to shew a willingness to be pleased with their endeavours to please you, and to seize every occasion of doing justice to their many agreeable qualities.

One of the complaints urged against the English by the French, and indeed by most foreigners, is a superciliousness of disposition that inclines them to undervalue whatever they meet with abroad. More enmity has accrued to us from this than from any other cause. You cannot therefore be too much upon your guard against so prejudicial a failing. Acknowledge readily

readily what is good every where, dissemble small inconveniences, and take in good part all that is meant as such: this I have constantly found the surest method of conciliating affection and esteem, from persons of all characters and stations.

The French are peculiarly delighted with the praises which an Englishman bestows on their country: it would be very imprudent to refuse paying so moderate a price for the many civilities it will purchase.

As the late war has ended to their advantage, though not in the least to our dishonour, you will find them, on that very account, the more willing to accept of any compliments which you may occasionally think proper to pay them: winners are always in good humour; and little gains suffice to excite that of the French; though, to speak truth, they have in the present instance ample reasons to be satisfied.

LETTER II.

As soon as you are landed on French ground, renew the resolution I have often heard you make, of losing no opportunity of conversing with the natives in their own language, and upon subjects which relate to them.

You will find them surprisingly communicative and affable. They are peculiarly desirous of gratifying the curiosity of strangers, especially of the English, whose good opinion they are always earnest to obtain. I speak of the genteeler classes.

The common fault of our countrymen abroad, is to associate too much with each other, and too little with the people of the country they are in. This is an unaccountable turn in persons of understanding. To what intent did they go abroad? or, to ask the right question, had they any other than to seek out some new method of killing time, and relieving themselves from the burden of idleness through novelty of amusements?

LETTER III.

THE journey from Calais to Paris, will, on comparing it with that from London to Dover, furnish you with abundance of subjects for reflection. The respective aspect of each country, the appearance of the inhabitants, their looks, their attire, their habitations, all will afford a sensible Englishman powerful reasons for thanking Providence that he is one, as the philosopher did of old for being a Grecian.

As you approach Paris, you will see no cause to alter your sentiments. *Splendide Mendax* was the idea that always struck me, whenever I beheld rich cloaths or fine buildings on that route, as they are so strongly counter-balanced by the wretchedness of multitudes.

But

LETTER III.

But let us enter that metropolis, which you defign to make your abode, and the centre of your fpeculations.

The entrance into Paris is no ways prepoffeffing in its favour. Poverty and narrownefs of circumftances foon meet an experienced eye. Notwithftanding the partial appearances of fplendour that here and there prefent themfelves, it is eafy to perceive the general deficiency of plenty and profperity.

The dwellings of the inferior fort are poor and uncomfortable; the fhops are mean, and feem to want employment.

On the other hand, you will be ftruck with the grandeur of the public buildings, the churches, monafteries, and houfes of the great.

But it is only in their outfide they exceed the ftructures of the fame kind in
Eng-

LETTER III.

England, churches excepted, which are usually larger, and more magnificent than ours; the conveniences within doors are not to be compared with those of English houses.

These and various other remarks of the same nature I will leave you to make at your leisure. Of such objects I would wish you to be very carefully sollicitous.

My present aim is to lead you to the contemplation of these as well as of higher matters. They should affect deeply the minds of attentive people, as they relate so essentially to the immediate and solid well-being of the community.

Well do I know that the generality of travellers seldom think it their business to stoop to such concerns as these. Palaces, gardens, statues, pictures, antiquities, and productions of art, are the principal subjects of their curiosity: the others are
merely

merely collateral, and noticed only *en passant*, in a light and transient manner.

It is this frivolous turn of mind that renders so many books of travels totally unworthy of the perusal of serious people; who seek to instruct much more than to amuse themselves. But even in the light of mere amusement, it requires, one should think, no small share of patience, to wade through so many pages of descriptions of paintings and sculptures; which can be of no use but to refresh the memory of those who have seen them, and are at the same time tolerable connoisseurs of their merit. To all other classes of readers they must certainly prove very insipid.

A man who travels with views of substantial improvement, will rank such things in the secondary class of his observations. They will serve as amusements, but by no means as the principal objects of his inquiry.

I thought

LETTER III.

I thought it necessary to warn you against that rabies of admiration for statues and pictures, which is so commonly but a bare affectation. There are few real judges of them: for one that is truly qualified for such a task, there are crouds of pretenders. I could mention a variety of proofs how often the ignorance of such persons is ridiculed by artists. These are usually too polite to offend gentlemen, and it may be added, too wise to disoblige customers. From such motives many a man passes for a judge, who is very ill qualified for one.

There are so many other objects to employ your attention, and in which a man of sound understanding cannot be deceived, that I would always wish you to give the preference to these, and consider them as the chief sources of the benefit you are to derive from your travels.

LETTER

LETTER IV.

FROM the warmth with which I have reprobated the frivolous purfuits of the plurality of our travellers, I would not have you conclude that I am an enemy to elegant arts and amufements. I intend no more than to fet them in their right place, by prevailing upon you to view them in a light far inferior to the knowledge of thofe things on which the grandeur and profperity of nations are founded, or of thofe which are the caufes of their detriment and ruin.

It is reported of the famous Locke, that he was fo diligent in prying continually into the various callings and occupations of individuals, that he poffeffed a complete theory of all the principal branches of mechanical bufinefs; and could readily

con-

LETTER IV.

converse with tradesmen of almost every denomination, on the most intricate parts of their profession, and point out errors and improvements, of which they were not aware themselves.

It is not necessary that every gentleman should be as intelligent in these matters as Mr. Locke; but it is highly requisite that such as travel on the score of substantial improvement, should bring home with them, as much of foreign knowledge and experience in useful things, as is consistent with the line of life which they purpose to embrace. This would conduce to justify the expence this nation is at in the vast sums yearly laid out in tours to the continent of Europe.

Foreigners that travel, set us the example in this particular. Within these twenty years numbers of them have visited our island, prompted by views of deriving beneficial lights to their country,

from

from the various inftitutions and eftablifhments that have latterly rendered the Britifh nation fo renowned.

The truth is, that foreigners have much more rational purpofes to ferve by coming amongft us, than we have by going among them. Utility is generally their aim; ours is feldom any other than pleafure.

When you have ferioufly pondered on the pernicioufnefs of travelling for fo paultry an end, I promife myfelf from your good fenfe, and the pains you have taken to qualify yourfelf to appear abroad with credit, that you will not deferve to be counted among thofe who are continually imprefling foreigners with difadvantageous opinions of the natives of England.

I remember to have heard a Swifs gentleman of excellent capacity remark, that moft of our Englifh travellers were fent abroad much too young and inexperienced in the affairs of their country. Without a competent knowledge of which, he was positive in his conviction, that travelling became no better than a mere amusement. No man, till he had attained his four or five-and-twentieth year, was fit to judge with solidity concerning the transactions and business of his own country, much less of another, to which he was an utter stranger.

The only reasonable expectation to be formed in regard to a travelling youth, was the acquisition of foreign languages. Were it not to this intent, he would often say, that no people could betray more thoughtlessness and imprudence than the English, in suffering, or rather indeed encouraging their young gentlemen to make such long and expensive excursions.

Among other mistakes and negligences, of which English parents were guilty, he greatly blamed them for not endeavouring to train their children to some share of military knowledge: a campaign, was it no more, he thought absolutely requisite to perfect the character of a young man of rank and fortune.

He did not mean by this to turn our nobility and gentry into military men; but to infuse into them a manly spirit, and wean them from habits of indolence and effeminacy.

In this he asserted that he spoke from experience, and that he had always found in well-disposed young men, a wonderful aptitude to receive much profit by adopting such a plan. He mentioned several whose talents and dispositions had been improved, to the surprize of all that knew them.

Certain it is that a due portion of martialism elevates the soul in a remarkable degree. We never had a more respectable body of nobles and gentlemen in England than

LETTER IV.

than in the reigns of Elizabeth and Charles the First. Their education and their valour were both equally conspicuous, and has never been rivalled since.

In France, during the reigns of Lewis the thirteenth, and of his son Lewis the fourteenth, the French nobility were remarkably conversant both in arms and literature.

If we turn to Greek and Roman antiquity, we find all the principal personages of each of those celebrated nations, not less renowned for their courage and talents in war, than for their skill in polite knowledge.

I do not think it necessary to give you a catalogue of names by way of proof: you are sufficiently acquainted with the truth of what is asserted; and it were a shame that any gentleman of your age should require his memory to be refreshed on such an occasion.

Whether your friends will coincide with the opinion of this Swifs gentleman, is not the point in queftion; but one need not afk their permiffion to be convinced, that a young gentleman who has remained abroad three or four years, and has neglected opportunities to acquaint himfelf in fome meafure with fo neceffary a duty as that of ferving his country in time of need, is undoubtedly guilty of great indolence and remiffnefs.

It is highly probable that in a fhort time difputes will arife in fome parts of Europe. Thither I think it incumbent on a young gentleman of fpirit to repair. Of the two parties, let him join that which is the moft friendly to Britain, and facrifice at leaft a twelvemonth to the ftudy of war.

Poffibly an advice of this kind may not coincide with the ideas of many of our gentry. When people ramble abroad from mere curiosity, and the desire of varying their pastimes, such counsel is not acceptable; but hoping that you are determined to distinguish yourself from the bulk of our travellers, I have ventured to address you as a young man of sense and resolution, as one that means to travel in that character, and laying aside the frivolous occupations that have so long disgraced them, to impress foreigners with a new set of ideas in regard to the young gentlemen of England.

Hitherto, *riche comme un Anglois*, as rich as an Englishman, has been the compliment usually paid to our countrymen. It were to be wished that an epithet of a more honourable tendency could be substituted in its room. To be known chiefly by that, is almost to deserve no other.

LETTER V.

AFTER laying before you the foregoing general ideas, I will now endeavour to descend into such particulars as may render your journey of real advantage, and make it the foundation of much future enjoyment and utility.

As you propose remaining two complete years among the French, I think that in order to employ that time beneficially, you should begin by drawing up a plan of the manner in which you intend to fill it, and suffer no unnecessary avocations to interrupt it.

The great cause of so much time being idled away both at home as well as abroad, is that people are not sollicitous to make a previous distribution of it according to

LETTER V.

probable occurrences. An orderly mind is the foundation of all intellectual acquirements. Through regularity, the most immense and weighty business may be dispatched with celerity and ease; but every thing is too much for people who act without any rule.

I need not repeat the well-known story of Dewit, who was no less a prodigy from the talents he displayed in the management of public affairs, than from the astonishing facility and diligence with which they passed through his hands, owing entirely to the judicious arrangement of his time.

In imitation of so illustrious a precedent, let every hour have its particular assignment, and adhere to it punctually.

I pretend not to dictate what employments are most suited to the different parts of the day. I have observed that the

the notions and dispositions even of sensible persons do not always concur in this matter.

I have known some who began the day by reading or studying, others by writing and composing, reserving the other for the evening. But though such a method may be as advantageous as any to individuals who reside at home, and are masters of their own time, yet to a young gentleman abroad I imagine the morning alone should be sacred to the muses, and that he should constantly dedicate the after part of the day to society, from which he is to reap his principal improvement.

Without prescribing any particular method of dividing your time, I shall only advise you to be faithful to the division which you may think proper to make; and to be persuaded that unless one is made, time will insensibly steal away, without leaving any other remembrance than of its loss.

LETTER

LETTER VI.

WE are told that the proper study of mankind is man; to which let me add, that the proper study of a traveller is the country and people he visits.

It was judiciously done to carry over but a few English books with you: when I see large quantities chested up by our young travellers, unless it is with an intent to make presents of them, I am always inclined to suspect that either they mean them as a parade, or possibly to give them that reading abroad which they have neglected at home.

But let them not be deceived by fruitless expectations. He that has not read the good writers in his own language, before he left his country, is ill calculated to go abroad in the character of a gentleman; and cannot promise himself

himself much benefit from the literature of other countries.

To know little of one's own countrymen in that province, is an insuperable bar to improvement by the writers in other nations. It is too late to begin an application to one's own language, when the time is come for applying to that of others. If previous to travelling, a man could or would not perform one only of these tasks, it is hardly to be expected that while on his travels, he will either be able or willing to go through the fatigue of both.

No gentleman should, in short, venture himself abroad as a traveller, before he has laid in a sufficient stock of liberal knowledge, that of his own language especially, together with a reasonable tincture of those with which he will have occasion to form a more extensive acquaintance.

French and Latin are indispensibly requisite in a young man who proposes to mix

mix in elegant and respectable companies. While you are not deficient in these, you need not apprehend being undervalued; but without them, the second especially, I have frequently remarked, that the French are inclined to suspect one of being *un nouveau parvenu*, a lucky fellow of mean birth and breeding.

If Latin is necessary to preserve you from these suspicions, French is no less wanted to enable you to join company and conversation, and to render you acceptable in both.

Deficiency in this respect, though not so disgraceful as the former, is more inconvenient. The French have so long been used to look upon their language as the medium of genteel communication, that they learn no other, and expect that every person who forms pretensions to polite breeding, should speak it.

LETTER VI.

As you know enough of it to be at no loss upon any occasion, I congratulate you on the satisfaction you will receive from that circumstance. It is no trivial one in any country; but especially in one where the natives are seldom able to converse in any other.

To this let me add, that the French are charmed to hear a foreigner express himself with ease and correctness in their language. They look upon it as a tacit homage paid to the superiority of its merit, and at the same time as a proof of the taste of him that possesses it.

It is, in short, an accomplishment of essential weight with people of all characters in France, and for which they are willing to allow one very ample credit.

Next to Latin and French, let me recommend the intelligence of the Italian, for two reasons, first, because it is attained with

LETTER VI.

with facility by one that knows the two former, and secondly, as it is not improbable that you may be smitten some day or other, with a desire of seeing Italy.

To these two reasons one may add a third, the excellent authors in that language, and the number of Italians that repair to England.

A complete knowledge and skill in these three languages, will abundantly suffice, together with your own, to furnish you with copious means of information in all the divers branches of learning.

If you have not forgot your Greek, cultivate it with all care and diligence; but if you have, or never should have made much proficiency therein, I do not see of what service an application to it would prove at present. When turned of five-and-twenty, languages are but an insipid occupation to a solid, thinking mind. Unless they are
learned

learned in early youth, nothing but absolute necessity can justify a man's labours in so rugged and tedious a task.

Beside the fatigue that accompanies them, they cannot fail to preclude our attention to matters of far greater moment. What are they after all, but mere combinations of letters and sounds, different in one country from what they are in another, but expressive of the same thing, and productive of no idea that is not to be found in one as much as in all?

It has frequently raised my indignation, to see men profoundly skilled in the learned languages, totally unconversant in other knowledge. This is by no means an uncommon case. One would be tempted to imagine, that persons of this stamp had little or no turn for any thing else; which is perhaps too often the real fact.

I once knew a professor in a foreign university precisely in this predicament. He

LETTER VI.

He had a singular facility in the attaining of languages; but was a stranger to ancient or modern history, and almost to every other branch of knowledge. His fort lay entirely in his expertness as a linguist: he understood critically the meaning of words; but did not seem to relish the spirit and sublimity of the expressions of which he so well comprehended the sense. Whether he read Hesiod or Homer, Virgil or Silius, I apprehend his raptures were equal. Those who knew him were convinced of this, as well as that he held many of the best modern poets and other writers in a most unjust contempt.

This naturally leads me to warn you, to hold an equitable scale in those matters; and to consider that there are many men of excellent taste and discernment, who are unacquainted with, or have forgotten the Greek and Latin which they formerly learned at school; but are on the other hand

hand very extenſively read in the good writings of their countrymen.

The paſſion for languages is not however much known in France; leſs I believe than in any nation. As they abound in tranſlations, they ſtand in the leſs need of originals, and have the more time to employ on things themſelves.

To do them juſtice, they are uncommonly ready to peruſe the productions of other people, when clad in a French dreſs: it may be ſaid that there is hardly a work of any merit which has not been tranſlated into their language, and has not met with the moſt gracious reception.

They ſeem perſuaded that the time and pains beſtowed upon the learning of languages, will be much more profitably employed in peruſing judicious verſions. Theſe one is ſure to read with facility, and thoroughly to comprehend; whereas years are neceſſary to arrive at the exact underſtanding of an original. While people therefore are not under an immediate obligation of ſubmitting to ſo much toil, they not improperly ſtile it, *travailler pour l'Amour du Travail*, labouring for the ſake of labour.

You will, conformably to this opinion, find very few Frenchmen fond of other languages than their own: but then you will find excellent tranſlations among them, of almoſt every book worth reading, whether ancient or modern.

One of the moſt celebrated French tranſlators of Greek and Latin, was Monſieur D'Ablancourt: this gentleman was of opinion, that, hiſtory, laws, and ſciences excepted, which were in their nature progreſſive, and muſt of courſe furniſh a continual ſeries of matter for ſtudy and improvement, all other branches of literature were already sufficiently investigated; and that whatever the moderns might add of their own, would never attain the excellence of the ancients.

Instead of exhausting themselves in vain attempts to rival them, he advised the literati to content themselves with the works of preceding ages, and to employ their abilities in translating them faithfully and elegantly for the use of the present times.

He not only gave, but conformed to this advice with the most remarkable punctuality: his whole labours were devoted to the service of those who were unacquainted with the learned languages, and yet were desirous of benefiting by the excellent things they contained. His versions are incomparably the best extant.

After precautioning you against the needless study of languages, let me with the

LETTER VI.

the same breath intreat you to neglect none that you are a master of.

I will here use the freedom of setting before you the method used by a friend, in order to retain those of which he was possest.

Those pursuits and studies excepted, which demanded immediate and daily attention, he dedicated every week in rotation to one language exclusively; selecting for that purpose the best authors in each, and avoiding carefully to intermix the least application to any more than one at a time.

By such means, and with little more than an hour's space in the day; he preserved for years a competency of skill in the languages he had been taught in his youth.

You will find, in several of the coffeehouses, foreigners of great merit in this particular branch. I knew an Hungarian gentle-

gentleman, an officer of Hussars, who spoke most of the European languages with surprising fluency and correctness. He was a person of thorough education: he wrote and exprest himself in Latin in a masterly stile: I remember an ode of his composing to the honour of Voltaire; which connoisseurs esteemed equal in point of latinity to any production of the time. He conversed in, and, what was more remarkable, he pronounced the English like a native. Pope he knew in a manner by heart, and preferred him to all modern poets, Voltaire excepted, whom he stiled the reigning King of Parnassus.

This gentleman, to the best of my recollection, possest nine modern languages, the Polish, Hungarian, Turkish, German, Dutch, Italian, Spanish, French, and English.

I mention him as an instance of what may be accomplished through a regular course

course of assiduity, even by a man taken up with the business of the world, and wholly dependent upon his own industry for his success in life. He was turned of fifty when I knew him; and had experienced some trying vicissitudes, having during his youth been a captive in Turky, and met afterwards with other mortifications.

But in the midst of difficulties he always found leisure for improvement. His erudition was of a manly useful kind: ancient and modern history, fortification and tactics, he was allowed to excel in, and in all discussions of this sort his opinion was held decisive.

As nothing however should be undertaken *invita minerva*, I would very seriously admonish you, to beware of being seduced, by his example, into such an arduous attempt as that of compassing the knowledge of a multiplicity of languages.

An instance of such a nature is a phenomenon, exhibited now and then as a proof and specimen of the extent of human powers; but which while we admire, it would be fruitless to propose as an object of imitation.

Contenting yourself therefore with those languages I have already recommended, improve yourself in them; and be persuaded that more utility and credit will result from the perfect possession of two or three, than from an incomplete and partial knowledge of half a dozen.

The general rule is, that such as are conversant in many, are seldom masters of any. This is an old proverb, and as such deserves particular attention: as far as my experience goes, it is justly founded.

It is principally among illiterate people one meets with the greatest linguists. I have known sea-faring men at Genoa and Leghorn,

Leghorn, able to converse readily upon common subjects in almost every language of Europe.

I hope that you will in this branch of knowledge retain what you have got; but I do not wish you to obtain any more.

LETTER VII.

HAVING mentioned in my preceding, the likelihood of meeting in coffee-houses with foreign gentlemen worthy of notice for their skill in languages, I will also add, that you will have opportunities of becoming acquainted in those places, with some of the most sensible and knowing individuals in Paris.

In this respect the coffee-houses in that city have the advantage over those of our metropolis. In London no access is permitted

mitted without particular recommendation, to the affociations that are formed in coffee-houfes among the gentlemen who frequent them. Thefe excepted, the natural referve of the Englifh allows of little converfation in a coffee-room, unlefs it is upon the bufinefs officially as it were tranfacted there. Thofe adjoining to the Change, are for that reafon the only where much talking is heard and fubmitted to with patience.

But in Paris the leifure of numbers of the genteeler fort, being far greater than with individuals of the fame clafs with us, from that variety of caufes which it is not here neceffary to enumerate, the coffee-houfes of credit abound with perfons of merit and ingenuity. Their converfation not being fo tedioufly ingroffed by politics or bufinefs as that of our coffee-houfe frequenters, affords a much greater choice of fubjects for the pleafure, variety, and animation of difcourfe.

As

LETTER VII.

As freedom and affability reign confpicuoufly in the companies that meet in thefe places, ample encouragement is given to difplay abilities of every fort. I have been frequently entertained with learned and ingenious, as well as with amufing fubjects; and been ftruck with admiration at the variety of talents exhibited on thefe occafions.

Thefe places being often the evening rendezvous of perfons noted for their genius and capacity, are upon that account reforted to by numbers who feek for inftruction or pleafure. They are both fo well blended, that one is fure to mifs of neither.

It is here the nature and difpofition of the French is perfectly difcovered: polite yet warm, impetuous yet affable, full of life and vigour, and no lefs replete with obligingnefs and complacency.

Characters of all denominations abound here. Provided no ill-natured reflections be cast on the ruling powers of the state, and upon such matters as plain sense will tell one should not be meddled with, an unbounded freedom is allowed and taken in all things.

Quidquid agunt homines nostri farrago libelli, the whole circle of human actions comes into discussion before these assemblies; and it is impossible, considering the genius and experience of those from whom the dissertations proceed, that great utility, as well as enjoyment, should not result to the audience.

For these reasons you will, if you are wise, often repair to these houses; and lay aside that pernicious pride, which prompts so many of our countrymen abroad to disdain all company, but that of persons of the highest rank.

But

But let me requeſt it of you, ſeriouſly to reflect, whether ſuch a ſociety is in reality the moſt agreeable, or the moſt inſtructive.

More honour indeed accrues from an introduction to it, and a greater facility of admiſſion elſewhere; but is it of ſuch company the moſt brilliant and moſt meritorious characters were ever known to form the principal part?

People of very high rank are, with few exceptions, the moſt inſipid, and unacquainted with the world, and generally the moſt ignorant and uneducated. Were it not for the ſplendour that accompanies great riches, perſons born and bred to vaſt opulence, would poſſeſs but little attraction. The ſecret expectation of deriving emolument from their frequentation, is the chief motive that ſurrounds them with followers and adherents. Few are there among them whoſe acquired qualifications deſerve much

much notice or respect. If they are blest with a good character, 'tis in general purely the gift of nature, unassisted by art or culture. A proof of this is, that rarely do we see a superstructure raised on their native good qualities; as if those to whom they had been intrusted, were afraid they should be invested with any other superiority than that with which they were born.

So far as interest is concerned, it would be imprudent to neglect them; but if you seek for improvement, it is not there you will find it.

The chief, and indeed the properest motive pleaded for courting the presence of the great, is that it brings us acquainted with such persons of merit and reputation as frequent it from similar views: as to the principals themselves, they may be considered rather as the conveners, than as the authors and promoters of brilliant society.

society. I have said nothing, I believe, that is not in general tolerably true.

From the vivacity of your mind, I make no doubt you will embrace all opportunities of storing it with every kind of improvement. It is only by associating promiscuously with persons of all professions, that we can become acquainted with the reality of things. While a man therefore bears an unsullied character, think him not unworthy of your society; and if his station is genteel, though his circumstances should be unequal to his worth, let this alone have weight in your estimation; and make as much of it your own as you can by frequenting him, and participating the knowledge and experience he is willing to communicate.

The acquisitions made in this manner, are, next to those that are obtained through our own personal exertions, incomparably superior to those that arise from reading

and

and study. Men of abilities, arrived at a certain time of life, are wonderfully pleased with docility in their juniors, and always repay it by the justness and solidity of their instructions: as they are drawn from their own stock, they are built on practice, and may be relied upon. Happy will you be, if among the various individuals, whom accident may throw in your way, you chance to form a connection with one of this description. Should you be so fortunate as to meet with such a prize, I most ardently pray, first that you may be sensible of its value, next that you may feel an earnest desire to improve so auspicious an opportunity, and lastly, that no impatience or petulance on your side may deprive you of the benefits of such an acquaintance.

It is in the company of such men, that young gentlemen will form themselves, in a short time, without expence, and at no risk. These are three considerations that

ought

LETTER VII.

ought powerfully to weigh with them, when they recollect how often years are spent, money lavished, and frequent difficulties and dangers incurred by others, without obtaining an adequate recompence for the toil they have undergone.

I would wish you therefore to view such a fort of acquaintance as a real prize in the lottery of life. They are not so rare to be found as may be imagined. Unhappily there are many who find them as the cock did the diamond on the dunghill: not knowing their worth, they turn aside in queft of characters more in unifon with their own.

Were it not for this want of perception in fuch numbers of our young men of fortune, that part of their education which is by far the moft important, the finifhing part, would not ufually be fo miferably defective.

E Frefh

LETTER VII.

Fresh from the university, they are ushered into society, with the notion, that the knowledge they have acquired of the learned languages, and of the sciences, is the best and surest foundation of future improvement.

Abstractedly speaking, this notion is just and well founded. But then they should be apprized, that unless an expert conductor is provided to take them by the hand, experimentally conversant in the various scenes of life, and able to give them practical explanations of the precepts they have been taught, unless the theories, to which they have so long applied, are not illustrated by the instruction and example of real men of the world, they will remain ignorant in the midst of imaginary knowledge.

You have yourself oftentimes exprest your astonishment at the profound inexperience, in a variety of respects, of gentle-

LETTER VII.

men of rank, fortune, and even understanding. To what else think you could this be owing, than to the missing of that necessary requisite to men of their description, a person of capacity and expertness to attend their first progress, and initiate them in those pursuits and occupations that become their station in life?

Innocence of heart, integrity of morals, learning and genius are with reason deemed essentials in a tutor. To a gentleman that proposes *fallentis semita vitæ*, to pass his life in the shade, such a one may be sufficient. But it is ridiculous to seek for no other guide in favour of those who are destined to figure in the perplexed circles of worldly transactions and public affairs.

Intelligent foreigners are not a little surprised, when they behold our young gentlemen sent abroad in the company of persons doubtless of good character, but not unfrequently as new to the scenes they experience, as the very pupils intrusted to their care. I will make no comment upon such a text.

I have always been convinced, in conformity to the persuasion of the ablest men whom I have heard discourse upon this subject, that a travelling companion is far preferable to a travelling tutor.

The disparity of age, added to the idea of controul, must necessarily lessen that confidence and cordiality which ought to subsist between fellow-travellers. When the difference of years is not material, and they are both on a footing in point of authority, friendship is much less liable to interruption, as prudence is the only director they will have to obey.

But then I am supposing they are both young men of sense, discretion, and maturity. And are any others fit to travel? I also suppose that one of the two has already

ready been abroad, and that friendship induces him to accompany the other.

Whenever the system of travelling undergoes a reformation of this kind, I make no doubt this nation will soon perceive the difference between so beneficial an alteration, and the present mode of dispatching raw young lads abroad, to no other purpose than to see the raree shews upon the continent, and initiate themselves in foreign levities.

I will conclude this epistle by repeating what cannot be too much inculcated, that until the age of four or five-and-twenty, travelling is of little benefit. To travel with any reasonable hopes of improvement, the mind should be formed; which it cannot be, at least seldom is, before that period.

It may be added with equal truth, that unless we are accompanied by an experienced

enced friend, previously acquainted with foreign parts, we shall see them only by halves, and lose of course much time, money, and trouble, where they might otherwise have been usefully employed.

LETTER VIII.

WHEREVER curiosity, and the desire of information leads you, always keep those in your eye, in whom you perceive an aptitude and inclination to gratify your wishes. Shew them all deference and attention; and be assured that, next to charitableness and generosity, there are no characters in the world more deserving of respect and gratitude, than of such individuals as are willing to instruct and edify others at free cost.

France to its credit abounds with such characters. The French are in general extremely communicative. This renders people of knowledge and capacity among them, peculiarly agreeable to foreigners.

There are two claſſes of men in that country, that yield not the palm of ſubſtantial merit to any other denomination of men upon earth. Theſe are the Officers, and the Abbees.

Theſe two bodies contain a multitude of individuals of great worth and abilities. Abbees in particular are diſtinguiſhed by their wit, learning, and genius. The Officers by their experience and knowledge of the world, and the agreeableneſs of their manners and converſation.

Among theſe two claſſes endeavour to ſelect ſome of your moſt familiar acquaintance. The good humour and affability for which the French gentlemen are noted, will make it no difficult taſk. As they have uſually, the Officers eſpecially,

cially, much leisure upon their hands, they will readily spare you as much as you can want.

It is not however among the younger part of either of these classes, that I would counsel you to seek for a connection. Until a Frenchman approaches forty, his extreme vivacity is unacceptable to the temper of an Englishman. But nothing can exceed the amiableness of a French gentleman of sense and education, *Cujus octavum trepidavit ætas claudere lustrum,* when he has attained the above mentioned period of life.

His mind and body retain their full vigour: but then the fire and impetuosity of youth are spent; and the experience which years have acquired, has taught him to command his passions. The chearfulness of his disposition is left at full play, and is no longer subject to interruption

ruption from the warmth and unrulinefs that characterife the generality of young Frenchmen.

A circumftance attends the connections formed with moft of thefe gentlemen, which in the fcale of prudence will have confiderable weight. As they are not commonly in affluent fituations, they are ufually perfons of oeconomy in pecuniary matters.

I entertain not the leaft doubt that this circumftance may, in no fmall degree, have contributed to render them unfit company for many of our young travellers; who feem much more intent on making a parade of their opulence, than on ufing it as the means of improvement.

I was, at an early period of life, intimately acquainted with an old gentleman of excellent parts, and great good humour; who had, according to his own account,

led

led a most pleasant and agreeable life, and partaken of every enjoyment that a reasonable man could desire.

Among the various methods he had used to procure himself so much felicity, the liberality and friendliness of his temper had afforded him the most effectual.

He was an Irish gentleman of small fortune from his father's side, but his mother had a brother at Lisbon, who in the course of years raised an immense fortune by trade; which, having no children, he left to her, and she to her son.

He was at this time about thirty years of age. Having received an elegant education, and being of a lively facetious disposition, he met with an easy reception in the best companies, and soon became a favourite every where.

But the superiority of his understanding weaned him in a short time from that kind
of

LETTER VIII.

of society, which has no other merit than being composed of persons in genteel circumstances. This was not sufficient for a man who sought ardently for improvement, and was above sacrificing it to mere amusement.

Resolving to gratify his inclinations without reserve, he left England, where he had lived from his childhood, and went over to Paris, at the time the famous Mississippi scheme was in agitation, and had set so many heads to work in that kingdom.

His motive for quitting England was to make the tour of Europe, and to introduce himself to the acquaintance of people of conspicuous merit in all countries.

He visited accordingly the principal capitals in Europe; but soon returned to Paris; where, for particular reasons, he chose to fix his residence.

On his first arrival there, he had contracted an intimacy with a French officer of rank; whom, on his return, he found almost ruined by speculating in the scheme above-mentioned.

As the friendship he profest for this gentleman was solid and sincere, he assisted him in his distress, and enabled him so far to stand his ground, as to preserve his regiment, which he had been on the point of selling in order to pay his debts.

The gratitude of this gentleman made him ample returns. He procured him a numerous set of useful acquaintance: he represented him every where in the most advantageous colours: he became his confident and adviser on some arduous and critical occasions: and on succeeding to a large estate, and having no issue, he annually expended considerable sums in deference to, and conjunction with, his friend, in providing for young gentlemen of good family, but narrow means.

In

LETTER VIII.

In the mean time, as they were both persons of the very gayest frame of mind, they spent their lives in a continual round of merriment: but the basis of it was elegance and refinement. It was, if I may so express myself, an alliance between Epicurus, Anacreon, and Plato.

Those whom they admitted to their company and pastimes, were chosen for their merit alone, independently of every other consideration. Their society consisted of none but men of prime rate abilities in every department of science and genius, or of the most consummate experience in the various affairs and professions of genteel life.

As individuals of this description are not always treated by fortune according to their deserts, the notice they took of such as were in this predicament went much further than bare hospitality. Both the gentlemen were equally ready to embrace
every

every occasion of acting a friendly part, and of convincing their worthy guests, that they viewed them in a far more affectionate light than that of mere conviviality.

In this generous manner did they expend their revenue. Their houses were the constant resort of individuals of worth. They sought, they courted, they befriended them. Many a brave officer in distress, many an ingenious person under pressures, experienced their kindness, and through their countenance were brought forward, and placed in a way of prospering.

Notwithstanding the numerous deeds of munificence in which they were both daily employed, no men could ever more meritoriously claim the title of modest and disinterested. *Prodesse quam conspici* was the unvariable maxim of their lives. Had it not been for their hospitable manner of living, and the gratitude of those who were

bene-

benefited by their liberality, the worthiness of their character must have remained concealed; so truly averse they both were to all manner of ostentation.

I have laid this example before you, to induce you as much as possible, to cast off that sullenness of pride, which too much characterises our wealthy countrymen both at home and abroad.

You cannot be too intimately convinced of the irreparable injury done to society in general by this absurd morofeness. It keeps at an unfortunate distance people whose mutual wants should be a continual motive of approximation. It perpetuates ignorance and presumption in the great, by preventing them from associating with those who might have effected a cure. It is the principal obstruction in the road of prosperity, to those who by their education and parts deserve to prosper. It tends in short to render inimical to each other,

those

those individuals among whom a good correspondence ought principally to subsist, the opulent on the one hand, and people of ingenuity on the other.

It is only by mixing freely with these latter that the former can ever hope to command the respect of the public. Men of fortune that slight persons of worth, who are not in affluence, seldom fail to repent it. These have a variety of ways of exercising a just, and at the same time a liberal revenge.

The world knows too well the necessity of union and cordiality between men of rank and those of genius, not to unite in condemning with the utmost bitterness and severity the arrogance of such as have no other recommendation but their pelf. A man who prides himself on this account, and undervalues his superiors in other respects, is always sure of making those his most dangerous enemies, whom he might have made his most useful friends.

LETTER

LETTER IX.

IN expectation that you will neglect no proper opportunity of introducing yourself to the company of all without exception, who may improve you, I will venture to recommend to your notice a clafs of men who lately made a confiderable figure in France.

Thefe are the Jefuits. Whatever objections the ftate might have to alledge againft them in other refpects, it cannot be denied that they were the moft learned and moft ingenious of all the religious orders eftablifhed in France; and at the fame time the moft ufeful to the public, from the affiduity and diligence which they difplayed in the inftruction of youth.

The moft celebrated colleges in that kingdom were under their management.

More men of genius and literature were formed under their tuition, than in any others. They cultivated every branch of polite knowledge with the most splendid success. It may be confidently asserted, that they alone have produced more proficients in arts and sciences, than all the other orders of the Roman communion put together.

Considerations of this kind, which are founded on strict truth, have made it a matter of astonishment among the most sensible people in Europe, both Protestants as well as Roman Catholics, that so general a conspiracy should have been formed against them; as it does not appear that their conduct has latterly been more liable to reprehension than in preceding periods; or that their principles are altered from what they originally were at the time of their primitive institution.

But leaving the disquisition of these matters to those who may be better informed,

formed, suffice it to observe, that they are a striking instance of the instability of human establishments.

No class of men flourished with so much lustre, and enjoyed such reputation and credit. The first families in the kingdom prided themselves in the enjoyment of their good-will and predilection, and were happy to live in habits of intimacy with their principal members. Their colleges were filled with youths of the first rank; and they had the choice of the whole realm for the selection of those whom they thought proper to admit into their body.

This admission was regulated by the wisest maxims of policy. The qualifications necessary to procure acceptance, were birth, wealth, or capacity. From these sources they derived a constant succession of solid supporters of their prosperity. How they could, with so much foresight and precaution, meet with so mortifying a downfall, is truly surprising.

Independent of these prudential maxims in the formation of their own body, they had extended their interest among the great by one of the most influencing and forcible ties which the Roman religion could afford. They were father confessors to some of the chief personages in the kingdom. The king himself was their penitent: his confessor was officially a Jesuit. They had enjoyed this high prerogative ever since the reign of Henry the Fourth, during a space of near one hundred and sixty years.

With all these advantages they could not stand their ground. Let not their ruin, however, impress you with any unfavourable ideas of their abilities. It is impossible to contend with power. Their enemies were so numerous, so potent, and so

LETTER IX.

so implacable, that their destruction was inevitable.

Numbers of the French Exjesuits, as they are now stiled, are dispersed over all Europe. You will meet with some of the most intelligent people in France among them; and it will be entirely your fault if you do not derive much profit and entertainment from their frequentation.

You must perceive that I strongly flatter myself that you will set yourself above all prejudices, and seek for improvement wherever it is to be found.

With this view I would not have you neglect the society of persons of the other religious orders, if you can conveniently obtain it. There are individuals of great worth in monasteries and abbeys. Neither are they so secluded from the world, as one might be apt to imagine from the profession they have embraced. Some of them

them are in many respects perfectly acquainted with polite society, and it will not be a business of any difficulty to become acquainted with such of them as are deserving of it.

Too few of our travellers think these classes of men worthy of their notice. Yet they constitute a considerable portion of the community, in all countries where the Roman Catholic persuasion is established. Their rules and ordinances, the spirit of their institutions, the utility or detriment which they have occasioned to the places where they have been settled, the motives that gave them birth, with those that caused their dissolution, the individuals of note whom they have produced, all these are subjects worthy of attention to persons who do not run abroad for mere diversion; but who travel with a real view of informing themselves of the nature and situation of men and things in the countries which they visit.

Nil

LETTER IX.

Nil contemnere was the precept of a great modern philosopher; who was also no inconsiderable traveller. This was the celebrated Montesquieu; who used often to say, that nothing cured mankind so effectually of that reciprocal contempt with which so many nations are brought up for each other, as travel and inspection into each others ways and manners.

But to do this in a manner conducive to the intent which he proposed, we should, on setting out, adopt and practise his preliminary maxim, and resolve *nil contemnere*, to despise nothing; that is to say, to suffer no prejudices to lead our judgment astray, and to pass no sentence of contempt, but after an impartial examination of those things that deserve it.

Were this rule faithfully observed, what a different set of ideas and opinions would many of our travellers bring home? What a variety of objects would appear to them

them trivial, on which, from inattention, they are led to set a groundless value? and how many others would they prize, which, from inadvertency, or dissipation, they pass by without discovering their real worth?

LETTER X.

I AM now going to propose an undertaking to you, for which I am convinced, from your disposition, and the occupations which have latterly taken up a considerable part of your time, you are peculiarly calculated and prepared.

Nothing is more common in England, than to hear its political constitution extolled as the perfection of all government, and preferred to every other system extant.

Were

LETTER X.

Were one to stop short one of the many vague declaimers on this trite subject, and question him about the particulars of that inferiority, which he so readily ascribes to the government of other countries, it is much to be doubted, whether the zeal of more than one in twenty, would not be found greatly to exceed his knowledge.

That you may not incur such an imputation, on your return to your native country, my proposal is, that, as you have for these two or three years past applied yourself to the study of its laws and constitution, you would at present dedicate a convenient portion of your time, to the investigation of the actual system of legislation and domestic rule established in France.

Less than an hour allotted every other day to this purpose, will make it a pastime; and will give you at the same time

an

an infight into thefe matters, of which an Englifh gentleman fhould not be ignorant.

Books on this topic are found in plenty among the French, fome of them very elegantly written. I hardly know which to recommend as the beft: that which I read with moft fatisfaction, was compofed, if I remember juftly, about thirty years ago. It is anonimous: the exact title I cannot recollect; but *abregé du gouvernement de la France*, is fomething near it.

Another occupation not lefs material, is the political fituation of that kingdom, its population, the fources of its revenues, the ftate of cultivation in its various provinces, its domeftic and foreign trade. Thefe are objects of incomparably more importance, than thofe which ufually ingrofs the attention of moft of our young travellers; and, with fhame it may be faid, even of thofe gentlemen of maturer age,

LETTER X.

age, whom lassitude of doing nothing at home, carries so often abroad.

Treatises on these matters are very far from being wanting. The curiosity of the French is such, that notwithstanding the severity with which the press is controuled, lucubrations on all kinds of subjects, are secretly printed and vended, in spite of the vigilance with which they are watched.

While you are engaged in this career, let me remind you not to forget the living characters of the times. No people are so alert as the French, in discovering the transactions of the day: their prying disposition is ever on the wing: nothing remains long a secret: curiosity to enquire, and loquacity to reveal, form the very essentials of the life and occupation of the fashionable classes.

Anecdotes, in short, are the soul of conversation among them. Invention, to be sure,

sure, is often at work to entertain company; but a person of sagacity will, after some experience and practice in the ways of the people he frequents, learn to discern between an agreeable story-teller and another upon whom he can depend.

In order to render yourself acceptable to French companies, you must assume something of their manner, and endeavour to put on some appearance of their vivacity. Their chief complaint respecting us, is a defect of liveliness, and a taciturnity which they suspect sometimes of being rather affected. I need not however be sollicitous on your account; nature has given you life and spirit enough to face any Frenchman.

In the mean time, that you may fill your place with propriety in French companies, furnish your memory with as many anecdotes as you can procure, concerning the people of high rank and fashion in England.

England. The French, like the Greeks of old, delight in obtaining all kind of information. It is but juſtice to ſay, that they are not only willing, but deſirous to hear what paſſes worthy of obſervation among their neighbours, and extremely attentive to thoſe who are able to ſatisfy them in ſuch particulars.

You will ſoon perceive that they far exceed us in their endeavours to be acquainted with tranſactions and characters out of their country. This may appear extraordinary, when their backwardneſs to learn foreign languages is taken into conſideration: but their anſwer is, that facts exiſt independent of language, and are incomparably more entertaining and inſtructive.

This leads me to reflect, that while our people of education are at immenſe pains to ſtudy the French language, and become acquainted with their literature; they are

are

are unpardonably neglectful in that part of it which relates to their history and domestic concerns, though unquestionably the most useful and deserving of their attention.

The French, on the contrary, though much less conversant in our language, are much better read in the affairs of this country than we are in theirs.

I have observed of late years an indolence and supineness respecting foreign matters, very scandalous and disgraceful in persons of education. *Sua tantum mirantur* is too applicable to numbers of our countrymen.

No Branch of knowledge is less cultivated among those who profess an application to letters, than the historical. It is not uncommon to see persons not meanly versed in Greek and Roman literature, amazingly defective in this most beneficial of all gentlemanly acquirements.

LETTER X.

Our French neighbours form a remarkable contrast in this province. No people are more abundantly supplied with good histories of all nations, both ancient and modern, in their own tongue; some of them excellent originals, and the others very correct and elegant translations.

In addition to what has already been premised on that subject, it may be said that in this department of literature the French exceed most, if not all nations. If we except the translations from Greek into Latin, made at the revival of letters by the men of genius in Italy, and the English versions of the ancient poets, the French have not only translated a far greater number of foreign authors into their language, than any other people have into theirs; but they have done it in a stile and manner which admit of no competition in the generality of other translators.

This may be accounted for by adverting to the vast difference between those who translate in France, and those who perform the same task in other countries, in ours especially. Among the' French they are usually persons eminent for knowledge and literature, and who chiefly propose the acquisition of fame. But elsewhere, in England and Holland particularly, they are too frequently unhappy gentlemen who engage in such business from necessity; and who from the same motive are more intent upon dispatch than perfection.

In this description we must not however include those members of our universities, who have given us versions of the Greek and Roman classics. Their performances have incontestable merit. But then they were in much the same predicament as the French above-mentioned: hurried by no pressures, and at leisure to polish their work.

It

LETTER X.

It is chiefly upon translations from modern languages, and from the French in particular, these strictures are made.

For this reason I would never advise any gentleman that wishes to enjoy a good French writer, to peruse him in a translation; unless indeed his avocations are such, as absolutely preclude him from the probability of ever having time sufficient to bestow on the learning of French.

I must not finish this epistle, without remarking, that of late the French have begun to apply themselves with uncommon fervour to the study of foreign languages. The English in particular is now become a capital requisite among their literati. The revolution that has deprived us of America, will in all probability render it for obvious reasons very popular also in the commercial world.

LETTER XI.

THE French have, within these thirty or forty years, addicted themselves to philosophical speculations with more zeal and passion than at any former period.

By philosophical speculations, I mean the investigation of human nature, and that review of events and transactions, which examines and appreciates the utility or detriment resulting from them to mankind.

Numbers of ingenious performances on subjects of this nature, have made their appearance within the fore-mentioned period. Some of them indeed are of the supremest merit, and have done the highest honour to the French nation.

Certain

LETTER XI.

Certain it is that a spirit of enquiry and examination has arisen latterly in France, which has made, and continues to make an astonishing progress.

L'esprit philosophique s'est emparé des François, says one of their writers, a philosophical turn has taken possession of the minds of the French.

This inquisitive disposition however meets now and then with some obstructions. The clergy are no friends to it, for this plain reason, because it is no friend to the clergy.

They look upon it as an inveterate foe, resolutely determined to operate the destruction of all power, and of all institutions that are not founded upon reason.

They are conscious at the same time, that according to the ideas inculcated by this new system, much of their authority and importance is called in queſtion: this of courſe alarms them, and awakens their jealouſy.

Happily for the adherents to the notions that begin to prevail among ſome of the moſt enlightened individuals of the French nation, the clergy has loſt much of the influence it once had among the great. The government ſupports them no longer with that blind ſubſerviency, which charactiſed the æras of ignorance and ſuperſtition.

The diminution of their credit appears in the diminution of their numbers. Much leſs conſiderable than twenty years ago, is the appearance of the ſecular and regular clergy at this day: one meets with fewer in the ſtreets and places of public reſort than formerly; one hears leſs about them; people alſo ſeem to think leſs of them: all this portends an inward decline, as it ſhews a viſible decay.

The

LETTER XI.

The French are not a little elated at this revolution in the intellectual empire, as they term it; I mean those who embrace this new system. It cannot be expected they should as yet be numerous enough to form an open decided party: they speak and write however with no small determination: some productions have lately seen the light, inferior in boldness to none that were ever written on speculative subjects in any age or country.

The study of nature flourishes at present in France, as much as in any part of Europe. We had the honour of leading the way; but the French have followed us very successfully. What I comprehend by the study of nature, is what is usually called natural philosophy. In this the French no less excel than in the investigation of those moral truths and duties which bind society together, and of those ideas and tenets concerning abstruse matters, which have so long busied the minds of men.

The French began in the last century to shake off the yoke of intellectual despotism. The celebrated Descartes had the courage, at an epocha when ecclesiastical power was yet very formidable, to rise up in opposition to the doctrines maintained in the schools and universities, respecting a variety of subjects.

He had a mighty name to encounter, and powerful obstacles to surmount. The one was Aristotle, who had for centuries been in possession of the scholastical kingdom, and reigned with unrivaled sway in every university throughout Europe. The others were the influence and authority of the clergy, who were the absolute directors of every seat of learning, and dreaded innovations in all scientific matters.

But his resolution was invincible. In spite of long standing prejudices, in defiance

LETTER XI.

fiance of those who abetted them, he found means to introduce a system entirely opposite to that which had so long prevailed; and which, after an obstinate defence, has at length been totally expelled from France, and almost from every other country, where it had so long domineered, to the exclusion of solid knowledge and sound reasoning.

It is not solely in physical studies that Descartes opened a new method of proceeding: in points of a profounder nature he also set an example, which has been copied by numbers to a bolder extent, it has been said, than he ever intended.

He was the author of that methodical doubt, as it is stiled, which has ever since been applied to every part of philosophy. From doubting according to form, people have at last proceeded to doubt in reality. This, as it might well be expected, has effected strange alterations in many things.

LETTER XI.

The French pretend, not without reason, to have produced as illustrious philosophers and speculators as any nation; and that human nature is no less indebted to their researches, than to those of any other.

It is with equal gratitude and pleasure an impartial man will acknowledge their claim. No names in the republic of science and literature are superior to some that France can mention.

Two performances have lately been given to the learned world in that country, which do it peculiar honour, from their universal utility, as well as from the masterliness of their execution, and the immensity of the undertaking.

The one is the Encyclopedia, the other is the History of Nature. The first is the joint composition of the most able, ingenious, and learned men in France; and is a universal depository of arts and sciences, of whatever, in short, is worthy of commanding the attention of man. It is compiled with infinite labour and judgment, and digested in the most elegant and interesting manner.

The second is chiefly the work of a single individual, the famous Buffon, now dignified with the title of Count. It is written with a gracefulness, perspicuity, and precision, that recommend it no less than the importance of the subject.

Both these performances merit your purchase and your study: they certainly have nothing superior in their kind.

As you travel from sincere views of improvement, and propose to embrace every opportunity of acquiring useful knowledge, I feel no repugnance in exhorting you to unite a vigorous application to books with the study of mankind. Far from proving a mutual embarassment, they are in fact the

stanchest

stanchest and most effectual support to each other. If you examine those among your acquaintance who know the world best, and make the most splendid figure in it, you will constantly find, that they are men who have applied themselves no less to the lucubrations of the closet, than to the occupations and pastimes of social life.

It is from the consciousness of the motives that lead you abroad, that I expatiate so largely upon all that relates to literature.

You will find it, if not in greater request, upon a more agreeable footing in France than among your own countrymen. I do not think, from what I have heard elderly persons in England express on this subject, that there is the same demand for literary talents among our great people as formerly. The rage and violence of parties is a malady attended by many

many more evil consequences than men are in general aware of. It not only banishes candour from political affairs, but it extinguishes the propensity to polite knowledge; and renders individuals insensible to all other merit than that of being able to assist them in the pursuits of faction.

To this inauspicious disposition of the times, is owing the decline of that warmth with which letters were once cultivated; and that indifference for their encouragement, which is become notorious even in the perception of judicious and observant foreigners.

Voltaire takes notice somewhere, that in England *on n'écrit gueres que par esprit de parti*, little is written but from spirit of party. This stricture is rather too severe; but he might have asserted with great truth, that unless a writer knows how to render his pen serviceable in the

cause

cause of party, he will seldom rise to any considerable degree of fame and prosperity.

I do not by these reflections mean to impress you with a notion, that literary men should forswear the discussion of political subjects: on the contrary, it is shameful in a gentleman of learning not to be well conversant in such matters. What is the purport of education, but to enable men to think, speak, and write judiciously on all points of importance, and what is more important than the welfare and interests of the community at large?

It is not therefore an application to political knowledge that is reprehended; it is the exclusive encouragement given to the zeal and dexterity that are manifested in the cause of party.

In this unhappy cause it sometimes happens, that a man may render himself extremely

extremely serviceable without possessing any talents of real utility to the public. Little or no knowledge is required, but of the respective designs and circumstances of each party, their schemes, their manœuvres, the particularities respecting their heads and leaders: with all this an individual may be acquainted without any material acquaintance with any thing else.

True it is that party writers may be, and often are men of real unquestionable abilities in a variety of instances: but still it is not in this light they are brought forward, and meet with success: it is purely for having laboured in that field, which requires no other talents to cultivate than those that are above mentioned.

LETTER

LETTER XII.

PURSUANT to my expectation that you will engage with due warmth in the prosecution of gentlemanly knowledge, I will venture to review the names and characters of some of the principal personages in the French literary world; in order that you may be at no loss in selecting those whom it concerns you to make a part of your library.

At the head of French literature stands incontestably the name of Voltaire, *quem dixisse sat est.*

The French are justly proud of this celebrated man. No country ever produced a more universal genius. In history and tragedy none of his countrymen surpass him; and in epic poetry none equal him.

Corneille,

LETTER XII.

Corneille, Racine, Crebillon, and Voltaire, are the four greatest tragic poets in France, as Shakespear, Otway, Dryden, and Rowe, are esteemed in England; with this difference however, that while Shakespear enjoys undisputed supremacy with us, the French are divided in their opinions whom to prefer.

A French wit thus appreciates their merits: *Corneille peint les heros tels qu'ils devroient être; Racine tels qu'ils font; Crebillon tels qu'ils ne devroient pas etre; et Voltaire tels qu'ils fouhaiteroient de paroitre.* Corneille paints heroes as they ought to be; Racine as they are; Crebillon as they should not be; and Voltaire as they would wish to appear. This you will say is a concise method of characterising them. It is not however ill-founded; and agrees with one still shorter: *Corneille est fort; Racine, tendre; Crebillon, terrible; Voltaire, brillant.* Corneille is nervous; Racine, tender; Crebillon, dreadful; Voltaire, splendid.

Of the numerous plays written by Corneille, only six are ever acted at this day. I will mention them, that you may give them a perusal, as they are masterpieces: Le Cid, Cinna, Pompée, les Horaces, Polieucte, Rodogune. They are written with a majesty of stile and sentiments that has long charmed all Europe.

The tragedies of Racine, one or two excepted, are still acted with the highest applause. As they amount to no more than ten, read them all with attention. For purity of language, elegance and dignity of thought, and regularity of composition, the unanimous opinion of the world pronounces him second to none.

The tragedies of Crebillon and Voltaire merit no less an entire reading. Each in his peculiar line is full of beauties. The former enters deeply into the passions, and by the terrible subjects he has chosen, excites rather terror than pity. The latter
fur-

surprises, through the variety of characters he has brought on the scene. He displays every where a profound knowledge of human nature. No writer is more copious, eloquent, and pathetic. He describes men and things in the strongest and most vivid colours, and shews himself a complete master in the science of the world. It is needless to recommend such an author to your perusal.

These are the four pillars of French tragedy; *les quatres pilliers de la tragedie Françoise*, as one of their countrymen stiles them: those which form the basis of its merit and glory; and whom they scruple not openly to prefer to Sophocles and Euripides; in short, to every tragic writer either of ancient or modern date.

There are other authors of merit in the tragic line, such as Marmontel, Gresset, and Delaplace; this latter has translated Venice preserved, and other English plays.

Notwithstanding the French tragedies are all in rhime, yet I never found it obstructive of my attention to the design, the characters and action of the piece. Reflection teaches us that people do not speak in verse, much less in rhime; but if the language is otherwise unaffected, we presently forget those particularities, and attend to the main scope of the representation before us.

A favourable circumstance accompanies this method of writing. It obliges an author to polish and refine his diction much more than if mere prose were allowed. If this holds with respect to blank verse, it is still more observable in regard to rhime. Nothing can be more finished and correct than the language in French tragedies: perhaps indeed they have more correctness and refinement than is suitable to tragedy; which being the language of the passions, does not require so studied and laboured a stile.

But

But on the other hand they have this advantage: they entertain you in the closet almost as much as on the stage; and sometimes more, from the leisure you have to examine and admire the beauties of diction. The fine passages too are more easily retained.

I will not enter upon a discussion of the respective merits of the French and English tragedies. They are both excellent in their kind, as they are both adapted to the genius of the two nations. Their taste is not less different in this than in many other instances; and the English have no more right to censure that of the French, than the French that of the English.

I have sometimes been inclined to select the most beautiful passages in the French and English tragic writers, that corresponded in subject and manner of being treated. Such a selec-

selection would afford the completest opportunity of comparing them, and of tracing the national genius of both people, in the various light they view and describe events and characters, and in the feelings and sentiments to which these give rise.

The French, notwithstanding they are so gay and airy, seem to delight in tragedy more than the English, who are so much more serious and grave. The reason may be, that persons of this latter cast are more in want of some lively pastime than the others; whose native jocundity of disposition stands less in need of refreshment and support.

The French comic writers are amazingly numerous. Two of them however excel the rest beyond all comparison. I need not tell you that Moliere is one. The other, though not so well known in England, is no less esteemed and popular in France. This is Regnard; whose plays,
though

LETTER XII.

though inferior in number, yield not in merit to those of the former.

Wit, gaiety, life, merriment, and humour, fill the compositions of those two writers: not only the French, but all who understand their language, are inchanted with them: their excellencies are so various and striking, that one knows not in what either of them has any superiority. If one may venture to assign their peculiar merit, Moliere is the greatest moralist; and Regnard the greatest exciter of mirth.

I must intreat you to read them both with particular care. They will give you an ample theory of the French character in social life; and enable you to raise with ease and pleasure, that superstructure of practical knowledge, which can only arise from company and conversation.

There are also others besides these two, who have written comedies that have met
with

with vast applause. Among the foremost of these are Destouches, and La Chauſſée. This latter is the inventor of a new kind of comedy, called by the French *la Comedie larmoiante*, corresponding exactly with what we call sentimental comedy.

As I would not burthen your memory with more than is absolutely necessary, or highly useful, I think you may content yourself with reading *La Prejugé a la Mode* of *La Chauſſée*, and *le Philosophe Marié*, with *Le Glorieux* of *Destouches*; being their best productions.

The numerous plays of Boiſſy, and Marivaux, are all of the light and mirthful kind. You will see them often enough, as well as other dramatic performances of the same cast, chiefly at the Italian theatre, so called by prescription, but where all the merriest French pieces are constantly acted.

You

You will not repent however the reading of *Le Mechant* by Greffet, and *La Metromanie* by Piron, both admirable comedies.

I began with the theatre, becaufe I imagine it is the place where you will firft begin your endeavours to perfect yourfelf in the knowledge of the French language. As the *utile* concurs with the *dulce* in this fchool, I recommend it in preference to any other.

Before I clofe this prefent, I will fay a word or two on a paftime, which is in much higher requeft in France than has hitherto been its fate in England.

The French tragic opera, however deficient in mufical merit, is the firft in Europe in refpect of poetical. In proof of this, one need only mention the names of Quinaut, Fontenelle, Voltaire, and Marmontel.

Quinaut is worth your perusal. There is a softness and harmony in his versification, and a gracefulness in his ideas and sentiments, that captivate all who have the least turn for compositions of love and tenderness.

The comic opera in France is the most diverting of all elegant amusements. The native genius of the French for mirth and pleasantry, shines here in all its glory. The compositions of Vadé, Piron, and Favart, are the very summit of all that is joyous and laughable.

LETTER XIII.

BESIDES dramatic poetry, you will meet in France with excellent performances in the other Branches of that delightful art.

In lyrics, in satire, and in fables, the French have no superiors among the moderns.

moderns. Boileau, Rousseau, and La Fontaine, are classics of the first rank, whether we consider their language or their matter.

The good sense, and energy, the correctness, and elegance of Boileau, equal him to any of the ancient satirists; and his art of poetry is a work that has no superior in its kind: it rivals Horace in fire and judgment, and surpasses him in order and method. His Lutrin is the model on which the Heroi-comic poems produced since his time, have in a great measure been formed. It claims, with the Rape of the Lock, the honour of being one of the two most beautiful originals in that species of composition, written in any language.

The odes of Rousseau are the noblest performances in that line since the days of Horace. Dryden and Pope have each greatly distinguished themselves by their

cele-

celebrated ode: but allowing them all the merit which they have a right to claim, it were highly unjuſt to place them on a level with a man who has compoſed ſo large a number of odes; every one of them excelling in all the requiſites of that branch of poetry; correctneſs, elegance, copiouſneſs, and ſublimity.

La Fontaine is the favourite of all who are able to read him. He may be ſtiled the poet of nature. Eaſy, flowing, unaffected, full of wiſdom couched under the pureſt ſimplicity, and moſt inſtructive where moſt entertaining.

Read or rather meditate theſe three authors. They are the propereſt of any for promiſcuous peruſal at any time; as their ſubjects are unconnected, and the longeſt of them may be ſoon diſpatched.

I now come to that poet who has reſcued France from the reproach of not having produced an epic poem.

This

This poet you readily comprehend to be Voltaire. The French, and many beside, have long considered him as having written upon the most useful topic he could have chosen. The design of the *Henriade*, is to teach mankind the necessity of legal obedience, the calamities arising from religious dissentions, the evils concomitant on faction, and the horrors of civil war.

One of the principal beauties of this noble poem, is, that the faithfullest homage is paid to truth throughout the whole. The precepts and lessons it offers are enforced by facts, and illustrated by realities; and the embellishments are strictly consistent with the taste and ideas of the times.

It is not only an epic, but an historical poem of the most meritorious tendency; as it treats of the most important period, not only in the History of France, but in that of all Europe.

The impartial energy with which it describes the actors and transactions of that stormy period, the judicious light it throws upon events, the strict justice it does to the celebrated characters that come under representation, all contribute to interest the reader much more than the most ingenious fiction could possibly have done.

It is in this particular that Voltaire has raised himself so many adherents and admirers. He lived in an age, when the minds of men began every where to shake off the fetters of religious prejudice and fanaticism. Nothing therefore could be more acceptable to them than a work wherein the miseries originating from thence should be exposed with strength and vivacity. He also saw that the temper of the times required instruction to be blended with entertainment, and that the

universal

universal turn to politics among the European nations, would be peculiarly delighted with a performance formed on their favourite plan.

How well he has corresponded with the disposition of his cotemporaries, let the prodigious success of his work testify. He was the more praise-worthy for coinciding with the general inclination, as it was manly and laudable. Mere fiction, however decorated by genius, was no longer able to please. The accompanyment of truth was demanded, in order to render it palatable to men of thought and judgment.

Conformably to these maxims, his poem is in some measure a continued lecture of the soundest policy. It inculcates every maxim necessary to form the statesman, the hero, and the good citizen. If history is philosophy teaching by example, the *Henriade* is certainly one of the noblest
of

of all philosophical instructions, as it employs so forcibly the united advantages of history and poetry.

Of all French poems, look oftenest to this and to the excellent notes with which it is accompanied: they breathe a spirit of sense, virtue, and judiciousness; and they contain abundance of interesting and curious anecdotes.

Voltaire has written a variety of other poetical performances, all of unquestionable merit; but the Henriade, and his tragedies, are what I chiefly commend to your perusal.

Next to those I have been mentioning, you may dedicate some of your leisure hours to *Gresset* and *Racine*, son to the famous tragic poet of that name. This latter is author of two very remarkable poems, on religion, and divine grace: the subjects are

are very serious; but he has treated them in a very elegant and pleasing manner.

While we are engaged in this review of French poetry, it may not be amiss to say something of the poetical works of the famous philosopher of *Sans Soucy*. This, I suppose, you know to be no less a personage than the King of Prussia.

Though not a Frenchman, he has written a number of excellent things in prose and verse in the French language. It is incumbent on every gentleman to be acquainted with the sentiments of such a man as the King of Prussia; not because he is a king, but because he is a great king, one of the greatest that ever existed.

But independent of his exalted rank, his works are worthy of a royal pen. He writes as he governs, with wisdom, power, and majesty. His thoughts are like his

actions,

actions, great, uncommon, surprising; and denote every where an extraordinary character.

LETTER XIV.

THE French have long been noted for romances and novels. They overflowed the last century like an inundation; and vitiated during a considerable time the taste of almost all Europe.

When people of curiosity and leisure, are at the pains of perusing some of the voluminous productions of that sort, which were in such request at that æra, it cannot fail to astonish them, that compositions so wild, so absurd, and so bombastic, should find such multitudes of readers.

There are none of them deserving the least attention. In fact, they are totally forgotten at this day. The taste of the French

French nation has long since undergone an entire alteration; and will admit of nothing that is not correct and regular.

But though they reject the turgid and unnatural romances of former days, they are willing to admit of novels written with elegance of stile and probability of incidents.

Some of the most approved writers in this line are Marmontel, Crebillon, son to the celebrated tragic author, Marivaux; and Prevot, known for his numerous translations from the English.

Among the novels of prime note must be classed *les Memoires de la Vie du Comte de Grammont*, by Hamilton. It is an original in point of stile and of method; full of wit and pleasantry; and keeping truth in view in the midst of laughter and merriment.

As time is precious, especially to a traveller, stint yourself chiefly to these: or if you cannot refrain from others, consult the most judicious of your French acquaintance, which have the vogue of the day; that being usually the principal merit of such productions.

From the severity of this stricture, I am bound however, by all the laws of criticism, to except *Gil Blas*, and *le Diable Boiteaux*, both written by Le Sage. Never was a truer and more entertaining picture of human life and manners exhibited than the former, nor a keener and more witty satire on vice and folly than the latter. His *Bachelier de Salamanque* may deservedly keep them company.

I cannot deny that there are abundance of other ingenious performances in the same line, written in French: but I am at the same time so desirous that you should apply yourself to something more solid

LETTER XIV.

solid and profitable, that I do not chuse to enlarge upon this subject.

You will meet but with too many opportunities of sacrificing time to such amusements. Numbers of the gay world read nothing else but such books. You will find them too often on the tables of the literati, and the toilets of both your male and female acquaintances at their country houses; for here the French of all ages and denominations deem themselves at liberty to think of nothing but mere pastime and pleasure.

There are two works in the French language, which some have thought proper to mention in the catalogue of romances: but they certainly deserve a higher place: these are Telemachus, and the Travels of Cyrus.

The first, though written in prose; is unquestionably the beautifullest poem in every other respect that ever appeared in the French Tongue. The second is an exquisite selection and arrangement of historical facts, connected together by a judicious fable, tending to form and enlighten the understanding, and at the same time to enrich the memory with a large portion of useful knowledge.

No modern production has met with more applause than Telemachus. It has indeared the name of Fenelon, its illustrious author, to the whole world. But the Travels of Cyrus have not, if I may venture an opinion, been sufficiently diffused in the literary circles of Europe.

On their first appearance they had some enemies to encounter in the field of criticism: but their defects were so slight, and so readily rectified, that they soon gained their author, the celebrated Ramsay, a prodigious reputation. The ingenuity and erudition so judiciously blended in this perform-

LETTER XIV.

performance, render it of the most extensive utility, and afford equal pleasure and instruction.

It may not be improper to take notice, that this is another instance of a foreigner producing a work of prime merit in the French language; Mr. Ramsay being a native of Scotland.

I will conclude this short epistle by advising you to compare the French translation of Tom Jones by Monsf. Delaplace, with the English original. Study the various dictions, examine the different turns of both languages: this will give you a complete idea of their respective idioms; and enable you upon occasion to translate with facility and correctness.

LETTER XV.

I NOW come to that branch of literature wherein the merit of the French is confessedly very eminent.

This branch is history, till very lately too much neglected in England, but long since cultivated in France with great assiduity and success.

The first French book of this kind I would earnestly wish you to read, is *Discours sur l'Histoire Universelle*, by Bossuet. It is a chronological account of the world until the close of the eighth century. It is written with great eloquence, and is full of learning and instruction.

Les Discours sur l'Histoire Ecclesiastique, by Fleury, is another object I must point out to your attention. They are the very pith and essence of all that is worth knowing on this matter. Peruse them with care and diligence, and do it more than once.

His *Traité des Etudes* claims also your notice. It is an historical abstract of the ancient methods of studying, with excellent directions what books, and in what manner to study.

The History of France, by Father Daniel, is the best extant. I do not propose him as a faultless writer: but he is copious, exact, and, considering his situation in life, more impartial than could almost be expected. His stile is correct and flowing; and though not remarkable for energy, is clear, unaffected, and altogether very pleasing.

A work which, for its intrinsic and evident utility, claims a high consideration in the republic of letters, is the Ancient History,

History, by Rollin. If any man deserved well of youth, it is certainly he. No one has so greatly facilitated the means of that knowledge which becomes a gentleman. He wrote with an eloquence and dignity befitting his subject; and well deserves the words I have seen under a print of him, *Lege et relege*. Forget not Crevier, the elegant continuator of his History of Rome.

Rapin Thoiras should be read by an Englishman on two accounts: he has written the history of our country; and he has done it with impartiality. His stile is rather dry and frigid; but his judgment and penetration make ample amends.

Father Orleans has treated of the same subject in a far more entertaining manner. As you have years and discretion sufficient to think for yourself, you may peruse him without any danger to those principles

LETTER XVI.

which ought ever to be uppermost in an Englishman.

Vertot is a writer whose diction is equally correct and eloquent. He is full of entertainment; and few authors are more in request with their countrymen. His Revolutions of Sweden and of Rome are highly esteemed, the latter especially.

The History of the famous League of Cambray against the Republic of Venice, by Dubos, is a performance of singular merit: it displays a fund of political knowledge, very curious and interesting to such as are desirous of being well acquainted with that important and celebrated period. It is written in a noble and elevated stile, and has met with the universal acceptance of all Europe.

A composition of peculiar merit is the Life of Henry the Fourth of France, by Perefixe. It was designed for the instruction of Lewis the Fourteenth, by the author, who was his preceptor. It abounds with excellent paſſages, and is incomparably the beſt account of the reign and actions of that great monarch: it is a book which every prince ought to read.

There is an abridgment of the French hiſtory, written of late years by Monſ. Henaut, a man of uncommon abilities and ſagacity: it is extolled as a moſt perfect and finiſhed performance.

St. Real is an author whoſe hiſtorical pieces have met with extraordinary praiſe. The Spaniſh conſpiracy againſt Venice is unanimouſly allowed to be a maſter-piece.

The learned Tillemont's Hiſtory of the Roman Emperors, is written with an exactitude and care, and with a correctneſs and prĕciſion of ſtile that have procured him the higheſt reputation.

All

LETTER XV. 123

All these writers, I doubt not, you will bestow the utmost diligence in perusing. I could have mentioned many others very deserving; but these are incontestably the first upon the historical catalogue.

If I have omitted the celebrated Abbé Raynal, it is not because I have forgotten him; but that his writings are of a particular class, being a mixture of history and philosophy, blending and supporting each other in a manner that renders him an original in this sort of composition.

I recommend him to your most attentive perusal. His head and his heart seem of the purest and sublimest frame. No writer appears more sincerely zealous for the common happiness of society; none more determined to promote it by the uniform tenour of all his writings.

Another historical performance of an original nature, is the Considerations on the

the Rise and Decline of Rome, by the illustrious Montesquieu.

I will not have the vanity to say any thing in praise of a work that is above all commendation. The concurrent testimony of all Europe has long pronounced it to be the noblest monument of historical wisdom that ever yet appeared. It is read by all nations as a book of oracles; and has left nothing to be added on the subjects it has treated.

A person of great rank and dignity, and of no less discernment and sagacity, has intitled this famous performance The Roman History, written for the use of Kings and Ministers of state. This is a compendious but fully expressive elogium.

I will close this review of the principal historians among the French with Voltaire. He is by accurate judges esteemed not only one of the best, but the very best historian

historian that nation has produced. He excels in all the qualities required in that province; imagination, fire, elocution, judgment; he possesses them all in perfection: his language is elegance itself, and his stile is full of grandeur and energy: his characters are drawn to the life; and his descriptions are pictures that strike the eye, and turn his readers into spectators.

His History of Charles the Twelfth of Sweden, and that of Lewis the Fourteenth of France, have immortalized them together with himself. You cannot be too much conversant in both these admirable performances.

Will you permit me to add a word in favour of three compositions, from which, as I have derived much pleasure, I flatter myself you will do the same. These are the History of Lewis the Eleventh of France, by Duclos, that of Sobieski, by Coyer, and the Life of the Emperor Julian, surnamed

surnamed the Philosopher by some, and by others the Apostate, written by Lableterie.

Of all branches of polite knowledge, history is the most useful, as well as the most ornamental to a gentleman. It is that which teaches him the science of states and nations, and fits him to make a figure on the great theatre of the world.

An English gentleman should be particularly versed in history; not only that of his own country, but those of as many others as he can possibly spare time to read and study. It is chiefly by an application of this kind that he will become of public utility: he will learn what courses to avoid, by contemplating the calamities they have occasioned; and what measures to pursue, by considering the benefits they have produced.

Men

Men of rank and fortune in some other countries, may doubtless attain the same knowledge; but in them it will prove inactive and fruitless: it is only in states blest with liberty that such a science is not a dead letter to the possessor.

Study therefore history beyond all other subjects. It will bring you most honour and profit: it will enable you to shine in public deliberations, and to act upon necessary occasions. It will, in short, supply the demands of both theory and practice.

But were you destined to spend your life at a distance from the busy scenes of the political world, still it is highly becoming an individual of condition above the vulgar in this land of liberty, to qualify himself to judge of what passes on the stage of public transactions.

In this light, history is an amusement and a benefit: it relieves our leisure hours, and

and teaches us at the same time what to applaud and what to condemn: it is attended also with another consequence of still greater weight: when people in power know that their conduct will undergo the examination of an intelligent public, able to weigh their actions in the scale of historical comparison, and to judge of the present by the past, they will certainly pay more deference to its opinion, and will endeavour to deserve its approbation by the rectitude of their measures.

History however can never be again on the same footing of splendour it was in ages of old.

Whatever historians France, or any modern nation may have produced, let us not imagine they bear any proportion in point of merit to those of antiquity.

Two reasons concur to decide in favour of these: they were born and bred in republics,

publics, and enjoyed an unlimited freedom in the manifestation of their thoughts; and they wrote in a superior language.

Should any one object the examples of Livy and Tacitus, let them recollect that the first wrote at a time, when tho' liberty was opprest, it was not extinguished. Augustus did not wish to appear its enemy; on the contrary, he always spoke with the utmost respect of the sovereignty of the Roman people: hence a great degree of liberty remained, not only in appearance, but also in reality.

Tacitus wrote under the Emperor Trajan, the greatest friend to the rights and liberties of mankind that ever sat upon a throne.

But the historians of modern ages have not had the same advantages. To say nothing of the inferiority of their language, which however is a weighty consideration,

K they

they were the subjects of monarchs, and had measures to keep.

From these two causes, we never can expect such historians to arise again as those of Greece and Rome. One alone of these causes is sufficient to rank them above modern writers; and one of them is sure to subsist, were the other to cease.

Whatever degree of liberty may become the portion of mankind, there is no likelihood that in any future age a language will be formed equal to the Greek or Latin.

In this respect we must be content to yield perpetual precedence to the ancients: happy if we can compensate this deficiency, by equalling them in that exquisiteness of sense and judgment, for which they are not less conspicuous than the unrivaled beauty of their language.

LETTER

LETTER XVI.

AFTER viewing the ſtate of hiſtory in France, let us next proceed to that of their oratory.

The ſame reaſons aſſigned for the inferiority of their hiſtorians, are equally concluſive for the inferiority of their orators.

In this department, from the frame of our conſtitution, we are unqueſtionably much ſuperior to the French.

Nature has given them undoubtedly as brilliant and as ſolid faculties as to any other nation: this fully appears by the excellence of their productions on thoſe ſubjects where they have nothing to fetter their abilities.

But

But even in the field of eloquence, as it confifts of various parts, they fhine occafionally with undeniable luftre.

This field is very fpacious. It is not therefore to be expected that any fingle capacity fhall fill it completely.

The vaft variety it affords muft of courfe open various careers to range in. Not to lofe ourfelves however in too indefinite a view, let us confine our examination to the principal branches of this wide fpreading tree, in order to afcertain with precifion thofe which the French have cultivated with moft fuccefs.

Oratory may be comprehended in fix divifions, the fenate, the bar, the pulpit, the academy, the ftage, and common difcourfe.

In the firft of thefe we cannot imagine that any people will diftinguifh themfelves, selves, unless they enjoy a free constitution. Debates on public matters, carried on with the utmost freedom and unrestraint of sentiments, are the only soil where this noblest species of eloquence will prosper.

Until therefore a revolution happens in the government of France, the French must resign all pretensions to figure with any distinction in this line.

In the second, a people, without the possession of constitutional liberty, may appear with much splendour; but not however with as much grandeur and dignity, as if the laws alone had the supreme decision.

Hence, notwithstanding the correctness and elegance that characterise the pleadings at the French bar, they are evidently deficient in that fortitude and resoluteness of expression, which attend causes here wherein the state is in any wise concerned.

As both nations profess the same religion, one would think they would resemble each other in the manner of inculcating its doctrines and morals: yet even here the native disposition of the two people is remarkable. The French are warm, impetuous, and strongly swayed by imagination: the English cool, sedate, and chiefly guided by reasoning.

Impartiality requires it, however, to be acknowledged that appearances are in favour of the French. Whether their preachers possess greater talents than ours, or whether the French are more easily moved, you will often see an audience almost universally drowned in tears, on occasions which admit of the pathetic. This neither you, nor I, nor any person of my acquaintance, I am positively certain,

tain, from having asked the question, ever saw in England.

The honours of academical eloquence, to speak the language of card-players, may be divided. I have read a pretty good number of orations spoken at the university meetings, and college-solemnities, in both countries, without finding myself inclined to adjudge the prize to either of the parties.

The elocution of the stage is a very disputable point. In all countries there seems a standard of speaking, calculated to please the natives, and none else; or only such as have by long residence naturalized themselves to the place. It is not equitable for this reason to pronounce definitively upon this subject; as it is not the matter spoken, but the manner of speaking it, that is in litigation.

It may however be surmised, that as the French plays are mostly in metre, this cannot fail to influence, in some measure, the pronunciation of the actors, and to make it appear more studied than if they were in prose: this is visible in our tragedies in England; where notwithstanding the versification is less fettered than in France, being only in blank verse, whereas the French is in rhime, still there is a stiffness of speech, of which even the best of our actors can seldom divest themselves.

The agreeableness in the discourse of people of education in France is well known. Their conversation pleases not only from the chearfulness of their disposition, but equally from its elegance, and their choice and command of words and phrases.

In this latter species of eloquence, I apprehend you will find the French uncommonly expert. The vivacity and quickness of conception which characterise them, are no where more perceptible than when engaged in a tête-a-tête discussion: their manner

manner on such occasions is very prepossessing; and the people of other countries, besides our own, have often experienced to their cost, how much the French excel in the science of carrying their point, whenever it is to be effected by the arts of persuasion.

We have now gone through the ostensible divisions of oratory. But it is made up of many other parts, small indeed and almost imperceptible, but very effectual and conducive to the ends for which they are employed.

A word sometimes is worth a long oration. Even the look or accent with which it is pronounced, has been amazingly decisive. I appeal to those who have seen variety of scenes in life: they best can tell how often affairs have been decided by such means.

In

In these instantaneous exertions of thought the French are admirable. If therefore they are deficient in the grander and more striking parts of eloquence, let us frankly allow them to be complete masters of this one; which is perhaps of more diffusive utility in the general affairs of private life.

After saying thus much on a subject, which I thought it necessary you should examine with some attention, let us now proceed to enquire into the merit of those individuals in France, who have distinguished themselves by their eloquence, as far as their subjects enabled them, and other circumstances permitted.

I have already observed, that none of that eloquence which flourished in the popular assemblies at Rome and Athens, can be found in France.

LETTER XVI.

But in default of this, the French courts of judicature have produced speakers of great eminence in judicial matters. The printed speeches and law dissertations of the late Chancellor D'Aguesseau, are highly deserving your perusal. He was unquestionably a man of the sublimest parts, and one of the most perfect and complete orators ever produced in France. It is a real detriment to literature, that so few specimens remain of his talents for oratory: his compositions were looked upon by his cotemporaries as master-pieces; and you will, I doubt not, be of the same opinion when you have perused those he has left. What has been said of D'Aguesseau may with equal justice be applied to the illustrious Lamvignon, first President of the Parliament of Paris a century ago.

The lawyer in France, who has been principally celebrated for introducing regularity and method into the business of pleading, is Patru. Read him with attention:

tention: he will teach you, together with elegance and purity of language, many particulars relating to the French laws, very deserving of your knowledge.

The famous Pelisson, known for his other performances, has written a defence of the unhappy Minister of state, Fouquet, his friend and patron, which is esteemed a piece of eloquence inferior to none in the French language. Read it together with his explanation of the institutes of the Emperor Justinian, the best that was ever written, and containing an excellent collection of moral and political reflections.

If you can prevail on yourself to search with patience into the mass of law tracts and speeches, with which France abounds at least as much as England, you will meet with some excellent productions to repay your trouble.

Should you find yourself thus inclined, the interval between the death of Lewis the
Thir-

Thirteenth, and the conclusion of the civil feuds during the minority of his son Lewis the Fourteenth, will furnish you with the most interesting materials.

In pulpit oratory the French have long made an illustrious figure. Bourdaloue, a Jesuit, was the first who regulated and methodised the art of preaching. He is nervous and solid, and reasons with great justness and dignity. He is the Tillotson of France.

In the same line shines with great splendour, Massillon; whose sermons many prefer to those of the former, on account of his more intimate and practical knowledge of the polite world, and the less degree of austerity contained in his doctrine.

You can surely dedicate a few spare hours to read such of their sermons as are upon subjects of a generally interesting nature.

LETTER XVI.

There is a species of pulpit oratory which has been more succesfully cultivated in France than in any other part of Christendom, that of funeral orations. Nothing approaches the grandeur and magnificence of those composed by Bossuet and Flechier. A pathetic sublimity of sentiments reigns in both, conformable to the gravity of their subjects. Force of language, beauty of images, elevation of thought, richness and vivacity of description, all conspire to fill their readers with pleasure and admiration. Doubtless you will be one, after such an account of them; which is no more than strict truth.

Of the academical orators I will only mention one, Porée; some of whose Latin orations have been translated into French with as much correctness and elegance as in the language he wrote them. He is full of wit and beautiful sentiments; and well deserves your perusal; were it only to give you an idea of that sort of eloquence

quence which is the taste of French universities.

I need not, I suppose, touch on the article of stage elocution. You will see enough of it to judge for yourself, besides that it is of a nature to admit of no other judgment.

On the dexterity of the French in the art of ingratiating themselves by the agreeableness of their conversation, enough has been already said. I will only add, that you will find it no loss of time, should you study to imitate those among them, whose excellence in this particular, you may have occasion to observe. The way to imitate them is to frequent their company, and attend to their manner of discoursing. A footing of intimacy, and an earnest desire to profit by their example, will hardly fail of accomplishing this aim; as we generally resemble those whom we esteem, and with whom we continually associate.

I will

I will conclude this article by advising you to hear the best preachers and pleaders. It will prove, you may depend upon it, a very agreeable recreation. I speak from experience. You will find the audiences of both composed of the most intelligent people; a proof that they are deserving of your attention.

LETTER XVII.

I HAVE in a preceding epistle mentioned the progress that philosophical studies have made in France.

I will now give you a list of those whom I think it your interest to peruse. In this I intend to be concise, and to lead you no further into this province, than will prove of essential service. Superfluity in these matters is of great disservice to a man who means to take an active part in the world.

I shall

LETTER XVII.

I shall therefore restrain myself to those who will powerfully contribute to the improvement of your mind, and to the necessary increase of your knowledge.

Neither shall I speak of physical or mathematical writers. As you have acquired as much of those branches, as it is your intention to be master of, I shall not needlessly enter into an enumeration of the many useful performances of that kind that have been composed in France.

What I chiefly propose, is to lay before you those productions which investigate the operations of the mind, and cultivate the faculties of reasoning; together with such as teach us to examine with a philosophic eye the various transactions in civil and moral life, and enable us to draw just conclusions from facts and occurrences; such, in a word, as conduce to the formation of a solid system of thinking and judging of what passes in the world.

L Among

Among the moſt uſeful publications in the laſt century, is that, entitled *l'Art de Penſer*. It is the beſt compendium of logick that ever was compoſed; clear, methodical, and though profound, remarkbly intelligible and entertaining. Set apart ſome portion of your time purpoſedly to give it a thorough and attentive reading.

Another book much anterior to this, but equally excellent in its kind, is *La Sageſſe*, by the famous Charron. It is an orderly and ſagacious deſcription of human nature, and of all that conſtitutes its happineſs or miſery. The language is obſolete; but full of life and energy. With the aſſiſtance of ſome of your French acquaintance, you will ſoon be able to comprehend it with eaſe.

You muſt not forget a cotemporary of Charron, the ſtill more famous Montagne. He is in the lively and facetious, what the other is in the ſerious and grave. In the multiplicity of ſubjects he treats of

with

with so much wit, sense, and learning, you will find a perpetual fund of amusement as well as of instruction. Long has he been the delight of all intelligent readers; and I doubt not he will be yours.

La Bruiere and Rochefoucault I need hardly remind you of. You know their worth too well to be without them. The first has drawn pictures from the life with a truth and exactness that procured him the unanimous admiration of all who knew the originals.

The second has depicted, with a discernment and energy that were never exceeded, the nature and operations of the human passions, their causes and effects, their dominion and tyranny over the heart and mind. This he does in so lively and agreeable a manner, that while he seems to have no other end than to amuse, he conveys the most solid instruction.

The philosophical works of Alembert, Diderot, Maupertuis, and Voltaire, claim your particular notice. They are worthy of the reputation of their authors; and treat of subjects highly interesting to mankind.

Those of Bayle are perhaps too voluminous to recommend to you for an entire perusal at present. Keep him however in petto. The time will come when he will prove a source of the highest entertainment. With all his failings, he is a striking proof, that wit, vivacity, and the talent of entertaining, are reconcilable with the most immense erudition.

Fontenelle is a writer with whom you must not neglect an acquaintance. Beside his mathematical works, he has written a variety of others; out of which, select for your reading, *Dialogues des Morts, Histoire des Oracles, Eloges des Academiciens, Pluralité des Mondes.*

De

LETTER XVII.

De l'Esprit, by Helvetius, is an equally profound and agreeable explanation of the influence exerted over the minds of men by the various events and circumstances of life. It is the natural history of the internal and intellectual faculties of mankind, as they are set in motion by the force of inclination, the power of education and prejudice, the concurrence of accidents, the caprice of fortune, and the torrent of the times.

The celebrity of Rousseau of Geneva, will undoubtedly engage you to read his works. He is in every respect an original. He thinks and writes alone, and props himself on no other man's doctrine or authority: his ideas and his arguments flow from his own mind; and you will have the satisfaction of knowing the opinions of one who borrows none, and who freely imparts without fear or favour, the notions he has formed of men and things. Doubtless he deals much in speculation; but the thoughts of so extraordinary a person will always deserve weight. Having gone through a variety of scenes, and encountered many hardships in the course of his life, he must have seen much, and necessarily performed an active part on many occasions. His lucubrations therefore may be reasonably deemed equally the fruit of reflection and of experience.

I hesitated whether I should, while speaking of speculative writers, mention two that are very eminent in the logical and metaphysical class; Malbranche and Crousas. The cause of my hesitation was my aversion to fatigue your mind with such profound disquisitions. But as you have gone through Locke's Essay on the Understanding, I will not discourage a survey of these. You will find Crousas the most solid and satisfactory. Let these, however, be the *ne plus ultra* of such abstract studies. I am no friend to them: they demand an uncommon share of labour;

LETTER XVII.

bour; and after a great deal of toil, one is not properly repaid; as they leave us in the fame ftate of uncertainty in which they found us.

For thefe reafons you fhould be careful not to intangle yourfelf in purfuits of this kind: when begun, the very difficulties attending them are a fpur to a ftudious mind. We are loth to give over an attempt founded on a confidence in our capacity. Pride produces perfeverance; and perfeverance expence of time to no purpofe. After much trouble, to ufe a vulgar but fignificant expreffion, we have nothing to fhew for our pains. For what other name can we give to mere opinions combated by others; and which we have no more right to infift upon, than opponents have on theirs.

I fpeak experimentally on thefe matters. I wifh you therefore to adopt the determination I have taken; to wafte no more time

time in vain researches. There are things so inscrutable in their nature, that the world ought long since to have stigmatized those who investigate them, as idlers, and authors of the detriment occasioned by the misemployment of abilities that might have been converted to pursuits of real and visible utility.

LETTER XVIII.

IN the present epistle I intend to offer to your consideration, such miscellaneous writings as come under no particular denomination, and can only therefore be classed in the general list of polite literature.

Rollin's *Belles Lettres* claim the first mention. A work translated into all the languages of Europe.

A performance which has deservedly met with a most gracious reception every where, is the *Lettres Persannes*, by Montesquieu.

It was his *Coup d'Essai*, his first trial of skill; and prepared the world to expect those master-pieces that flowed afterwards from his pen.

The design of this work is obvious on perusing the first pages. It procured him enemies among the narrow-minded; but all the sensible people in Europe were charmed with that ingenious review of the manners and notions of the times, and with those instructive and well-founded strictures, with which it is so judiciously interspersed.

The principal production of this extraordinary genius is *L'esprit des Loix*. It is incontestibly the noblest original in its kind that was ever produced by the wit of man. It has had the fate of all such works, to be commended by the world at large, and attacked by envy, malice, and ignorance.

But

But there is no necessity for expatiating on a performance of which the vast utility is so widely acknowledged. Allowing that some faults may be found in it, they are but thinly scattered: its perfections will meet you in every page. You will be charmed with his stile, astonished at his learning, and every where improved by the profound wisdom of his observations.

Let this book be your constant companion. Meditate its contents, and consult it on every occasion, as you would do the instructions given you by authority.

Next perhaps in national utility to this immortal work, is that intitled *les Memoires de Sully*. The ground plot was prepared by that great minister; language and order have been added by the Abbé Deleclufe. You cannot prize it too much in its present form.

Mabli's

LETTER XVIII.

Mabli's *Droit public de l'Europe* will not improperly follow the perusal of the last. It is a publication of great utility in the political world.

The French hold in high and just esteem that performance of Dubos called *Reflections sur la Poesie, la Peinture, et la Musique.* It is a learned, philosophical, and truly curious dissertation on each of these arts.

Madame de Sevigne's Letters are the most pleasing account extant of the court of Lewis the Fourteenth. They are the completest models of the epistolary stile; full of elegance, vivacity, and politeness: no language affords a more entertaining collection: they will give you a complete idea of the stile of living, and manners of the people of rank in France during the last century.

Another cotemporary writer is peculiarly worthy of your notice. This is the famous

mous St. Evremont; who spent a great part of his life in our island, and enjoyed the good-will and esteem of all the literati, as well as the people of fashion, in his time, both in France and England. His stile and manner are that of a gentleman. He was well acquainted with all the great characters and transactions of his days, and has transmitted many of them to posterity in masterly colours. He has written on a variety of subjects, and displays every where the profoundness of a philosopher, no less than the gaiety of a man of the world: he abounds with curious anecdotes; and is, on the whole, one of the most entertaining writers in the French language.

Among the French critics, let me remind you of Bossu, and Bouhours: read the *Traité sur le Poeme epique* of the first; and as much of the last as you can: no man writes purer French, nor with more taste.

The

LETTER XVIII. 157

The works of Rapin the jesuit may be classed with theirs, and deserve no less your perusal.

Of the many memoirs that abound in France, those of Cardinal Derets, and of Gourville, hold the foremost rank. The Cardinal wrote as he lived, with force and grandeur, but with much irregularity. *Nil fuit unquam tam dispar sibi.*

Gourville is the precise contrast. Cool, orderly, under an appearance of simplicity one discovers a man who measures every step he takes, and weighs every word he speaks; he never swerves from this rule; and you will find him constantly *qualis ab incepto.*

Permit me to conclude what I have already said concerning Voltaire, by desiring you to except none of his writings from your perusal. Prose or verse, read them all, and you will read them more than once.

In

In this eulogium of Voltaire, and perhaps in the commendations given to some other French writers, it is not meant to recommend indiscriminately every part or design of their writings; it is on the contrary much to be lamented, that an author so very esteemable in other points, should in religious respects be so dangerous, especially to his young readers.

La Condamine's *Journal d'un Voyage a l'Amerique Espagnole*, together with his other travels. Le Blanc's *Lettres d'un François sur les Anglois*, and most of the publications by the Marquis D'Argens, will afford you instruction and entertainment.

Add to these, Muralt's observations on the French and the English Nations, and upon travelling, a truly philosophical performance.

Deshoulieres, La Fayette, and Lambert, are three ladies who deserve commemoration in this catalogue. The poetry of the first
is

is much esteemed; the second wrote the first sensible and elegant novels that ever appeared in France, *la Princesse de Cleves*, and *Zayde*; and the third distinguished herself by several pieces written with great delicacy and judiciousness.

Madame de Graffigny, author of *Lettres Peruviennes*, is not unworthy of their company.

Were I inclined to set before you all the French writers worthy of your perusal, I should swell this list to much larger dimensions: but as I propose only to lead you to the acquaintance of the most necessary, useful, or entertaining, I think the present number will answer this end. If you can, within the compass of the time you intend to remain in France, read over even the principal of these, it will be an effort of application, of which few, if any of our modern young travellers, would willingly admit the idea.

To the books of amusement above mentioned, let me, however, add two of rather a studious complexion; but which you must not omit purchasing, and often consulting, if you seriously mean to make yourself that complete master of French, which you have often declared was your fixed determination.

These two books are *la Grammaire Françoise* by Restaut, and *les Synonimes François* by Girard. They are the two performances of most solid utility for the perfect attainment of the grammatical purity, elegance, and precision, of the French language. The great pains taken by those two gentlemen in the composition of their respective performances, are well known, and have not been lost: they are clear, methodical, and copious without redundance; and may be proposed as models to those who in other nations are inclined to undertake works of the same nature, for the benefit of those who study their language.

Re-

LETTER XVIII.

Reſtaut is excellent in his kind; but being tied down to the uſual form preſcribed in treating of grammatical matters, he will prove more inſtructive than amuſing: but Girard is a writer of a very peculiar claſs; in giving you the preciſe ſignification of words, he will at the ſame time furniſh you with a variety of ideas; many of them profound and philoſophical, and all of them beneficial and entertaining.

I will cloſe this epiſtle, by adviſing you to read the tranſlation of Quintus Curtius by Vaugelas in one hand, and the original in the other. I have found eſſential benefit by this method of ſtudying the French.

Do the ſame by Ablancour's Verſion of Cæſar's Commentaries, and of Tacitus. You will find no great labour in all this, but experience will ſoon teach you the utility reſulting from it.

LETTER XIX.

FRANCE is the country which first gave birth to those periodical productions in the literary world, that afford a stated amusement and instruction to the lovers and cultivators of learning.

Le Journal des Savans is the most ancient, and by numbers esteemed superior to the others in point of merit, as well as of antiquity.

Le Mercure de France followed it; but *non passibus æquis.*

Le Journal de Trevoux began with the present century. The Jesuits had the conducting of it, till their final dissolution, and acquitted themselves highly to the satisfaction of the intelligent public.

Le

LETTER XIX.

Le Journal de Verdun commenced much about the same period, and has always subsisted with reputation.

Le Journal Oeconomique is of about forty years standing; and has its share of merit as well as the rest.

I should have told you, the two first made their appearance about the seventieth year of the last century.

The motive for making this enumeration, is that you may, at your leisure hours, look occasionally into each of them. They will serve to convey an adequate idea of the manner with which the French conduct undertakings of this nature.— They will at the same time enable you to form a comparison between the merits of their literati thus employed and those among ourselves who follow the same occupation. But above all, it will empower you to take an extensive view of the taste in learning and literature of the French nation at large. You will feel the pulse of their present capacity and inclination for study: you will discover in what branches they chiefly delight: you will weigh in the surest scale of comparison the number of meritorious performances that appear in France and in England; and you will have a clear sight of those studies which respectively preponderate in both nations.

This latter consideration is of the highest importance to such as make it their business to examine the different characters of people, in order to strike the balance of their actual worth.

Nothing is more common than to appreciate nations by their former merits; but surely nothing is more erroneous and absurd: all have had, or will have their days of splendour: to judge of what they are by what they have been, is not admissible, fible, therefore, according to the rule of found reafon.

It happens very fortunately for the prefent times, that thofe nations whom it is of moſt importance to know beſt, are the moſt forward to make themfelves known.

The French and the Engliſh, indifputably the firſt nations upon earth, are continually employed in elucidating every thing that concerns them, and in laying before the world the whole fyſtem of their proceedings. There is nothing fo minute but what has undergone an inveſtigation; nothing fo fecret, but what has been brought to light. Their government, their politics, their trade and commerce, their national advantages or deficiencies, have all been expofed to the univerfal view of their neighbours. All Europe indeed has fo well profited by their endeavours to render themfelves noted, that their fituation and circumſtances are as well known in other countries as in their own.

But while they have been so busy in laying themselves open to the public, they have been no less industrious in prying into the state of others. There is no country in Europe, or rather in the four quarters of the globe, which they have not inspected, and of which they have not described the peculiar excellencies and defects, and examined whatever had any reference to themselves with the utmost acuteness and diligence.

From the rivality long subsisting between these two nations, it is natural to infer that they have been especially attentive to all that concerned each other.

Nothing accordingly deserving of the least notice has been omitted in this reciprocal inspection. Virtues and vices, great and good qualities with their opposite blemishes, public transactions and private occurrences, events of the highest consequence and matters of the least, all have

have been examined and scrutinised on both sides with surprising minuteness.

In a revisal of this kind, such things as were most accessible to their mutual curiosity, must of course have been subjected to the strictest scrutiny.

Among these the learning and literature of both people were the most susceptible of discussion. These are no where accounted *Arcana Imperii*, secrets of state, improper to be divulged; on the contrary, they are held out as proofs to the world, of the merit and prosperity of those nations where they flourish, and as motives to gain them esteem and respect.

Every step has therefore been taken to display their eminence in these particulars. It has been said, that in the triumphant days of the Roman empire, there were individuals employed in recording *Romanorum acta diurna,* the daily transactions of the Romans. The spirit of such an institution has been completely fulfilled by the various compilers and examiners of all that is done, spoken, or written, in France or in England.

But the latter being the fairest and clearest object of discussion, it has consequently attracted the notice of the majority of speculators in both countries.

Notwithstanding the literary pursuits of a nation may not strike at first, as leading to any material discoveries of its actual state in points of importance, yet to the clear-sighted, they will probably appear to contain very essential information.—Though they may not ascertain the designs and prospects of persons in power, they shew what is of far greater weight, the temper, disposition, abilities, and exertions of the bulk of a people. As it is on them the grandeur of a nation depends, their neighbours are deeply interested in

the

LETTER XIX.

the knowledge of what they are prosecuting, or inclined and able to perform.

This knowledge may be obtained with great precision, by consulting those periodical productions, that take a general review of all that passes in the whole circle of arts and sciences; in short, throughout the extensive empire of wit, ingenuity, and invention.

It is in this light that I have thought it very proper to recommend to your attention, the literary journals, and similar performances, that will so often occur to your sight: no depth of application will be necessary to make them subservient to the purposes I have mentioned.

LETTER XX.

BESIDES the journals I have indicated in the preceding, there are a variety of others very much deserving your notice,

tice, and that will completely enable you to form a just and adequate idea of the turn and disposition of the French, at present.

The most useful and popular of these periodical publications, is, in my opinion, *Le Journal politique et litteraire.* It contains the general news of all Europe, both political and literary, and is published thrice a month.

Le Journal de Paris is a minute and curious detail of what passes in that metropolis.

Le Journal ecclesiastique is an account of all things relating to the clergy, such as preferments to benefices and dignities in the church, books published and opinions maintained, characters and anecdotes of eminent divines. It is in short a chronicle of all daily occurrences in the ecclesiastical world. An occasional glance at it,

from

from time to time, will give you proper notions of the policy of the French court, with regard to that immense body of men which composes the secular and regular clergy in France. It will also teach you what opinion to form of this class of individuals, not only in that kingdom, but in all the Roman Catholic countries.

Le Journal Encyclopedique is a regular account of scientific and useful performances, dissertations, and inventions.

La Gazette universelle de Literature des Sciences et des Arts, published twice a week, is a repository of real utility in the line it professes.

La Gazette du Commerce is also published twice a week, and is of use to those who are desirous of speculating in commercial affairs.

Le

Le Journal d'Agriculture is a monthly publication. Its object, which is the cultivation of land, is of late years become a favourite one over all France. There are at present, if I am rightly informed, upwards of thirty societies in that kingdom, for the improvement and encouragement of agriculture, under the sanction and patronage of royal authority.

I neither advise nor wish you to apply yourself in a particular manner to the perusal of the performances above enumerated; but on the other hand, they deserve your observation, especially such as have a reference to national objects. Periodical productions of this latter species you must not omit consulting with attention: they will enrich your memory with essential information, and they will empower you to judge with solidity and discernment of the progress which the French are making in those things, in which it behoves the English not to be surpassed, and, if possible, not equalled.

We

LETTER XX.

We cannot be too obfervant of the improvements taking place in that nation. Though by the laws of honour and humanity we are bound to efteem and refpect them for their many noble and excellent qualities, yet prudence directs us at the fame time to caft a watchful eye on all their proceedings. They are, it is true, a great and illuftrious people; but they are no lefs a dangerous neighbour. They are our rivals in arts, in fciences, in all that dignifies human nature, and renders nations famous; but they are likewife our ancient and inveterate enemies, ready to feize every opportunity to diminifh our power, and reduce us to diftrefs: their vigilance is equal to their enmity; and they have given conftant proofs of their expertnefs in converting all our errors to our immediate and utmoft detriment.

Such a people fhould not be vifited by way of recreation. That is the laft idea which Englifh travellers fhould admit of; but

but unhappily it is their first. Were France the country of our best friends and allies, we could not testify more ardour and partiality in its behalf.

After doing the French that justice which they deserve, you will, I am confident, remember that you are an Englishman, and endeavour to preserve yourself from the general contagion that infects our countrymen abroad, inattention to every thing but diversions and amusement.

It is principally from the well-founded conviction that such is the disposition of those multitudes who run over to France, that the French are so willing to shew us every encouragement to visit their country.

They know from incessant experience, that notwithstanding the determinations adopted by our legislature, in order to discourage whatever tends to benefit France, the folly of individuals will always defeat the wisdom of the state.

Laws

LETTER XX.

Laws in this respect may be compared to a trumpet, which may sound to battle, but does not inspire men with courage to fight.

The French are perfectly convinced, that, as a nation, the English entertain as rooted an ill-will to their prosperity, as they do to ours: but then they are equally sensible, that men in their private capacity are entirely ruled by fashion and caprice, and that public measures have no influence over the inclinations of people in their ordinary intercourse.

Add to this the infatuation of the light and fantastic part of society in this island, in their absurd preference of French devices and inventions, not on account of their superior propriety, but merely because imported from France.

It is from the ridiculous propensity to imitate that people, so common among us, that every effort fhould be made to reclaim thofe who go among them.

The true and only method of compaffing this defirable end, would be to perfuade every young gentleman who propofes to travel in that country, that he fhould in fome degree confider himfelf as commiffioned to take a view of an enemy's territory; that he ought therefore to examine its ftrength and weaknefs, and lofe no occafion to mark every advantage it poffeffes, and every defect under which it labours.

Were thofe principles carefully inftilled, our travellers would then go forth upon plans of infpection and enquiry. Inftead of returning home, fraught with the frivolities of the continent, they would employ their time and money in collecting that knowledge, and making thofe obfervations, which would amply repay them for their trouble and expence.

LETTER XXI.

I WILL now take a survey of those institutions, that have done so much honour to their founders, and proved of so much utility in the advancement of learning and literature.

Next to the foundation of universities, the most beneficial in the republic of letters, is that of academical societies.

The French will tell you that Charlemagne was their first institutor, and that he maintained in his palace, at a very liberal expence, a considerable number of the most learned and ingenious persons of that age.

Without determining the precise manner which that great monarch and conqueror

queror adopted for those laudable purposes, it will be sufficient to acknowledge that he was one of the greatest promoters and benefactors of learning; and that had his example been followed by his successors, the ignorance of subsequent ages would have been obviated.

The miseries and desolations that afflicted France, during the course of two or three centuries after the demise of that celebrated Prince, left no room for the cultivation of learning.

After the elevation of the Capetian family on the throne, the internal quiet of the kingdom becoming less liable to interruption, letters begun to experience a more settled and regular cultivation: but it was not until the reign of Francis the First that they flourished with any distinguished lustre.

Lewis the Ninth, by the French stiled St. Lewis, had befriended them as much

as

as could be expected at that illiterate period, which was the middle of the thirteenth century; a time when all Europe was plunged in the abfurdities of what was called the Ariſtotelian Philoſophy.

That excellent Prince contributed by his private bounty, and public authority, to the eſtabliſhment of ſundry uſeful regulations in favour of learning. Among other foundations, he promoted that of the Sorbonne, the moſt famous divinity ſchool in Chriſtendom.

But it was reſerved to Francis to merit the title of Reſtorer of Literature. He was not only the patron of all kind of learning, but he cultivated ſome of the politer branches with particular predilection.

His munificence to literary men, and his zeal in promoting the liberal arts, gave a new turn to the French nation. A taſte

taste for polite knowledge became general among the upper classes; and they who before had bewildered their minds in the unintelligible sophistry and jargon of the schools, applied themselves to the useful and elegant study of the Greek and Roman authors.

From an application to these, they naturally proceeded to cultivate and polish their own language. It received considerable improvements during the period that lasted from the times of Francis, till those of the civil wars on account of religion, which involved all France in scenes of blood and devastation for many years.

The pacification that ensued on the settlement of Henry the Fourth upon the throne, revived the ardour with which learning had been prosecuted. Being himself of a witty facetious disposition, and expressing his thoughts with remarkable pointedness and energy, his courtiers were, as usual, emulous in the imitation of their master.

This of course effectually contibuted to improve the French language. We find accordingly in the works written from the commencement of the seventeenth century, to the epocha of Cardinal Richelieu's ministry, a gradual and perceptible alteration both in its words and phrases, and even its grammatical construction.

There are in France, as elsewhere, warm partisans of all that favours of antiquity, *miranturque nihil nisi quod libitina sacravit*, and who cannot prevail upon themselves to admire the performances of men that have not been long since laid in their graves.

To such individuals the above changes did not prove acceptable. They complained that nothing was gained by them in perspicuity and elegance, and that much was lost in strength and concisenefs.

The altercations that took place on this subject lasted a considerable time. They were carried on with much warmth on both sides, and cannot be said to have entirely subsided.

The favourers of the new methods of speaking and writing, urged the propriety and necessity of polishing a language that had so long been used by an ignorant and illiterate people for the mere purposes of common intercourse, and in which hardly any thing had been written of a scientific or liberal nature.

They quoted the precedent set to them by Francis the First, who, in order to encourage the amelioration of the French language, had ordered it to be thenceforward employed in all public acts and deeds,

deeds, which had theretofore been written in Latin.

This had doubtless advanced the improvement of it which was thereby intended; but much remained yet to be done: the confusions that had happened since the reign of that Prince, had retarded the progress he had so auspiciously begun. Latin was still in possession of the pens of their best writers, from the suspicion they entertained of the deficiency and inaptitude of the French tongue in the matters of which they treated. It was therefore incumbent on those who were desirous to see it employed by men of superior abilities, to bring it to such a standard of purity and perfection as might induce them to make use of it.

The opponents of these innovations, as they called them, insisted on the other hand, upon the inutility of changing old words for new which were not more expressive

pressive nor yet more harmonious: they contended for the ancient phrases, as possessing equal clearness with those that were substituted in their room, and not yielding to them in point of energy.

They cited at the same time several productions in vindication of their arguments. Among these were the writings of Amyot, Montagne, Charron, and divers others.

It was not an easy matter to refute people who came armed with such authorities. Amyot's translation of Plutarch's Lives, is deemed a master-piece in France even at this day: other translations of that famous work have been attempted in French; but they fall infinitely short of that done by Amyot.

The language of Montagne charms the readers of all nations from its liveliness and agreeable simplicity. Ill would certainly betide any man who should presume to dress

him

him up in modern French. I have heard that an essay was once made; but that the maker did not dare to produce it. This proves how much merit there is in the style of Montagne.

That of Charron is remarkable for the forcibleness with which it conveys the vast variety of ideas that abound in his excellent treatise on human wisdom. No French writer displays a greater extent of thought, nor flow of language.

It would ill become any one but a native of France, consummately versed in that language, and who had given public acknowledged proofs of his ability, to assume the decision of so long and obstinate a controversy.

But as opinions may be ventured, provided they are delivered with modesty, one may on this occasion follow the example of Horace; in whose time the literati at
Rome

Rome were split into violent parties, respecting their ancient and modern writers.

That great critic, as well as poet, does not seem to have sided with the antiquarian party. No man certainly knew better the merits and pretensions of either side: yet as he evidently inclines to the moderns, we may reasonably infer that the same motives which influenced his judgment, guided the ideas of the French critics, who in the like manner decided in favour of their modern against their ancient stile and phraseology.

This decision does by no means detract from the excellence of those who used it, any more than that of Horace did from the real deserts of the old Roman authors. Both the decisions go no further than to affirm truths that cannot impartially be contradicted. As the writers to whom he gave the preference soon obtained it from the generality of people, so have the variations

tions introduced into the French language, given it, in the opinion of most persons, a manifest superiority over that of preceding times.

A corroboration of the soundness of Horace's judgment, is that at the distance of eighteen centuries, the learned world as unanimously coincides with it, as it has done during the whole duration of that long space.

This could not happen through partiality: nothing but conviction of the rectitude of his ideas could prevail upon mankind to espouse them.

In the same manner all Europe has long since joined issue with France, in allowing its language to be highly improved in a variety of respects, in comparison of what it was at the commencement of the last century.

When

When the forecited authors are therefore adduced, as equal in the beauty of their diction to any of those that have since appeared, the answer is, that they carried the powers of language as far as it was possible for their time; but still would have shone more conspicuously, had it possessed the same degree of elegance and refinement as at this day.

Hence it may be said, that what we admire in them, is not their language, so much as their manner of using it. Like an indifferent utensil in the hands of a skilful artist, it executes great things; but would have executed still greater, had it been more complete.

These discussions employed much of the attention of the literati, when Cardinal Richelieu began to act that part in the world, which has rendered his name so famous. As he aspired at all kind of glory, he resolved to obtain the reputation

of

of being the greatest protector of literature in his age.

Full of this determination, he openly espoused the cause of those who contended for the necessity of improving the French language, and conceived the project of founding a society for this purpose.

To this was owing the institution of the *Academie Françoise*, as it is denominated, a society of individuals who make it their duty and business to exercise their abilities in perfecting and maintaining the purity, and the true standard of the French language.

Its institution took place in the year one thousand six hundred and thirty-five: an epocha when Cardinal Richelieu was at the zenith of his power, when he had subdued faction at home, and was extending the influence and reputation of France over all Europe.

It

It consists of forty members; which number was never augmented. They are always persons of indisputable merit in some, and often in many branches of literature.

To speak with justice of this celebrated society, it has always been composed of the most illustrious writers in France. Almost all the famous names that have rendered the age of Lewis the Fourteenth so conspicuous, have belonged to it.

There is no association of the kind, containing such a number of persons of the first rank. I have seen a list, wherein among the fellows for the time being, I counted two Marshals of France, both of them Dukes, three other Dukes, one Cardinal, one Archbishop, and four Bishops, beside other persons of high rank in church and state.

Cardinal

Cardinal Richelieu's intention has been fully anſwered by this happy mixture of ranks. Knowing that merit without patronage ſtands no chance of being rewarded, he wiſely ordained that a conſiderable proportion of the academy ſhould, if poſſible, conſiſt of individuals of quality. In this he had two motives in view; to promote an application to letters among the upper claſſes, and to procure a ſufficient number of protectors to literary men.

The King is their immediate patron, and no inefficient one. A decent penſion is ſettled upon every member that is ſuppoſed to need one; and ſuch as manifeſt an aptitude for political employments, ſeldom are neglected.

In order to render their ſituation and buſineſs reſpectable, an apartment is aſſigned them in the Louvre; where they hold their meetings, and are often honoured with the preſence of the firſt characters in the

the state, and with the visits of the first personages in Europe.

To show at the same time that all men are equal in the republic of letters, and that merit alone has a right of conferring distinctions, a President is annually chosen by plurality of votes, to whom the title of director is given, and who has the chief management during that time.

The regulations concerning this academy are too many for an epistolary notice: be careful however to obtain a sight of them. As they were drawn up by men of genius, they cannot but contain many particulars worthy of your knowledge. Some of them will possibly appear unnecessary, and even frivolous; but there were reasons for them, which, upon investigation, may not prove altogether so deserving of censure, as it has frequently been surmised.

LETTER

LETTER XXII.

THE literary society next in point of seniority, is that intitled *l'Academie Royale des Inscriptions et Belles Lettres*.

The purpose of its institution, is to cultivate polite literature in all its various branches; to explain and elucidate the dark and difficult passages in ancient authors, and the inscriptions upon monuments; to examine the remains of learned antiquity, and to perpetuate the memory of great national events by medals, emblematic devices, and public inscriptions.

The number of members belonging to this society is about sixty. They are divided into three classes, honorary, pensioners, and associates.

LETTER XXII.

The first are all persons of high distinction, Ministers of state, Dukes, Bishops, and other great dignitaries.

The second are men of noted eminence for their learning and genius, usually indeed the first of the kingdom in their different lines.

The third cannot be said to differ from the second in any thing but rank, appellation, and salary: in substantial merit they are much the same.

Besides these, there are veteran associates. These are gentlemen whose age is supposed to preclude and absolve them from any further labour in the field of literature, and who are intitled by the merits of their former years to enjoy both rest and remuneration. The celebrated Fontenelle, who lived to the age of a hundred, was one of this venerable class.

There

There are also members of this academy under other denominations; but the former only can be strictly deemed of that body.

The date of its institution was in one thousand six hundred and sixty-three, under the ministry and auspices of the famous Colbert.

Influenced by the example of Cardinal Richelieu, and the instigation of the illustrious Seguier, Chancellor of France, and a warm friend to literature, he availed himself of his master's propensity to signalize his reign by remarkable transactions, to infuse into his mind the salutary idea of emulating such of his predecessors as had distinguished themselves by their patronage of learning.

As Lewis the Fourteenth was a Prince ambitious of every kind of praise, he was readily induced to embrace a proposal that

that flattered his disposition in so agreeable a manner.

Three years after the institution of this academy, he founded another, well known in the literary world under the name of *L'Academie des Sciences.*

The object of this society is to cultivate and improve natural philosophy, mathematical, and mechanical knowledge, physic, surgery, and anatomy, chymistry and botany, whatever in short relates to the study and science of nature.

The members of this society are distinguished by four denominations, honorary, pensioners, associates, and pupils.

The first are all personages of the first distinction in the kingdom, and are looked upon as the friends and protectors of the institution, and of those who compose it.

LETTER XXII.

The second are the efficient and acting members, and must reside at Paris, in order to attend the business of the institution.

The third are much in the same predicament, with this difference, however, that eight of them may be foreigners, and remain in their respective countries.

The fourth, like the second, must every one be settled at Paris, and are expected to give punctual attendance at the stated meetings of the society.

The King appoints yearly a President, and has the nomination of the Secretary and Treasurer, both which places are for life, as is also the Secretaryship of the Academy of Inscriptions and Belles Lettres, and that of the French Academy.

Both these societies have an apartment in the Louvre for their meetings, as well as the French Academy.

The

The academy of sciences has also its veteran members. The illustrious Fontenelle had the honour of being on this list, as well as on that of the academy of inscriptions.

You will readily perceive that the academy of sciences is the most useful of these societies, and the most beneficial to society at large.

For this reason the French have, in imitation of that at Paris, established several others in the principal cities throughout the kingdom.

Those that have come to my knowledge are the following: the academies of Rouen and Caen in Normandy, of Nancy in Lorain, of Marseilles in Provence, of Touloufe and Nimes in Languedoc, of Dijon in Burgundy, of Lyons in the Lyonnois, of Bourdeaux in Gascony, of Rochelle in Aunis, of Arras in Artois.

LETTER XXIII.

Besides these, there are others which I do not recollect. The number of them all together amounts to twenty, if not more. They are unequivocal proofs how much the French are addicted to learning and literature.

LETTER XXIII.

BESIDES the academies already enumerated, there are three others deserving of mention.

That of surgery, which I name the first on account of its evident utility. It was instituted in one thousand seven hundred and thirty, and is certainly as useful an establishment as any during the late king's reign.

It consists of sixty members, all of prime eminence in their profession. You will observe that the French pride themselves greatly for the progress and improvements they have made in this art. They esteem themselves indeed the first who brought it to any degree of perfection.

It must be acknowledged, that their claim is justly founded. Whatever may be the present merit of the English, or of other nations, in this neceſſary branch, France undoubtedly led the way in most of the ameliorations it has received, and in the fabrication of most of the numerous instruments it employs in its many operations. None, it is said, were made in England, before the time of the late Cheselden, reputed the first surgeon among the English in his day.

Surgery in France is on a respectable and scientific footing. None are admitted to practice without a competency of liberal scholarship. They must have attained the degree of master of arts, and undergone a public examination of their abilities.

It

LETTER XXIII.

It were to be wished that in this particular, an imitation of what is done in France were adopted by those that follow that profession in England,

The next academy in point of utility, is that of architecture, established in the seventy-first year of the last century, at a time when France was at the highest period of its glory, and arts and sciences met with every kind of encouragement from the ministry of Lewis the Fourteenth.

This academy is composed of about thirty members, divided in two classes, between which however there is no material distinction.

The gentlemen of whom this academy consists meet in the Louvre, and have in general the care and inspection of the royal houses and palaces. Most of them are very eminent in their art, and they must all have given proofs of their capacity

either

either in France or in other countries, this being indeed a condition of their admittance.

The French however excel most in military, and naval architecture. A numerous list is continually occupied in the study of means to give them respectively all the degree of perfection of which they are susceptible. I have heard judicious and knowing Frenchmen assert, that the flourishing state the French marine was brought to, in so short a space after the late peace of Aix la Chapelle, was owing much less to the sums expended on it, than to the ingenious management and contrivances of those whose talents for such purposes were properly noticed by the persons intrusted with the important charge of forming a navy. Thus much is certain, that France produces the best engineers, and as skilful ship-builders as any country in Europe.

I now

LETTER XXIII.

I now come to the academy of painting, sculpture and engraving, instituted in one thousand six hundred, and forty-eight.

This academy consists of upwards of an hundred members. Twenty of them are honorary, about fifty are painters, and the remainder sculptors and engravers.

From the fondness of the French people of fashion for magnificence and decoration, and no less from the genius of the Roman Catholic religion, full of ornament and of shew, constant and profitable employment is found for most of the artists that excel in those branches.

It cannot be denied that they flourish in France with as much, if not more lustre than in any part of Europe. The list of French painters, sculptors, and engravers, for more than a century past, will afford a number of names equal to those of any nation during that period, and, in the
opinion

opinion of many, not Frenchmen but foreigners, far superior.

Acknowledging myself no connoisseur in these matters, I resign you entirely to the guidance and instruction of those who are. You will find enough at Paris. To them I will leave the care of shewing and explaining to you the beauties of the many pictures, statues, sculptures, and engravings, that abound in France, as much as in any country in Christendom, both in churches and public edifices, and in the houses and private collections of individuals.

I shall only add, that no people display more willingness to exhibit their stores of this kind than the French, especially to foreigners. They consider themselves as bound in a particular manner to satisfy the curiosity of such as visit France.— Looking upon these exhibitions of their artists, as proofs of the superior ingenuity

nuity of the natives, they are defirous you fhould carry away with you an ocular conviction how much they excel all other people.

You will foon difcover this propenfity of the French to rank themfelves foremoft in this as in every other lift. They will indeed allow the Italians to have been the revivers of thefe fine arts, and even to have produced the nobleft fpecimens of modern genius. But that æra of Italian perfection, they now fay, is no more; France is the country which has inherited it, and where all thofe arts appear at prefent in greateft fplendour.

As you will find frequent opportunities at Paris, of converfing with intelligent foreigners of all countries, you may confult them on thefe pretenfions of the French. Notwithftanding the partiality with which almoft every man efpoufes the caufe of his nation, you will be fully able to

gather

gather from their respective judgments on these subjects, a sufficiency of materials out of which to form your own.

I will finish this epistle by advising you, while your attention is employed on these objects, to read Fresnoy's Latin Poem on the Art of Painting. The universal esteem it has so long enjoyed, is a sufficient recommendation.

Another poetical performance in the same language upon sculpture, has been written by Drouessin a Jesuit. It met with a very favourable reception from the public, and well deserves your perusal.

LETTER XXIV.

I SHOULD have told you that an easy access may be procured to the academies I have been describing, on their stated

stated days of meeting, for any persons of genteel rank and character.

After visiting these, one of the most entertaining pastimes in the literary line, is the liberty allowed to all individuals of decent appearance, of entering at pleasure, as often as they think proper, a considerable number of rich and magnificent libraries, very justly for that reason known by the appellation of public.

The first on every account is that called the king's library. It is a noble and spacious building, containing a number of large and elegant rooms, wherein are deposited near eight hundred thousand volumes of print, and upwards of sixty thousand volumes of manuscripts in every language that is written.

This library is of long standing; but the time when a royal collection of books was first made in the Louvre, has not yet been ascertained.

A royal

LETTER XXIV.

A royal library subsisted in the reign of Charles the Fifth, surnamed the Wise. It consisted of about nine hundred volumes, a noble collection for that time.

As the art of printing was not discovered till a hundred years after, they were all manuscripts, and from the rarity of books in that age, it was with much difficulty they had been collected.

The contents of this library would at present appear very paultry. It was chiefly made up of French and Latin bibles, mass books, breviaries, psalteries, and the like. They were richly bound, and curiously ornamented with figures coloured and gilt in the taste of those times.

Besides the above, there were a few of the ancient fathers of the primitive church. But to compensate for the deficiency in this article, there was a good quantity of legends, and lives of saints male and female.

LETTER XXIV.

Of books of learning and literature the number was inconsiderable. There were some treatises on geometry, but many more on judicial astrology, and other methods of divination, which were sciences highly in vogue at that æra, as they always are in proportion to human ignorance and imbecility.

There were also numerous treatises of physic, mostly French or Latin translations from Arabian authors; a great many historians of the Gothic ages, but a far greater proportion of romances in prose and rhime; with some writers on law and jurisprudence.

The most capital defect was the very small number of classics: there were only three of the old Latin poets, Ovid, Lucan, and Boetius, if this latter may be accounted a classic.

LETTER XXIV.

Of those authors in prose, who figured in the days of Roman eloquence, there were but few: of Cicero in particular there was not a single copy.

From this review one may judge of the taste of those who were employed in the formation of this library, unless we are to suppose, what may possibly have been the case, that no other books could be procured.

I cannot refrain on this occasion from reflecting on the immense disparity between the knowledge and literature of this period, which was about the middle of the fourteenth century, and the flourishing state in which they were among the Greeks, about three hundred years before the Christian æra.

If you will be at the pains of comparing the respective characters of Charles the Fifth of France, and of Ptolomy Philadelphus

LETTER XXIV.

ladelphus King of Egypt, you will find a remarkable likeness in their love of learning, and respect for learned men. Had Charles lived in a more enlightened age, he would probably have been an excellent scholar. It is recorded of him, that in the midst of the weightiest business, he dedicated constantly a portion of each day to the improvement of his mind by reading and study.

Yet with all his efforts, and with an expence that was confiderable for the time, it appears that he was not able to collect a thousand volumes to compose his library.

How different was the success of the Egyptian prince, when he undertook to compile a royal library! Instead of one single thousand, procured with infinite trouble, he was able to furnish the sumptuous edifice he had erected for that purpose,

pose, with between two and three hundred thousand volumes.

Leaving you to ponder on the causes of the prodigious difference between these two epochas, I shall proceed to counsel you to make use of the opportunities you will have in your visits to this library, to examine with due attention the great variety of remarkable books and manuscripts it contains.

I do not mean that you should read them. That were impossible. But it is by no means impracticable to take a cursory survey of the principal, according to the order of time they were written.

The number of excellent performances, and I only speak of such, is very moderate. By surveying them in the manner I have recommended, you will obtain a chronological knowledge, as it were, of the progress and improvement of the human

LETTER XXIV.

man mind, and be able to judge of the respective abilities of nations in different ages.

This advice I hope you will not neglect. You will never be able to follow it to greater advantage than on the spot in question. You may repair to it twice a week, and oftener, if you chuse to ask permission.

My intention however is not to convert you into an *Helluo Librorum*. A devourer of books, like a devourer of victuals, seldom can digest them. I therefore repeat the caution I have already mentioned; let none but the best claim your attention in the proposed review; and then you may be sure it will not be burthened with too many.

Besides the printed books and manuscripts, you will find there a most superb collection of medals and other antiques. In the revifal of thefe, affociate if you can with fome learned acquaintance, otherwife you will only fee them by halves, and carry away but a fmall fhare of their utility and merit.

Forget not the cabinet of prints, and of miniature paintings on vellum, of animals and plants to the number of fix or feven thoufand. Here too you fhould be accompanied by a connoiffeur, to enjoy thefe fights properly.

To go through all this may feem a laborious tafk: but if you regulate your time judicioufly, and adhere punctually to the regulation you make, it will not only feem, but prove in reality a mere paftime.

LETTER XXV.

I HAVE dwelt on the royal library somewhat circumstantially because it is certainly one of the completest and most useful in Europe, if indeed it may not altogether challenge the preference over any.

The next public library in point of richness and utility, is that of the abbey of *St. Germains des Prés*, so called from its former situation before the enlargement of Paris.

It is in the possession of the Benedictine order, the most ancient, the most wealthy, and what is much more to its honour, the most learned in all France.

You will not do amiss in forming a literary connection with some of the conventuals of this abbey. Should you be desirous to visit any of the most noted monasteries and religious houses, you will find them extremely ready to oblige you with letters of recommendation, and these you will experience to be highly serviceable in more than one respect.

The library of this abbey is open every day of the week. It abounds with magnificent editions of the Greek and Latin fathers of the church, and with a large quantity of manuscripts written during the Gothic ages. I mention these in particular, because you will find them no where else in such good order and such high preservation.

I need not remind you of the great obligations which the learned world is under to the Benedictine order. To the extraordinary care and diligence with which they transcribed the works of ancient authors, at a time when printing was unknown, and writing no ordinary accomplish-

LETTER XXV.

complishment, we are in a great measure indebted for the renovation of polite literature.

Besides a variety of books on all subjects, in addition to those already observed, this library possesses some very fine pictures, highly esteemed by good judges, together with a noble collection of medals and antiques, and another of natural curiosities.

The other public libraries are those of the Abbey of St. Victor, occupied by Canons regular; an institution by some ascribed to St. Augustin, Bishop of Hippone, a place not far from Carthage; in which case they would be more ancient than the Benedictines, by near a century, as that celebrated Bishop flourished not far from the middle of the fifth century, and the others were not instituted till near the middle of the next.

The library of this abbey is well supplied with all kind of books, and is continually

nually increasing from the funds assigned to that intent. The conventuals are polite and well-bred men, several of them extremely conversant in the world, and abundantly civil to those who are introduced to their acquaintance.

The famous Santeuil was of this abbey. He was an original in his character and manners; but still more for his prodigious talent in Latin poetry. He composed a collection of hymns, which are now used almost universally in France; they are full of elegance and sublimity; you will find them thoroughly suited to the occasions for which they were intended. Were I inclined to make a comparison, I would call Santeuil the Buchanan of France.

The Abbey of St. Genevieve, possessed also by Canons regular, has another public library full of choice and excellent books, with a noble collection of antiques and natural rarities.

But

LETTER XXV.

But what peculiarly distinguishes it, is a curious series of ancient golden coins and medals. They are the gift of the late Duke of Orleans, a Prince of great learning and sanctity of life. He chose this abbey for his abode in his latter years, and spent his time in continual study and devotion. I have heard such accounts of his manner of living, as will often rather surprise than edify thinking people. He was a prodigy of penitence and austerity: he denied himself every comfort of life, and seemed to consider his existence chiefly as the means of perpetual mortification.

You will naturally ask what he had done to condemn himself to so much penance and self-denial; but that is a question which may be rationally proposed to many others as well as him. The fact is, that they who lead such wretched lives, are usually persons who have the least to answer for.

Excesses

Excesses of this kind are much more frequent in Roman Catholic than in Protestant countries. It is a great pity that worthy and respectable individuals should suffer themselves to be lead away by such unreasonable and groundless ideas of religious perfection: I make no doubt that premature death has oftener than noticed, been the consequence of so erroneous a conduct. Such characters ought to be reminded of the saying, *sapias ad sobrietatem*.

This Abbey of St. Genevieve has produced several men of great learning and abilities; the celebrated Bossu, author of the treatise on epic poetry, was one.

There is a very large library belonging to the Advocates and gentlemen of the law. Beside books on other subjects, it is the best repository for those who wish to become well acquainted with the feudal law, and with the system of jurisprudence that prevailed

vailed in the Gothic times. Among a variety of tracts upon these subjects, you will select the best, and examine those parts that will strike you as most deserving of knowledge. You will easily find some one to direct your choice. I met formerly with such a work in French; but I forget the title and the writer: it was a quarto close printed, the language elegant French, and the matter entertaining, considering the subject: it was written about the close of the last, or the commencement of this century. These are the sole indications that I now recollect.

There is in the *Maison de la Doctrine Chretienne*, a very considerable library open to the public. Among other works it is remarkable for its abundance of excellent editions of historians, chiefly those of antiquity. The gentlemen of this house are secular Priests, who live in a collegial manner, and are noted for their learning, and regularity.

The *Hotel de Ville*, that is to say the Guildhall of Paris, is also in possession of a library for the use of the public. It is kept in a spacious house formerly belonging to the Jesuits, and contains a very large number of books in exceeding good order, and chiefly French.

The college founded by Cardinal Mazarin, and stiled *Le College des Quatre Nations*, is endowed with a very numerous library of excellent books.

This famous Minister had little or no learning; but much of natural wit and readiness of thought. He erected this college and library in compliance with the example of his predecessor in the Ministry, Cardinal Richelieu. As the munificence of this latter had won him the praises and attachment of the literary world, Mazarin hoped to procure himself by the same means the favour of that class of society, and to atone thereby in some measure, for
the

the illaudable ways and means he had used in the amassing of the immense riches, which exposed him to so much reproach.

To all the fore-mentioned libraries, individuals of genteel appearance are admitted on stated days of the week. Herein the convenience of the public has been so judiciously consulted, that you are sure of admission every day to one or more.

The intention in granting this access to the public at large, seems not so much to furnish them with books to read, as to enable studious persons to examine and transcribe passages out of such as they cannot otherwise procure. Another useful purpose is, that by inspecting these libraries, people are directed what books are principally deserving of their attention and perusal.

But beside these libraries, there are several others; to which, though not professedly

fessedly public, entrance is never denied to men of letters, and persons of any character.

Among these, that of the Sorbonne holds the first place. It is noted for a very considerable number of ancient manuscripts, and is well stocked with books of divinity, composed by people of all persuasions.

The Doctors of the house and society of Sorbonne, as they are denominated, form a very learned and respectable body. It is the most ancient of all theological institutions. Its authority in cases and discussions of this nature, is almost supreme in France, and very great in all countries professing the Roman Catholic religion.

There is another society of Doctors in divinity, not so ancient nor considerable, but which has nevertheless produced many persons of extraordinary merit in that line. It is stiled the Society of Navarre, and
was

was founded in the sixteenth century by the royal family of that name, which afterwards acceded to the throne of France in the person of Henry the Fourth.

They too are in possession of a very fine library, full of old manuscripts, and no less noted for a large and curious collection of those editions of ancient authors that first came out on the invention of printing.

A society known by the name of *Congregation de l'Oratoire* possesses a very numerous library, containing among other literary curiosities, a valuable collection of manuscripts in the eastern languages.

The members of this society are in high reputation for their proficiency in sciences and literature. Characters of the first eminence in these respects have belonged and still belong to this body. It is composed of secular clergymen, who differ no otherwife from others of the same denomination, than by living together in a conventual manner, and pursuing a stricter course of studies.

The library of the Celestins is a very numerous one, and remarkable for a large quantity of manuscripts written in the Gothic ages.

The Celestins are a Monastic institution: its first appearance was about the latter end of the thirteenth, or beginning of the fourteenth century: their rules and manner of living are much like the generality of other religious orders.

The library of the Convent of Dominicans, situated in the *Rue St. Honoré*, is noted for its excellent collection of Arabian, Turkish, and Persian manuscripts, and has also a curious assortment of natural curiosities.

LETTER XXV.

The Dominicans seem to be a medium between the strict monastic orders, and the secular clergy: their life is less recluse, and they mix more in society; the chief purport of their institution being to preach and instruct.

I have now gone through the best libraries that I can recollect. See them all, but not in a formal pedantic manner. I have known some persons so absurdly devoted to their contemplation, as to spend the best part of their time in looking over every book they contained: I know not with what intent, unless from the silly vanity of being able to say that they had seen them all. But even this was next to impossible considering their prodigious number. One thing however is certain, that no profit can be reaped from the superficial review of meer title pages, which is the utmost that can be done by those who take the ridiculous resolution of looking at them all.

The

The right method of proceeding in this immense laybrinth, is to resolve beforehand upon what branches to fix your attention. In every library a particular place is allotted to them: when you are in it, remember the precept, *lege fed elige.*

By adhering to this rule, a selection is soon made of what is really worth perusing. It is not assuredly by vast reading that great geniuses are formed, or even much solid learning acquired. Books are frequently, if not most commonly, a repetition of each other: they often serve to confuse and perplex, instead of affording elucidation.

How many things are there, which not to know, is, in the words of Pope, a praise: beware how you indulge curiosity; it is a more pernicious passion in those who are covetous of knowledge than they are usually aware of: unless a person possesses not only strong intellects, but a strong constitu-

LETTER XXV.

constitution too, an extensive application to reading and study, will fatigue more than improve, and by impairing the last will certainly affect the first.

Endeavour therefore to make learning as much as possible an object of amusement and pleasure: this you will compass without much difficulty, provided you apply yourself only to what suits your capacity; a few trials will soon decide which way it lies; when you have made this discovery, be satisfied with the talents allotted you; *non omnia possumus omnes.*

It is by pursuing the path pointed out by this auspicious discovery, that men of genius have acquired all their fame. The vulgar proverb says with great truth, that what is labour to one man is play to another. Conformably to this, when our faculties are employed in a proper direction, we proceed with smoothness and ease: it is only by striving to force nature, that we involve ourselves in difficulties.

LETTER XXV.

Do you imagine that Locke or Newton did not derive much pleasure from the pursuit of their respective lucubrations? abstruse and profound as they appear, and are to the generality of men, they were to them like the even surface of the sea, over which the propitious gales of their superior genius wafted them without perplexity or storms.

A great proportion of the recompence of men endowed with uncommon parts, is that satisfaction which accrues from their very exertion. You will invariably observe that the talent in which they excel, not only commands their warmest attention, but exercises an attraction which they prize beyond every other enjoyment.

This perhaps is more conspicuous in men of literary genius than in any others. We see them at all times enamoured with the objects of their respective pursuits, in a manner that fully convinces how highly they value them, and what delight they receive from their profecution.

To the fore-mentioned inftance of our two celebrated countrymen, may be added that of two late geniufes not lefs famous, Rouffeau and Voltaire. Their attachment to letters was fuch, that the life of both may be faid to have been fpent in their fervice. They died as it were with a pen in their hands, efpecially the latter, whofe end was abfolutely accelerated by the fatigue he underwent in the perfecting of his laft dramatic piece, working at it day and night, at the age of eighty-four, with the fame affiduity and indefatigablenefs as if he were no more than thirty.

Neither of thefe illuftrious writers were compelled by neceffity to exercife that inceffant application for which they were both fo remarkable. Voltaire was rich; and fo might Rouffeau have been had he chofen. It was pure inclination and choice that

that led them to devote themselves to continual study: the pleasure they found in it, repaid them amply for the neglect of what might seem to others, much more conducive to recreation and enjoyment.

Summon therefore all your attention, and dive as it were to the bottom of your disposition, in order to find out for what nature has designed you: to know that is of the highest consequence for your welfare, since on that knowledge depends contentment and serenity of mind, without which, no happiness can be attained.

Should your option prove erroneous, it is not in the power of human efforts to second it. Talents, unless directed to their proper object, are useless, and only occasion loss of time and labour. Until you have explored the province in which you are to act, you will appear to disadvantage, and will necessarily be displeased with a situation, wherein, as you can make no figure, you will experience no satisfaction.

But

LETTER XXV.

But the worst is, that exclusive of the mortification accruing from want of success, you will be a total stranger to that internal ease which arises from the fitness of our abilities for the employments in which they are exercised. The facility with which we move when placed in a proper sphere, counterbalances a multitude of inconveniences. It produces a constant flow of spirits, which enables us to bear with trials and disappointments; it is the source of chearfulness and equanimity, the two richest presents that nature can bestow, and the absence of which all the gifts of fortune are not able to supply; it converts our occupations into scenes of delight, and signally verifies the common saying, that a contented mind is a perpetual feast.

Observation and experience will soon teach you the truth of what has been asserted. Among your acquaintances have you not found those to be the happiest, who

who were engaged in businesses corresponding to their parts? have you not your own self, when employed suitably to your capacity, felt an alertness within you, that conveyed the highest satisfaction?

This inward placidity is the summit of a wise man's desires; but to attain it, we must not wander from the path wherein our talents enable us to tread with security.

LETTER XXVI.

AFTER having given you those informations respecting the libraries at Paris, which I thought might be serviceable, I shall now proceed to such a review of the churches as I would wish you to take.

In this article Paris claims a decided pre-eminence over London. What the churches

churches of this immense metropolis were before the dreadful fire that consumed such a number, is not very clear: they do not appear however to have been very spacious.

At Paris, exclusive of their magnificence, there are many parish churches vying for dimensions with the noblest cathedrals. This perhaps you will call a needless and ostentatious expence: it may be such; but it is an error of a splendid sort; it contributes to the formation of excellent artists, and employs a multitude of hands, which otherwise might possibly have wanted occupation.

When we recal to our minds the situation of the European world, at the time when the major part of those vast cathedrals were built, on which we look at present with so much admiration, we shall find that many, most indeed of those almost numberless trades and occupations
that

that give bread to the present race of men, were then either totally unknown, or confined to very few hands.

In ages so barren of those businesses that contribute to the pleasurable and expensive demands of luxurious society, it was happy for the indigent and laborious classes, that some motive existed from whence to derive a beneficial employment.

This motive in the days of ignorance was, it cannot be denied, religion ill understood; but it proved not only a harmless, but a useful and salutary mistake. Those edifices that were in so many parts of Europe constructed through devotion or through repentance, drew those sums out of the chests of the wealthy and powerful, which, but for those causes, might have remained there unemployed, or possibly might have been brought forth in the support of feuds and contentions.

It

LETTER XXVI.

It is almost fashionable among some people, to mention abbeys and monasteries as monuments of the folly of those who founded them: I hope you will suspend your condemnation of their founders, till you have better arguments to alledge than those whom I have heard expatiate on this trite subject.

In the first place, it is evident that their intentions were highly meritorious; and that knowing no other method of signalising their zeal in the cause of virtue and religion, more approved and applauded by the public, they complied with the reigning taste of the times.

In the second, it is equally clear that their money was by no means expended uselessly: besides the maintenance of the multitudes already mentioned, the erection of these numerous edifices either revived or kept alive the knowledge of architecture, and of sculpture, of both

which

which little was employed in any other kind of buildings.

In the third, learning was preserved and perpetuated in these places, and no where else. In this light these foundations, so heavily censured by the unthinking, were the auspicious means of securing to the present generation the knowledge and literature of the past.

I need not apprize you that in those dark ages, as they are called pertinently enough when compared with ours, hardly any individuals applied themselves to the commonest part of letters, but churchmen; and of these the secular clergy were often scandalously remiss.

The regular clergy, by which is understood the various orders of monastics, were incomparably more assiduous and diligent in the prosecution of their studies. None of them could be considered as entirely lost

to

to the community of letters. They whose turn or capacity did not incline, or enable them to make a figure in school divinity, or philosophy, which were the prevailing taste, were usually taught Latin enough, if not to relish or understand, at least to transcribe the writers in that language.

Until the art of printing was discovered, they were the only possessors, or compilers, of any kind of libraries. Notwithstanding the additions made by their pens to literature are of little or no value in many, if not indeed in most respects, yet in some they are not contemptible. Several of their historical compositions especially, are far from devoid of merit, either in matter or in manner.

It is unfair and ungenerous so readily to cast a slight upon men and times, for being less fortunate than our own. Had not printing come to the assistance of mankind, there seems no reason to presume that men
would

would have thrown off the shackles of ignorance. Barbarism and prejudice had taken such profound root over all Europe, that long after that propitious invention, numbers of such as ought to have known better, still continued obstinate in errors and absurdities of the grossest complexion, and often of the most fatal tendency.

Abbeys, monasteries, and other foundations of that sort ought therefore to be viewed as the refuge of the small portion of learning remaining in unenlightened ages. This is paying them no compliment; it is the strict truth, and it becomes every impartial man to acknowledge it, though he should thereby incur the displeasure of such as, from incompetency to compare and judge of the merits of men according to different periods, indulge themselves in the most unreserved and illiberal condemnation of those who built and endowed, and of those who inhabited those places.

Let

LETTER XXVI.

Let us not then triumph too unfeelingly in the superiority we boast over our forefathers in knowledge, in literature, and in the polite arts: they are the result of fortunate casualties, but not in the least of our deserts.

The fervour with which they applied themselves to the pursuit of learning was far greater than that of succeeding and happier æras. The number of colleges founded since the epocha of printing, is less than of those that were founded before.

Neither does it appear that the number of students is greater in them at present. The records of former times represent them occasionally so numerous, that on comparing them with the numbers that are usually found in the European universities at this day, they seem out of all proportion.

It is out of place to alledge that their studies were nugatory, and mere lofs of time and pains. They were partly fuch undoubtedly; but this we are to afcribe to the misfortune of the times, and not to the difpofition of thofe who profecuted them: we ought rather to admire the zeal and feduloufnefs of their application, and the infinite labour with which they cultivated the barren foil appointed them.

You will not blame me, I hope, for endeavouring to refcue our forefathers from the cenfure fo frequently and fo unjuftly caft upon them. Were the prefent age as deftitute of advantages and means of intellectual improvement, as thofe which it ridicules and fatirifes with fo much warmth, it is much to be apprehended, that confidering the frivoloufnefs which characterifes it, we fhould fall greatly fhort of our anceftors in literary qualifications, and incur much more defervingly the accufations urged againft them with fo much impropriety.

A pro-

A proemium of this kind appeared altogether not unneceſſary to precede ſo copious an article as that which churches and conventual edifices ſo commonly prove in the deſcription of things abroad. Many perſons are apt to vent ill-natured reflections on their inſpection of ſuch places, and to aſſume a kind of traditional privilege to exerciſe the ſevereſt ſtrictures upon all that relates to them. Hence it was fit and reaſonable to examine how far they were juſtifiable.

After this preface, I will next proceed to lay before you ſuch ideas and obſervations as have occurred to me upon viewing thoſe objects of public curioſity that are uſually pointed out to the attention of travellers.

Though I acknowledge myſelf no profeſt connoiſſeur, yet I never was diſpoſed to yield up my judgment implicitly to thoſe who are deemed ſuch. A true connoiſſeur ſhould have

have a feeling and capacious mind, susceptible of those impressions which arise from a lively imagination and an exquisite judgment, the first implanted by nature, the second resulting from an extensive fund of liberal knowledge. According to this rule, which is I presume well founded, the number of connoisseurs is nothing so great in reality as in pretensions.

When you are introduced to the sight of the various objects on which connoisseurs display their remarks, lose not if possible a word of them; but compare them with your own; and be not afraid to differ from them, when you cannot bring your sensations to correspond with their endeavours to excite them.

You will often find them in rapture at objects that will give you no emotion. I will not be so presumptuous as to affirm their raptures were affected; but whether it was want of perception in me, or the uninterestingness of the subject, while good manners extorted a feigned approbation, I have often felt an invincible repugnance to coincide with their sentiments.

There are many individuals whose feelings no subjects can reach, unless they are of a great and striking nature. I knew a gentleman of excellent understanding and education, who never exprest the least pleasure at the most mirthful scenes that pencil could describe, and yet never failed being charmed at those that were grave and pathetic. I have also known persons of no less merit, who were of quite a contrary disposition.

Hence we should distinguish between two things that are often confounded, taste and temper: *non omnes omnia juvant*, we are not all pleased with the same things; even in beauty we differ; what charms one is insipid to another.

Let not connoisseurs therefore pass their sentence of condemnation too hastily upon people for not conforming to their notions of excellence: with many, if not most men, the subject is an essential motive of admiration or of indifference. It is recorded of Lewis the Fourteenth, who was a prince of the most refined taste and discernment, that he could not endure with patience the sight of objects of grotesque and low life buffoonry. Does it follow from thence that he wanted judgment and feeling?

Grandeur and magnificence are found to please all men. There is something like authority and power imprest upon them, which commands respect and veneration. For this reason undoubtedly, though there may be numbers unmoved at the sight of the most excellent productions of painting or sculpture, yet a noble piece of architecture is always sure to make a due impression on every beholder.

Archi-

LETTER XXVI.

Architecture may be esteemed therefore the noblest of these three arts, as it is unquestionably the most useful. There is a natural beauty attending it, of which the power is felt universally, even by such as are hardly capable of being made sensible of any other.

It is mentioned in the memoirs of the time, that the four Indian chiefs who came over to England in the reign of Queen Ann, testified no emotion of surprize or of admiration at any other objects, but those of St. Paul's and Westminster Abbey. Most certainly they were not taken particularly with the exactness of proportions, nor with the regularity of the building; neither could it be the dimensions alone; it was the effect produced by the combination of all three, that formed in their minds an idea of greatness and sublimity.

As the merit of architecture is so much beyond that of the other arts, as to be perceivable even by the most common and vulgar eyes, it is a reason why you should attach yourself peculiarly to the contemplation of the many noble structures, that you will find in France, and in the other countries which you may visit hereafter.

Nothing decorates a country, and does more honour to the taste of the inhabitants, than magnificent edifices. The triumphant æras of nations have always been marked by architectural splendour. It is the pride and occupation of all men of eminent character, and proves in some measure that they are worthy of the great things which fortune may have done for them.

In the prosperous days of ancient Greece, we find the most polite and discerning among that celebrated people, no less intent on the cultivation of architecture, than on signalising themselves by their prowess and skill in military and civil affairs. Pericles,

cles, perhaps the greatest name at Athens, employed his credit and authority so effectually in the embellishment of that city, that it became the wonder of the times, and drew strangers from all parts to behold it.

The Romans, in imitation of the Greeks, were equally zealous in the decoration not only of Rome, but of every principal city throughout their empire. All the famous personages among them, in the days of their grandeur, were uncommonly diligent in procuring and encouraging the ablest architects. They not only erected splendid edifices for their private use, but expended immense sums on those magnificent and vast piles of architecture, of which the very ruins fill us with astonishment at this day.

Rome in fact was not more the metropolis of the world by its power, than by the prodigious number and surprising splendour of its public and private buildings.

ings. Among the promoters of this taste for magnificence, we may count the most illustrious of the Romans, Sylla, Lucullus, Pompey, Cæsar, Augustus, Agrippa, and various others whom it is needless to mention.

There was a noble emulation among all the people of high rank at Rome, who should contribute most to adorn it: this was one of the most popular methods of rising into favour and fame: every man that could afford it, thought himself in a manner bound to do something of that nature for the public: it was equally the passion of the greatest warriors, and of the wisest men. Cicero in particular had formed several plans of this kind. Some of his letters to his friend Atticus are full of noble and extensive projects, which he would undoubtedly have executed, had circumstances permitted him.

This laudable disposition was inherited by the Roman Emperors, and exercised
upon

LETTER XXVI.

upon the most sumptuous and expensive scale. *Lateritiam inveni marmoream relinquo*, were, it is well known, the words of Augustus in his old age. A prince that was able to say, that he found Rome built of brick, but that he left it of marble, stood in no apprehension of being exceeded by any of his successors.

But though they did not equal, they imitated him, however, with great success. Domitian and Trajan, two men of very different characters, resembled each other conspicuously in their propensity to embellish Rome; and, next to Augustus, distinguished themselves more than any other emperors.

Until the decline of the Roman empire, and almost indeed to its final destruction, the cultivation of architecture continued more or less to be a favourite object at Rome.

It

It may even be said to have survived the downfall of that mistress of the world. While the rest of Europe, and even Italy itself, was overrun by barbarians, they could not entirely subdue the knowledge and practice of that noble art: it remained in honour and request; and though it did not flourish in its ancient splendour, it was on a footing much superior to that of most other countries.

During the Gothic ages, notwithstanding the stile of architecture differed essentially from that of Greece and Rome, yet we ought to acknowledge, that in many parts of Europe a spirit of generosity and grandeur arose among the princes and superior ranks of men, that has never been surpassed, if equalled, by their descendants.

Their taste, it must be allowed, was inferior to the present, but far greater was their zeal and liberality in the construction of those numberless structures, which are
still

LETTER XXVI.

still considered as the noblest ornaments of the places where they have been erected.

Almost all the cathedrals in Europe are monuments of the piety and munificence of our ancestors. Whenever the period of their dissolution arrives, should it happen in such an age as the present, it is far from probable they would be rebuilt upon the same plan of grandeur and dimensions, on which they were primitively founded.

The stile of Gothic architecture seems peculiarly adapted to religious edifices.— There is a solemnity, a weightiness, if you will indulge me with such a word, in all that appertains to them, which inspire veneration and seriousness in the beholders.

It has been constantly observed, that the sight of our Gothic cathedrals excites a variety of pleasing, though grave reflections: we view them, as it were, like public legacies left us through the bounty

of

of our forefathers for the moſt ſublime purpoſes: ſuch an idea fills us at once with gratitude and reverence: we enter and examine them with an awful curioſity and ſatisfaction: all that meets our eye reminds us of ſomething either agreeable or inſtructive: the various objects wherein the workman, or the artiſt has diſplayed his dexterity or genius, afford a copious fund of entertainment to thoſe who delight in tracing the riſe and progreſs, or the revival and improvement of arts, and in comparing the taſte and notions of former ages with the preſent.

What greatly adds to the venerableneſs of theſe ancient ſtructures, is the recollection of thoſe countleſs multitudes that have by turns filled them during a ſucceſſion of centuries.

If the admirers of the old Greeks and Romans, can experience ſo much content on treading the ſame ground where Solon and

and Numa, Demosthenes and Cicero, Homer and Virgil, Alexander and Cæsar, formerly lived and flourished, with how much more pleasure must we find ourselves on the very spot, where such numbers of our progenitors have so often assembled, where the most sacred and solemn actions of their lives have been performed, where their thoughts have so frequently been taken up with considerations on that posterity which now occupies the places where they stood, and fixes its contemplations on them as it were by way of return.

Such reflections naturally occur in those ancient and venerable piles: we respect them for the sake of those several motives; and are always much readier to visit them, than those of modern construction.

An advantage of this kind is by no means to be overlooked. The devotion of men will sooner be kindled by such
recol-

recollections than without them: an eloquent and pathetic preacher may bring them very efficaciously to his assistance: they are truly what the philosophers call arguments *ad hominem,* and never can fail to make a profound impression.

I knew a clergyman so thoroughly persuaded of this, that he always preferred an old church to a new one, whenever the subject of a sermon was deep and moving. As he possessed the gift of speaking in an eminent degree, he was never at a loss in converting every circumstance of time and place to its proper utility: this he could do with the more readiness and facility, as he preached almost extempore, and without any other preparation than twenty or thirty words written on a card: he never used any other notes, and with the help of these would furnish out a long discourse.

He spoke with great deliberation and distinctiveness; and excelled in that which

is

LETTER XXVI. 257

is by judges esteemed the essential quality of a good speaker, the art of selecting with justness and discernment those words and passages on which to lay a particular emphasis: this he did in a manner remarkably striking, and yet so easy and natural, that it seemed to flow from, and to be dictated by, the subject.

But the talent in which he was most conspicuous, was that of availing himself of those objects which were present or actually existing: of such he made an admirable use; he employed them with surprising skill in fixing the attention and calling forth the sensibility of his auditors: a picture, a statue, a tomb, the transactions of the times, the reports of the day, all contributed in his mouth to affect the passions, and to excite those sensations which he intended.

From the description of this preacher, you will naturally suspect that he was not a native a native of England; or if he was, that he did not exercise his profession there. Neither of these indeed was the case. He was a Frenchman, a country curate in Normandy: his erudition was great, and his natural genius not less. He began the world by being preceptor to a young man of distinction; but disliking the subserviency required of him in the family of his pupil, he left it; and after a variety of those struggles with fortune, which men of merit who want patrons are always sure of encountering, he obtained at last the retreat above-mentioned.

In England a man of his character would not succeed in the pulpit. Reasoning alone seems to please the generality of English congregations: some of the best French sermons translated into our language, would appear no better than mere declamations.

Foreigners acquainted with the disposition of the English, are often struck at the

LETTER XXVI.

the contrarieties of which it is compounded. But the warmth and vehemence with which an Englishman enforces and supports his rights upon all occasions, forms in their apprehension the moſt remarkable of all contraſts, when compared with the cold and frigid method ſo generally uſed in the compoſition and delivery of diſcourſes made in churches.

Some attempts have been made in France to introduce a cooler manner of ſpeaking and arguing in theſe matters: but orators of this kind are only acceptable *raris auribus* to the few, and will never bring about an alteration of that vivacity and impetuouſneſs of ſtile which characterizes French preaching, and by having ſo long been annexed to it, ſeems to claim a right of preſcription.

LETTER XXVII.

IT is now time to enter upon a review of those churches and religious edifices that have given occasion to the preceding reflections.

The grandest and most noble church in Paris, is unquestionably the cathedral of *Notre Dame*. It is a stupendous pile in the true Gothic taste; but the inside is full of modern decorations, almost all of them very recent.

The most curious monument of a Gothic nature, is that which meets your eye on entering. It is the well-known figure of St. Christopher. He is a saint that seems to claim an ancient right of standing at the door of all capital churches: he is always represented bearing Christ in the

the shape of an infant upon his shoulders: hence he derives his name.

The reason for making him of so gigantic a size, is that in the days of ignorance, the credit of this saint was so great, that a bare sight of his image was reputed a preservative against sudden death and all sinister accidents. In order therefore that all people might enjoy a full view of it, great care was taken to make it a Colossus. That of Paris measures near thirty feet in height.

The nave of this vast cathedral is remarkably spacious and majestic; and from the number of large and costly pictures arranged on each side, affords a considerable fund of entertainment.

Notwithstanding the general massiveness of this structure, the roof is remarkably light and airy, especially above the choir. Around it is a roomy and agreeable gallery, from whence spectators may enjoy a clear view of the many ceremonies performed upon high festivals, and hear the music below to the greatest advantage. It is esteemed the finest of any church in France; the choristers being the best that can be procured for money.

In this, and in every Roman Catholic church, never omit seeing the treasury. Nothing teaches a man of sense what to think of times past, so completely as the contents of these repositories. Were it only for that reason, examine them thoroughly, and hearken with patience and politeness to the long details that will be given you concerning the heads, arms, legs, fingers, and bones of saints, and whatever else may be shewn you appertaining to, or relating to them.

But independently of what they contain, many of the shrines themselves are valuable pieces of curiosity, as they ascertain

tain the degree of expertness and elegance in workmanship of the times when they were made.

Observe with due attention from the same motive, the various other objects that will be offered to your inspection; such as crosses, croziers, chalices, pattens, crucifixes, candlesticks, censers, mitres, copes, vestments, and the numerous appurtenances of the Roman method of celebrating divine service.

The review of some of the principal vestries in countries of the Roman persuasion, is on these accounts extremely entertaining. To the Virtuoso and Antiquarian they display a world of articles to gratify their curiosity; to the Philosopher and man of reflection they serve as memorials of the opinions and ideas of mankind, and of the changes and revolutions to which all things are subject, that are not founded upon solid ground, and possest of intrinsic stability.

From the plan which I adopt in the examination of the subjects before us, you must perceive that my intention is not to go into any detail. I leave that to your guides and conductors. Besides that it would prove an anticipation of a heavy and tedious nature, I mean not to excite in you too warm a propensity for such amusements. I wish you to view all these things with a cool and philosophic eye, and by no means whatever *con amore*.

Leave such a disposition to the frivolous, the idle, and the dissipated. It is perhaps the most harmless and profitable manner in which individuals of that description can spend their time. But to a mind desirous of looking deeper than the surface of objects, they only appear in the light of instruments of thought and reflection upon matters of a far higher nature.

The

The mere ocular satisfaction which arises from viewing the productions of art, is the *ne plus ultra* of inferior capacities; but men of superior genius see them with quite different eyes: while the first are intent solely on the work of the artist, the others, exclusive of their attention to such particulars, carry their contemplations much further: the rudeness or the elegance, the ignorance or the knowledge, the infatuation or the wisdom of the times that produced the works they behold, become through those a subject of instructive and useful meditation.

It is in this frame of mind you should visit public buildings, and all other objects of curiosity. I would not however have you neglect the examination of their ostensible merits: on the contrary, view them as critically as you are able; it will prove an additional help to investigate with success the more essential points of consideration, to which they will give rise

rise in the minds of those who are above stopping at bare exteriorities.

There are several tombs in the church of *Notre Dame* very deserving of notice, chiefly for their antiquity, and the persons whose remains they contain.

Of all improprieties, none is more deserving of censure, than that of burying individuals of no substantial merit, in places that ought to be set apart for perpetuating the memory of those who have done real honour and service to their country.

When we see persons noted for nothing but their wealth entombed among those from whom a nation derives its glory, it raises a just indignation in every bosom that feels for the dignity of the public.

But it produces a much worse effect in the opinion of all discerning men. It
extin-

LETTER XXVII.

extinguishes that thirst of fame which is the most powerful incentive to signalize themselves in men of great minds and extraordinary parts.

What vigour and alacrity can we suppose them to feel, when they see the same honours paid to insignificant as well as to exalted characters, when they see the most deserving individuals laid in the same dust with those, whose pecuniary worth alone could purchase the breaking of ground for their reception.

People should be peculiarly vigilant in preventing this reward of public merit from being liable to such manifest prostitution; it is often the sole recompence bestowed upon individuals, to whose abilities, heroism, or genius, a nation owes much of its grandeur and reputation.

It is hard therefore they should share it in common with such as have no pretensions fions to it. Public honours are a property which ought to be more facred after the death than during the life of fuch as have a right to them: it is all that national gratitude has in its power to confer: it belongs to them exclufively; and it is the higheft injuftice to allow any others a participation.

Long has it been the complaint that monuments are not always what they fhould be, teftimonials of the worthinefs of thofe to the memory of whom they were erected. For this reafon none fhould ever be fuffered, without the fanction of public authority, in thofe places that have through cuftom and prefcription been appropriated to the burial of eminent perfonages, and no private body of men fhould have the privilege of granting permiffion of interment in them at their own option.

The *Jus Imaginum* was in this refpect one of the wifeft laws among the Romans.

By

By the same rule that they were not allowed to set up the images of their ancestors without having obtained a licence for that purpose, it were to be wished that no statues, representations, or memorials of any kind, should have admittance upon any spot consecrated to national uses of this nature, until it had been publicly decreed, that the deceased was justly intitled to such a remuneration.

LETTER XXVIII.

IN the examination of churches, after having taken a view of the other beauties of art, and curiosities they may contain, always remember to pay your last attention to the tombs and sepulchral inscriptions.

These latter you will generally observe to be more elegant than almost any other species of composition. For this, two obvious

vious reasons may be assigned; the first is, they are usually of no length, and being exposed to all the world, oblige the composer to exert himself. Secondly, they are on a subject that comes home to every body; and which excites those pathetic feelings that are easily described and communicated.

A review of monuments is peculiarly moving to a man of a lively imagination, and humane sentiments. It is, I must allow, a pastime of a serious complection; but it both softens and elevates our nature; none indeed but persons of delicacy and refinement are capable of relishing it: Tickell with great truth calls it a luxury to vulgar minds unknown.

As I do not range you in that class, I earnestly recommend to your inspection the many excellent epitaphs you will meet with in the churches of Paris.

Next

Next to that of *Notre Dame,* is in point of real grandeur the church of St. Eustatius. There is not in Europe a bolder, nor at the same time a more beautiful roof: it is of a surprising height, and appears still higher than it is, from the lightness with which the whole edifice is constructed.

In this church, among other tombs, you will find that of the celebrated Colbert. You will also find another not less worthy of remark; I mean that of the illustrious Chevert. A man whose whole life was a series of military atchievements, and who, as his epitaph justly insinuates, ought, for the honour of his country, much more than for his own, to have died a Marshal of France.

The church of St. Sulpice is intirely a modern building. It owes its erection to the indefatigable zeal and solicitude of the famous Languet, Rector of that parish. He lies buried in this church under a superb monument, which no man could have better deserved.

He was one of those extraordinary characters, that seem born to command the inclinations of mankind, and to render them subservient to their own designs. No man ever possest in a higher degree the talent of persuasion; it was to this he owed the perpetual supplies he drew from the purses of the great and the wealthy, for the support of the various undertakings, which his munificent disposition was continually projecting. He was himself a mirror of the most perfect disinterestedness, and made no other use of the extraordinary influence he possest over the minds of the first personages of the kingdom, than to render the most essential and most extensive services to the community.

Among a variety of laudable institutions, he was the author of one which deserves particular commemoration. This was a
house

house of education for young women of birth, but narrow circumstances. Instead of the fashionable accomplishments usually bestowed on females of distinction, they were taught the arts of good management and œconomy, and fitted for the cares and duties of a domestic life; when arrived at a proper age, they were dismissed with a genteel provision, perfectly suitable to their respective birth and pretensions.

In these and many other acts of beneficence, he generously expended his own fortune, and the immense contributions which his pious industry found means to levy upon the opulent and charitable part of society. Virtue and merit in distress were sure of a protector whenever he found them, and he made it his constant business to seek them out in every class and denomination of men.

So exalted and respectable a character should not be passed over with a slight and cursory mention: for this reason I have thought it expedient to give you this summary account of a man, of whom one may very properly say, *dignum laude virum musa vetat mori.*

The church belonging to the Carmes is esteemed one of the most elegant in Paris. Its dimensions are not large; but it is most magnificently decorated, and is one of the greatest curiosities in its kind that you will ever behold. The French call it *un Parfait Bijoux.* As it is situated in the street called Vaugirard, in the proximity of the Luxemburg, people often terminate their morning walk in that pleasant spot, by a visit to this church.

The Carmes account themselves very ancient. They derive their primitive origin from the prophet Elias, when he withdrew to the deserts and mountains, to screen himself from the persecution of Ahab King of Israel. But their first appearance

pearance since the Christian æra, may be fixed about the beginning of the fifth century, on Mount Carmel in Palestine; from whence they received their denomination.

Their pretence of originating from Elias has given rise to a remarkable *bon mot*, which has been put into the mouth of the famous Rector of St. Sulpice above-mentioned. This gentleman's piety, though very strict and exemplary, was by no means pedantic and austere; he was of an open chearful disposition, and occasionally very gay and facetious: this rendered him extremely popular, and procured him a number of adherents and well-wishers; from whom he was continually receiving donations and legacies for the carrying of his various enterprises into execution. It happened that among these was an elderly person of distinction and great opulence, who had long been a particular friend and benefactor to the Carmes. Finding himself infirm and sickly, and that his dissolution was approaching, he made a will, wherein he left to these good fathers, as the French term all the members of religious orders, an ample legacy, and a very moderate one to the Rector. This coming to the latter's knowledge, he hastened to the testator, and represented to him in so forcible and efficacious a manner, the impropriety of leaving so much to people who did not want, and the far greater merit of providing for individuals in real indigence, that the dying man was prevailed upon to alter his will in favour of the Rector, and to make over to him what he'had at first intended for the Carmes, to whom he assigned the portion designed for the other: on his leaving the gentleman's apartment, and going down the stairs, he met with two Carmes who were coming to visit their old friend: knowing who he was, they saluted him with great respect, and made way for him to pass; the Rector returned them the compliment

ment with equal politeness, and insisted on their passing first, adding in a jocose manner, that they were of the Old Testament and he only of the New.

This is not the only story of the kind, wherein he displayed his dexterity and facetiousness: he certainly had a copious share of both, and often met with occasions to exercise them.

In the street St. Antoine stands the magnificent church formerly belonging to the Jesuits. It is the burial-place of the celebrated Prince of Condé, next to Henry the Fourth the greatest man that ever sprung from the family of Bourbon.

A French wit speaking of this hero, says that all the atoms of intrepidity had met together at his birth, and formation; as it was formerly said of Epicurus, that all the atoms of wisdom and prudence were combined at his conception.

He was in every respect an extraordinary character; great in the field and equally conspicuous in the endowments of his mind: his speeches and repartees would fill volumes; they are often in the mouth of his admirers; most of them are of an original stamp, and equally bespeak a nobleness of sentiments and an acuteness of perception.

Let me on this occasion recommend a method of imprinting things on your memory, which I have experimentally found very effectual. When you have visited the tombs of famous men, while your mind is yet fresh from that occupation, and taken up with the ideas naturally arising from it, peruse immediately the best accounts of their actions and times that you can procure: you will soon be convinced of the utility of such a practice.

On the two sides of the high altar of this church are deposited the hearts of
Lewis

Lewis the Thirteenth and Lewis the Fourteenth, two Princes whose bigotted attachment to the Jesuits is sufficiently manifested by history, had they not, in the warmth of their predilection, bequeathed them this public testimony.

In the parish church of *St. André des Arcs*, lies buried the noblest historian that France ever produced, if one may not add, the noblest since the days of Augustus. This may without exaggeration be said of such a writer as Dethou; whose history of his own times yields not in point of truth and eloquence, the two pillars of history, to any that have been written since Livy and Tacitus.

Were it for no other reason, fail not to visit his tomb. It is the only object worthy of remark in this church. Dethou was not only a great historian, but one of the ablest politicians of his age, and what is more, a man of consummate virtue and inflexible integrity in the moſt difficult and worſt of times. All theſe motives conſpire to render him an object of peculiar attention and reſpect: ſuch men ought to be conſidered as luminaries of the world, as well as an honour to their country.

The church of *St. Genevieve* is of great antiquity. It belongs to the Abbey of Canons regular already mentioned. Beſides other particularities, it contains the tombs of ſeveral perſons of note; among others that of the celebrated Deſcartes, the deſtructor of the ancient and founder of the modern philoſophy.

But what will principally engage your attention, is the ſhrine of St. Genevieve, the tutelary Saint and patroneſs of Paris. Under this title ſhe has been recognized and held in the higheſt veneration in this city for a number of centuries. Her ſhrine is placed on the top of four marble pillars, behind the high altar, and incloſed in a

wooden

wooden chest, richly gilt and painted. It is never uncovered but on the day of her own festival, and upon extraordinary occasions, or to speak more properly in times of public calamity.

The confidence of the Parisian vulgar in the power and credit of this Saint is almost past belief: she is, next to the Virgin Mary, the refuge of all people in adversity; her intercession is implored not only by individuals in their private distresses, but by the whole corporation on public emergencies.

It is especially in dangerous excesses of dry or of wet weather, that her assistance is requested by all the magistracy in their formalities. Her shrine is then taken out of its repository, and carried in all the pomp of state through the principal streets of Paris, as the people of Naples bring forth the head of St. Januarius upon any alarming eruption of Mount Vesuvius.

There

There are several very large pictures in this church, representing the magistrates and citizens of Paris addressing themselves to this Saint, who appears on a cloud in the attitude of suing to Heaven in their behalf: these pictures have been set up in commemoration of benefits and relief obtained through her mediation: there is also in the choir a set of tapestry hangings very ancient, and for that reason very curious, exhibiting processions and other religious ceremonies on the same account.

My only motive for entering into this detail, was to give you a just idea of the modes of infatuation so long prevalent even among the most sensible and enlightened nations: neither should we speak of them in the past tense; nor is it the mere vulgar that bends before the altar of Credulity; there are numbers of the better sort, who would be highly scandalised at hearing any doubt exprest of the many miracles attributed to this Saint. I have seen a book

book wherein the author, a man otherwise of sense and learning, tells you very gravely, that the favours granted by Heaven through her intercession, occasion multitudes to have recourse to it.

Adjoining to the church of *St. Genevieve* is that of *St. Etienne du Mont*; they are built so close and contiguous, that a door opens from one into the other. This latter is the beautifullest specimen in Paris of that kind of architecture which holds a medium between the Gothic and the modern: there is an airiness and elegance in the inside of this church quite of an original cast; its painted windows are truly magnificent.

After seeing these two churches, obtain a sight of the spot where the late Duke of Orleans lodged, or rather had a cell during the last ten years of his life. It is rather a cavity than apartment between the walls of both churches, narrow, inconvenient,

nient, folitary, and out of the way of all human comforts.

You will not wonder at this uncommon choice, when you recollect what I have already mentioned concerning the character of this Prince, and the fyftem of life he thought proper to adopt.

Should you have an opportunity of converfing with the Conventuals of the Abbey of St. Genevieve, neglect not to inform yourfelf of what further particulars you are able to gather concerning him: they will teach you what ideas to form of that enthufiaftic devotion which people of weak minds and little reafoning account fo meritorious.

In the mean time juftice requires it to be acknowledged, that in the midft of this erroneous and abfurd plan of living, an excellent foul was difcoverable, and a fund of intrinfic goodnefs that made ample amends

amends for all mistaken notions. Charity, tender-heartedness, generosity, mildness, humanity, in short, without bounds characterised all his actions: his benevolence was universal, and his income was in the strictest truth the property, as far as it would go, of every man of indigence and virtue.

The church of the Carthusians has some very fine pictures; but those that attract chief notice are in the cloister. They are numerous, and contain the History of the Life of St. Bruno, the founder of this order. He is a Saint of the eleventh century, which is saying enough, when we reflect that superstition was then in its full vigour, and the minds of men susceptible of its strongest impressions.

Solitude and a total ignorance of what passes, and almost of whatever has past in the world, religious matters excepted, seem to be the basis on which this institution

tution is founded. You will naturally ask what purpose it can answer in society: the only reply that can be given, is that it has nothing to do with society.

The choir of the church of the Augustins is one of the finest in Paris: it contains some very valuable pictures, and strikes one altogether through its agreeableness as well as grandeur.

This order has many branches. It originated towards the close of the fourth century; but hardly made any appearance till about the end of the thirteenth.

In this convent are held the assemblies of the French Clergy, corresponding with our convocations. In it also are preserved the portraits of all the Knights of the order of the Holy Ghost since its first institution, by Henry the Third, King of France, in one thousand five hundred and seventy-eight. As the first Knights were
created

created and invested with the ensigns of the order in this church, it has been customary to present the convent with their pictures. They fill two spacious halls, and being exact likenesses, and very well executed, are deemed a great curiosity.

In the parish-church of St. Gervais are some very remarkable pictures: the structure is altogether very noble, and by Connoisseurs spoken of with great applause.

The famous Tellier, Chancellor of France, has a superb monument in this church: he was esteemed an eminent politician; but did not certainly shew himself such in the zeal which he displayed for the revocation of the edict of Nantz; the most fatal error ever committed by any of the Ministries of Lewis the Fourteenth. Neither was his character free from the imputation of partiality and vindictiveness, qualities in no small measure inherited by his son the celebrated Louvois.

One

One of the most elegant parish-churches in Paris is that of St. Paul. It has an air of decency and neatness superior to any others: this is due, in the opinion of judicious observers, to the agreeable mixture of simplicity and richness in its architecture and decorations. It has a variety of monuments and inscriptions to the memory of illustrious personages.

In the small but pleasing church of the Capuchine Nuns, you will see the tomb of Louvois, the flint-hearted Minister of the haughty Lewis the Fourteenth in the days of his grandeur. He had not a soul equal to his elevation, and could not bear the least shock of adversity. Grief at being harshly spoken to by that monarch sent him to an untimely grave.

Next to *St. Sulpice*, the most magnificent parish-church in Paris is that of *St. Roch*... Its architecture without, and sumptuousness within, are in the noblest taste;

taste; it is intirely modern, and is altogether an equally vast and conspicuous edifice.

I cannot pass over this article without taking notice of the apprehensions, which a celebrated Rector of this parish used to express for the reputation of its tutelar Saint. There lived in his time a famous critic, of profound learning, and equal intrepidity in applying it properly. This critic had, it seems, been very unfavourable to some Romish Saints, whose very existence he had called in question. The Rector, who probably was not over-persuaded of the reality of the patron of his parish, never met this gentleman without shewing him every mark of deference and respect, in order to engage him to be merciful to his Saint.

In the street of *St. Honoré* stands the collegiate church of that name. It is small, but the chapter is reckoned the richest in Paris.

LETTER XXVIII.

Paris. Here lies interred the renowned Cardinal Dubois, the favourite and Minister of the no less noted Duke of Orleans, Regent of France in the minority of the late King.

No man's character has been treated with more freedom. As he was the very reverse of a bigot, and addicted to all kind of licentiousness, he rendered himself odious to those who profess regularity and devotion, and became an object of universal scandal throughout the nation: but secure of his master's protection, he set all complaints at defiance, and continued in the pursuit and enjoyment of every pleasure that wit or money could procure.

Herein he was fully countenanced and seconded by his patron. No two men seemed more completely fitted by nature to fill jointly the same career. Their temper and disposition exactly corresponded, their ideas were similar on essential as well

well as immaterial objects. In their most serious occupations and most frivolous pastimes their abilities and taste perfectly agreed. Freedom of thought and libertinism of morals was the system they adopted in private life, equally determined to range at large in every gratification of body and of mind.

In public affairs this Cardinal was a man of extraordinary penetration and activity, a profound politician and an able negociator: in one particular he differed greatly from that description of a courtier, which Lord Chesterfield has drawn, as comprehending a full idea of what was necessary to constitute and complete such a character. The Cardinal was remarkably blunt and unceremonious both in his speech and manners, and yet, contrary to what might be expected from such a disposition, he possest the talent of persuading and even of pleasing.

LETTER XXVIII.

In the church of *St. Thomas du Louvre*, are magnificently entombed the remains of Cardinal Fleury, his succeffor in the miniftry at the diftance of a few years. No two men could lefs refemble each other: the latter was a model of politenefs, affability, and courtly breeding, regular in his life and edifying in his converfation; poffeffing at the fame time great fupplenefs and art, and uncommonly dextrous in the talent of infinuating himfelf into the good opinion and favour of thofe whofe friendfhip he was defirous to obtain.

A man far fuperior to both thefe lies buried under a moft ftately monument in the church of the Sorbonne. This is the great and juftly famous Cardinal Richelieu. It is by numbers efteemed the moft exquifite piece of fculpture in France, and inferior to nothing of the kind that has appeared fince the days of Lyfippus and Praxiteles.

This

This noble monument is in the middle of the choir. It was placed there in order to testify the gratitude of the society of Sorbonne, to which he was so eminent a benefactor. No figure can exhibit a stronger likeness of the person for whom it is intended.

It may not be amiss to take notice of the very different impression made by this almost animated figure, upon two of the most celebrated personages in the present century, Lewis the Fourteenth of France, and the great Czar Peter of Muscovy.

The former viewed it with the attention and discernment of a Connoisseur; his remarks were confined to the workmanship, and his praises to the artist.

But the second viewed it with the eyes of a King; he clasped the figure in his arms; would to God, said he, that I had such a Minister as thee.

I do not think it is possible to find in the history of these Princes, any passage that sets their respective characters in a stronger light. The one, though bred in Barbarism shewed he was born with the soul of a hero; the other, educated in the center of politeness and refinement, appeared in this instance in no higher a character than of an admirer and judge of the fine arts.

Without meaning to depreciate this character, is it not more becoming a man of rank and sentiments to have the feelings of a Peter, than the skill of a Lewis.

It is principally to improve your mind and excite an emulation of what is great and noble, that these various anecdotes have been occasionally interspersed. The beauties of statuary and of sculpture are of much less importance to a gentleman, than the knowledge of those to perpetuate the memory of whom they were employed.

These

These beauties when absent from the eye are easily forgotten; nor is it of any material consequence they should be remembered, provided our memory retains the transactions and the persons recorded by them.

The church belonging to the Abbey of *St. Germain des Prés* already mentioned, is a Gothic pile, venerable for its antiquity, and for the many tombs it contains. The most worthy of remark is that of John Casimir King of Poland, who resigned his crown in order to live his latter days in peace. There are several excellent epitaphs in this place, which being of dates very distant from each other, will exercise your penetration in discovering the respective taste and ideas of the times when they were written.

The church of the Celestins is not very spacious, but contains more tombs in proportion to its size than any church in Paris;

Paris; some of them are very magnificent: being so numerous they will enable you to trace the progress of sculpture from the ancient to the modern taste.

The churches of the Dominicans in the street called *St. Jaques*, who are thence called Jacobins, and of the Franciscans, alias Cordeliers, in the street of this name, are worth visiting on the same account.

This last is a very numerous order, consisting of a variety of branches. Its primitive founder was the famous St. Francis in the beginning of the thirteenth century, one of the most remarkable since the Christian æra for the institution, revival, or regulation of religious orders.

A church of which the situation is remarkably advantageous, is that of the female monastry called *Le Val de Grace*. It was built and endowed by Anne, Queen Consort to Lewis the Thirteenth and mother to Lewis the Fourteenth.

It is a truly magnificent edifice, ornamented without and within according to the modern rules of architecture. In it are depofited the hearts of many perfons of the blood royal, particularly that of the foundrefs.

She was a Princefs of a noble and generous difpofition, full of fprightlinefs and affability; fhe contributed not a little to diffufe a fpirit of elegance, and a dignity of manners among the French ladies, and to polifh and refine the modes of focial intercourfe between the fexes. Her court was in thefe refpects a model to all others, and was juftly efteemed the center of politenefs and good-breeding.

In the neighbourhood of the *Val de Grace* ftands the fmall but beautiful church of the Carmelites, ornamented in the richeft tafte; but for nothing fo remarkable as for belonging to the Convent, where the famous Duchefs De la Valiere retired
from

from the world, in the flower of her life and beauty, in order to spend the remainder of her days in doing penance for having been the miftrefs of Lewis the Fourteenth.

She was the moft lovely woman in France, endowed with every qualification that renders her fex amiable in the eyes of men: fhe was worthy of a more conftant lover than that Prince, who did not fufficiently feel the worth of fuch a woman, and forfook her for one that was far lefs deferving of his attachment. She compofed in her retreat feveral works of piety, one of which in particular is efteemed a mafter-piece for elegance of language, and fublimity of fentiments.

In many of the parifh-churches above-enumerated, there is what the French call a Calvary; it is always behind the high altar, and reprefents the fufferings and death of Chrift. Some of thofe calvaries are very curious and beautiful.

Another

Another particularity is the magnificent porches of several of these churches. That to which connoisseurs give the preference is *St. Gervais*: it is esteemed the most faultless and finished piece of architecture in its kind.

But there are others which I apprehend you will find equally striking, such as those of *St. Sulpice*, the new church of *St. Genevieve, St. Eustache, St. Roch*, and *Le Val de Grace*, all of them modern structures as well as the first.

The French pride themselves in the porches of their churches, as the English in the steeples of theirs. There is no country that offers such a beautiful variety of these as England: those of London are, in the opinion of judicious foreigners, one of its greatest curiosities.

I have now gone through as many of the churches at Paris, as I could recollect to be worthy of a traveller's notice.

In

In this review I have had it chiefly in my eye, to render them the means of conveying the knowledge of such men and such things as merited a place in your memory.

For this reason I would recommend a judicious perusal of the epitaphs of celebrated persons, and a due attention to the anecdotes concerning them that may be mentioned on such occasions: it is one of the most useful and profitable methods of acquiring information.

Viewed in this light the visitation of churches, and the examination of tombs and monumental inscriptions, may be compared to the study of ancient medals, and is of no less utility in the elucidation of past transactions.

I knew an Italian gentleman of extensive knowledge in historical matters, and uncommon accuracy in what related to

per-

LETTER XXVIII.

persons of figure and eminence. He often confest that the sources from whence he drew some of the most material information, were epitaphs. He had in his travels made a prodigious collection of them: I have heard him say that they had afforded him much more assistance in clearing up and ascertaining a variety of facts, than he had at first expected.

Curiosity alone had been the original motive for collecting them; but in process of time, being a man of great reading, he found them so serviceable, that what he began upon the score of amusement, he continued upon the footing of instruction.

It may be objected that funeral inscriptions are always partial to the deceased, and that one cannot therefore rely on what they say.

The truth of this may be admitted, without invalidating the propriety of considering

sidering them as general records of men and things. Is history any more? Does it necessarily exclude partiality? Perhaps on due reflection, we are more liable to be misled by this latter, which always professes to be impartial, than by the former, which we know and expect to be favourable to the dead.

This knowledge and expectation sets us naturally upon our guard: we read with caution, and mistrust what we are conscious has been written by the hand of friendship, or dictated perhaps by influence or authority.

These ideas necessarily accompany us in the perusal of epitaphs, and serve as a counterpoize to the praises with which they may be loaded; but it is not the same in the perusal of history; the impression it makes has quite another weight, and is usually, if not always, much more effectual in determining our belief.

LETTER XXVIII.

It is peculiarly remarkable, that many of those men who have had great honours paid to them after their demise, have been as much neglected during their lives. This reminds one of the Latin adagium, *Vivit post funera virtus.* You will agree with me in deploring the fate of such men, and that merit should so frequently have no other encouragement, than the prospect of living in the remembrance of mankind, when its unhappy possessor is no more.

Eminent merit is an invidious possession; it is a constant eye-sore to the mean spirited and narrow hearted, who, unfortunately for society, compose a numerous body, always intent on pulling down to their own level whatever rises above it. When people of this stamp prosper in the world, their selfishness is offended at the sight of such as are confessedly their superiors in the qualifications of the mind: hence they study by way of revenge, to dis-

discourage and deprefs them, and to undervalue those talents in which they excel.

Confiderations of this nature cannot fail to occur, when we furvey the tombs of illuftrious individuals, whofe lives have been filled with hardfhips and ftruggles. The envy and ill treatment they experience while living, and the applaufes beftowed upon them when dead, agree but too well with the complaint which Horace made long ago: *Virtutem incolumem odimus, fublatam ex oculis quærimus invidi.*

There is however a favourable peculiarity attending men of this character. As their circumftances remove all fufpicion of partiality to their memory from interefted motives, we may the more readily give credit to the good that is fpoken of them. Hence thofe epitaphs that are made for individuals of this clafs, may be read with very little fear of deception.

The

LETTER XXVIII.

The celebrated Charles the Fifth, Emperor of Germany, was particularly fond of contemplating the monuments of famous men. It was one of his most usual pastimes in the frequent travels through his extensive dominions.

I have heard a Polish gentleman assert the same of the great John Sobieski, King of Poland. It was an homage, that prince used to say, which monarchs ought to be the first to pay, as it was the powerfullest incentive with men of noble dispositions, to signalize themselves in their respective stations: it cost kings nothing, and effected a great deal: it was due to departed worth, and would produce an ample harvest of meritorious deeds among the living: let me, therefore, would he add, discharge a debt by which I can lose nothing, and may gain much: on these occasions he frequently repeated these words of Virgil, *his saltem accumulem donis et fungar inani munere*, meaning that the least he could

could do was to bestow admiration and praise where it was so justly deserved, and where it was all he could give.

LETTER XXIX.

BESIDES the remarks that have been made on churches, and what they contain, you will find various occasions to indulge your curiosity in other matters relating to them.

I will say nothing of the numerous ceremonies you will be witness of. These I shall leave to your private reflections. Whatever is well meant, it is ungenerous to censure: evil intentions alone merit condemnation: while no detriment results to society from religious formalities, it is equally absurd and iniquitous to quarrel about them.

What

LETTER XXIX.

What is particularly worthy of your observation, is the decency and decorum with which they are performed, and the orderly behaviour and exactness of those who are employed in the many branches of church duty.

I have been often surprised that so witty and ingenious a people as the French, could so long put up with such wretched performances, as many of the hymns that were used in churches before the introduction of those composed by Santeuil. My surprise is the greater, as more than a century and a half had elapsed before his time, since a taste for elegance and latinity had been restored in France.

This may be considered as one of the many proofs of the power of custom, and that men govern themselves by prejudices, even while they are acknowledged as such. Habit has long been found of more influence than the consciousness of the utility

that

that would result from an alteration, however proper and judicious.

Notwithstanding the superior beauty of Santeuil's compositions, there are still adherents to the old hymns, as in England we have many who prefer Hopkins and Sternhold's version of the psalms to Tate and Brady's, Watts's, or any other.

The best Latin translations of the psalms in verse, are those of Buchanan, of Johnston, and of Commire the jesuit. But notwithstanding their excellence, of the first especially, they have never been introduced into churches. The old pitiful version of the vulgate, as it is called, still maintains its ground in all the Romish churches, in spite of the universal conviction of its inelegance and barbarism.

Prudentius, who flourished in the fourth and fifth century, is author of the best hymns anciently used in the Gothic ages.
Se-

LETTER XXIX.

Several are ascribed to Hilary, Bishop of Poitiers, in France, and to Ambrose, Bishop of Milan, both his cotemporaries. Others have also contributed; but their stile in general, not excepting that of Prudentius himself, is far from being pure and correct: many of these compositions, such in particular as belong to the times subsequent to the writers that have been named, are absolutely devoid of all kind of literary merit.

What I presume will frequently attract you to their churches are the musical performances, and splendid processions on festival days. These, however, are not so magnificent, and do not return so often as they did formerly. The French are at present much less taken up with these matters than they used to be; and have greatly relaxed in this part of their devotion, to the no small concern of such as admire and extol the zeal and piety of preceding times.

You will neverthelefs be witnefs of as many as are neceffary to give you an idea of what they were, while the minds of men were plunged in ignorance and credulity.

The abfurdities of which people were then guilty, feem to thofe moderate and cool Proteftants who never faw countries of the Romifh perfuafion, to border almoft on calumnies and falfhoods; but they are credible enough to fuch as have feen Italy and Spain, where greater veftiges of them remain than in France.

It was principally in their proceffions the bigotry of the old Romanifts was moft vifibly difplayed.

The moft curious account of this nature that ever came to my knowledge, was of a proceffion made in honour of St. Peter. It was a very ferious and formal bufinefs, publicly authorized by the magiftracy and clergy

LETTER XXIX.

clergy of the place. In seasons of great drought, a solemn address was made to the image of this saint for wet weather. In order to make him the more sensible of their wants, and to urge him, as it were, the more pressingly, they carried him to the side of a river; there they sung to him, "St. Peter, help us in our distress; obtain some rain for us, once, twice, thrice:" the image making no answer, the populace insisted it should be plunged into the water, unless their request was forthwith granted: upon this the heads of the place represented to the croud, the impropriety of treating the saint so disrespectfully; that without coming to these extremities, they might be assured, that like a kind father, he would not fail to procure the rain they prayed for. After this representation, in order thoroughly to pacify the people, security was given to them for the performance of what it promised; and it never failed, it is said, on their accepting the security, to rain within twenty-four hours after.

This ridiculous ceremony was observed in more places than one. So confident was the multitude in its efficacy, that it was with difficulty prevailed upon to suffer it to be laid aside; and not until treatises had been written to prove its absurdity.

The most remarkable ceremonies that will occur to your notice in France, are those which annually return in Passion week. Among these you will observe the blessing or consecration of a very large and magnificent taper. It is of the finest white wax, and sometimes ten feet or more in length.

A motive for mentioning this in particular, is that according to a grave author of the Roman persuasion, it was anciently customary to distribute portions of this taper among the people, to perfume and keep in their houses, their fields and their vineyards, as a preservative against evil spirits and bad weather.

LETTER XXIX.

Whatever complaints may be made against the present generation in France, on the score of levity of behaviour in churches, the devotees who make them, can alledge nothing to compare with the strange liberties taken, and in a manner tolerated in these places during several ages.

An annual day was kept, called the Festival of Folly. It was solemnized in churches with abundance of ridiculous ceremonies. They who were concerned in the acting of this farce, chose one out of their own body, whom they created Bishop of Fools: this election was made on the first day of every new year: they arrayed him in episcopal robes, and he performed a mock service. His retinue in the mean while danced, eat, played, burned old shoes by way of incense, and committed other extravagances of the same kind. About the close of the twelfth century a bishop of Paris, in order to put an end to these absurdities, founded in his diocese a solemn celebration of the circumcision of Christ, on the first of January, the more effectually to exclude from churches the observation of this preposterous festival. But the good bishop's scheme succeeded only in part; the fondness for this extraordinary species of diversion, lasted yet a long time; and it was not finally abolished till upwards of two hundred years after.

A principal difference between a Protestant and a Romish church, is the number of chapels in the latter, every one of which has an altar or communion table, as we term it; whereas in our churches there never is but one.

Each of these chapels is dedicated to some saint, whose votaries have thereby an opportunity of paying their devotions to him in a more particular manner, whenever

LETTER XXIX.

ever their fervour is uncommonly warm, or their neceffities preffing.

Several faints being much more confpicuous than others, their reputation is vifible by the fuperior decoration of their chapels, as alfo by the numbers of thofe who frequent them.

It will afford you both paftime and inftruction to examine what is recorded of them in thefe places; peculiar gifts and powers are appropriated to divers of them: you will be diverted with the ftories of the wonderful events which they have operated; and by attending to times, places, perfons, and circumftances, you will foon teach yourfelf to find a folution for thofe wonders.

You will fometimes obferve pictures and tablets hung up, to reprefent and commemorate benefits received through their means: many are worth perufal either for their

their antiquity or singularity; I have read some in very elegant Latin. They are upon many accounts worth your attention, as they will give rise to many reflections, and lead to a variety of useful discussions.

The custom of lighting up small wax candles under the images of saints, is not so common as formerly; you will however see enough of it, especially on great festivals.

There are now and then some wags among the French, who amuse themselves with jesting on this invocation and patronage of saints: among the various tales I have heard, take the following as a specimen:

A surgeon of high reputation, for the cure of a certain disorder, went to view the curiosities of the abbey of St. Dennis: on seeing the statue of Charles the Eighth, King of France, he kneeled before it with

much

much seeming respect: a monk who was present told him he was greatly mistaken, and that it was not the image of a saint: my good father, answered the surgeon, I perfectly know what I am about; he may be no saint for you, but he is the best patron I ever had, since through him I am now worth thirty thousand livres a year: suffer me therefore to return him my sincere thanks.

To the expedition of this monarch into Italy, for the conquest of the kingdom of Naples, was owing the introduction of the venereal distemper into France, which has ever since proved so extensive and so profitable a branch of business in surgery. It retains to this day among the French the appellation of *Mal de Naples*, the Neapolitan evil. Soldiers, officers, in short almost his whole army was infected, himself not escaping. This fatal consequence of that celebrated expedition was, it may be added, in the words of the following distich,

distich, the only memorial remaining to the French of their temporary possession of that kingdom.

Parthenopes Regnum simul olim Galle luemque Cepisti, restat nunc tibi sola lues.

The catalogue of Romish saints is ample, I dare say, far beyond your conception. I do not know the precise number to which it may amount at present; but it must certainly be prodigious from the account I remember to have seen of those belonging to one single order, that of St. Bennet: they were computed at fifty-five thousand four hundred and sixty. This computation was made about the time of the holding the council of Constance, which was in the year one thousand four hundred and fourteen.— How many have been added since I cannot tell.

The right of canonising, that is to say of declaring any one a saint, and authorising

rising people to address their supplications to him as such, is vested solely I believe in the Pope. He is assisted by cardinals, and others whom he may judge proper to associate with him in this business; but the ultimate decision rests with him.

The Pope cannot, however, after the formalities of a canonisation have taken place, deprive the saint he has made of that title: like a British peerage, it may be given, but not taken away by the donor.

You will here observe an essential difference between ancient and modern Rome, in the powers assumed and exercised by both upon occasions of this nature. In ancient Rome they were extended to a far greater degree of latitude: the senate and consuls were sovereign arbitrators in these matters: they appointed the gods that were to be worshipped, and abrogated

gated them according to their own difcretion. Thus deities were made or unmade by a fenatorial decree, and the old in turn gave place to new; who, like their predeceffors, enjoyed but precarious honours and exiftence.

Before the high altar in the Romifh churches, and before thofe of fome of their favourite faints, lamps are burning night and day. They are ufually fufpended in veffels of gilt brafs, and often of maffive filver. The chief reafon for mentioning them, is that fome years ago, as I have been informed, a naturalift projected a renewal of that famous lamp of Callimachus, which was faid to burn a whole year without any frefh fupply of light, oil, or fewel.

This celebrated architect, befide inventing the Corinthian order, is reported among other ingenious difcoveries to have contrived a lamp of this nature, which

was

was placed in the Temple of Minerva at Athens.

A particularity will probably strike you on your Sunday visits to churches. While the French world at large is dissolved in pleasure, and rioting in all sorts of diversions and merriments, the pulpits are universally resounding with the warmest exhortations to avoid them, and the most dreadful denunciations of future punishment to such as neglect their warning. The contrast between what is spoken here and acted elsewhere, precisely on this day, is truly curious.

The truth is, that no preachers are more severe in their doctrines than the French. They labour with peculiar vehemence to give their audience a distaste and aversion for all the enjoyments and comforts of this life. I doubt not you will agree with me, in thinking that they outshoot their mark: by enforcing the necessity of adoping principles

ciples totally incompatible with human nature, their sermons often prove rather discouragements than invitations to piety.

This indiscreet zeal very ill accords with that liberty and countenance given to all manner of amusements, for which the French police is so remarkable: one would imagine from thence, that they who presided over this department, were conscious of their necessity, in order to keep the public in good humour, and entertained at the same time no respect for the opinion of those who combated them.

Certain it is, these advocates for a total renunciation of what they call the frivolous pomps and vanities of life, shew themselves miserably defective in the knowledge of what is essentially conducive to the well-being of society, and indeed absolutely necessary for the comfortable

able subsistence of the individuals that compose it.

Were the maxims inculcated with so much energy, to be reduced to practice, what would become of those countless multitudes who have no other means of earning their daily bread, but their skill in those that are called the arts of luxury?

These declaimers forget that vanity and luxury are but relative terms, and only applicable to such as live beyond their income: the more money is expended, the less men are liable to want and misery, which are never known where business is brisk and work is provided for the laborious. Instead of preaching therefore this apathy and disrelish for the things of this world, they ought on the contrary to exhort mankind, each according to his abilities, to afford all possible encouragement to activity and industry, as the only sources from whence the prosperity of individuals at large can reasonably be expected to flow.

In contradiction to the tenets maintained by so many of their preachers, a French writer says, that " it is through a peculiar Providence the reign of vanity has been permitted to succeed to that of charity, which has long been departed: three parts in four of the human race would die of hunger, were not the various branches of worldly vanity so many channels through which they are supplied with food: until the spirit of charity is revived, it were unwise to aim at the total destruction of vanity; such endeavours can only proceed from an ignorance of the character of the present times. The opulent should therefore expend their riches freely and abundantly among artificers, tradesmen, and people in business; instead of abridging their luxury, they are on the contrary bound in duty to continue it, for the employment and support of the

ingenious

ingenious and working claffes." This may not be the creed of enthufiafm and fanaticifm, but it is certainly the doctrine of found reafon.

Excefs of felf-denial and mortification is feldom, if ever, inculcated by the Englifh clergy: they are, highly to their honour, governed by more rational ideas, fuch as are confiftent with practicability, and tend evidently to the benefit and folid happinefs of mankind.

I need not tell you that whatever has a different tendency cannot be dictated by the fpirit of wifdom. The real teft of the truth or falfehood of all religious maxims and inftitutes, is their agreement with, or their repugnance to the felicity of man in his actual ftate, and in the vifible difpenfation of things.

Hear as many of their noted preachers, and fee as many of their religious ceremonies

nies as you can with conveniency: it is surely a pastime far preferable to that of lounging at home or elsewhere, which is too frequently the case of those whose minds are not sufficiently supplied with motives of activity.

Among others you will be much entertained with their funeral solemnities. An ode, or rather a series of Leonine verses in short metre, divided into stanzas, is always sung upon these occasions; it is called the the *Dies irae* from the two first words it begins with, and is justly esteemed one of the most beautiful productions of the Gothic ages. When sung in parts, it is a truly pathetic piece of music, and perfectly suitable to the occasion.

The French are much more solicitous to be buried in churches than the English. Such as can afford it, seldom chuse to be buried elsewhere; hence those places are crowded with graves.

It

LETTER XXIX.

It may not be amiss to observe, that this custom of interring the dead in churches and in cloisters, began chiefly to prevail about the seventh century: it was intended as an honorary recompence to those who had built or endowed churches or monasteries, and often proved an inducement to benefactions and legacies to both. The more considerable the donation was, the nearer the donor was laid to the altar.

In the primitive ages of Christianity, they seem to have confined burials to church-yards. Prudentius, in describing the honours paid to the memory of the deceased, mentions no more than the strowing of flowers and green boughs or leaves over the grave, and pouring odoriferous liquids on the stone that covered it: his words are

Nos tecta fovebimus ossa
Violis et fronde virenti,
Titulumque et frigida saxa
Liquido spargemus odore.

LETTER XXX.

WHENEVER men shall think fit to substract from Christianity what they have added to it, there will remain but one religion, as simple in its doctrine, as pure in its morals. Thus says a wit of the last century, and thus, I apprehend, will every man say that reflects on the ends and purposes for which it was instituted.

We are now verging towards the close of the eighteenth century since its foundation; but we do not perceive in the different sects into which it is split, any signs of a reconciliation in those opinions which constitute the difference between them.

Speculative men have often been at the pains of investigating the real causes of the religious

LETTER XXX.

religious disputes that have so long divided the world. With all deference to those who have already delivered their opinions on this matter, the most efficient cause is evidently the multitude of such as take upon them to teach and expound the doctrines of Christianity, some of whom spend their whole lives in writing notes and comments upon texts, on which, to use a vulgar but significant expression, the least that is said is the soonest mended.

They who dedicate their time to such lucubrations, cannot in the nature of things always agree about the explanation of difficult passages; but such is the pride and presumption of men, that when they have once made up their minds, to use the modern phrase, they are seldom, if ever, in the humour to unmake them.

Hence they adhere with invincible partinacity to the judgments they have formed, and deem their honour concerned in maintain-

maintaining them at all events and at all risks.

Were the authors of any particular opinions to stand single, were the notions they espouse confined merely to their own persons, they might with all safety pore over texts and make as many comments as they pleased; but the mischief is, that they are never satisfied unless the public is made acquainted with their ideas, and until they have gained favourers and adherents.

In the mean while, such as differ from them are no less eager in the procuring of proselites, and in defending their tenets with all the warmth and obstinacy which accompany theological disputes.

These, unhappily for mankind, are always carried on with more illiberality and violence than any other; and yet, upon cool consideration, there are none about which men ought to be more indifferent;
since

LETTER XXX.

since it is clear that before the subject which divides them, was brought into litigation, they were, to all the essential intents of religion, as safe and as knowing as any discussion of the matter will ever make them.

Well it is known that the more men dispute about religious points, the farther they wander from the purposes of religion: it was given to men as a guide and director of their actions; but they have converted it into an object of speculation.

Were the polemical works that have been written by the divines of all parties, to be consigned to the flames, it would abridge and improve the study of divinity by so many degrees as it would remove the seeds of contention, and leave nothing to be read and studied but what redounds incontestably to the benefit of mankind.

It

LETTER XXX.

It is principally to the Greeks we are to ascribe the origin of most religious disputations. They were noted of old for their subtile and inquisitive disposition: unfortunately for the world they applied it to objects inscrutable in their very nature: they treated religion as they had formerly done philosophy; they made it a business of endless argumentations; they investigated its tenets with the same spirit, and in the same manner as if they had been the categories of Aristotle.

But as the theory of true religion is founded on the purest simplicity, it could not fail suffering in such hands: they mangled and distorted it into a multiplicity of forms, and put it quite out of its original shape.

While the Greeks were taken up with quirks and quibbles, the remainder of Christendom was plunged in confusion and ignorance;

ignorance; the second resulted from the first, and they both equally co-operated in obscuring reason and defacing religion.

In this situation was Europe when the genius of monastic institutions began to rear its head. As they appeared the only refuge left to the little knowledge that remained in those barbarous times, they received the kindest welcome that people were able to bestow.

But as imaginary knowledge was copiously diffused and firmly established at that æra, it was implicitly adopted by those who profest an addiction to study, and soon found its way into convents and monasteries, and every other receptacle of the learning then in vogue.

Thus they retained and propagated the truths and errors they were taught, and were equally zealous in maintaining both.

As

LETTER XXX.

As ignorance is the parent of obstinacy, we are not to be surprised at the tenaciousness with which the various orders of monastics have invariably stood up for the doctrines and opinions that prevailed at the epochas that were so favourable to their foundation.

They were handed down successively from one generation to another, and were looked upon as a sacred deposit, which was not to be changed or diminished: their preservation whole and unimpaired seemed, in a manner, to be a kind of tacit condition and security for the existence and prosperity of those who were their teachers and propagators.

These were trained up betimes in a profound acquiescence and veneration for what had during so many ages been the creed of their predecessors; this duration, according to their ideas, added strength and authenticity to the established doctrines,

trines, and they could not with patience suffer them to be called in question.

Hence arose that inflexibility in religious controversies, which was the source of so many calamities in various countries, and still continues to render the different denominations of Christians so inimical and odious to each other.

We are not therefore to expect a cessation of hostilities in the field of religious contest, while they who are hottest in the dispute continue to keep their ground. Until the numerous host that goes by the name of regular clergy, is melted down into the common mass of their fellow-citizens, one of the greatest obstacles will remain to the general reunion of all Christians in a similar way of thinking.

Having thus briefly traced the origin and progress of the contradictory opinions subsisting among them, and of the antipathy

pathy which they occasion, I will conclude this epistle by advising you to run over at your leisure, the historical accounts of the principal orders of monastics in the Romish church. Fleury's ecclesiastical history is perhaps the best book you can consult to this intent.

I use the word consult, as I would not have you dive too deep into researches of this kind, while objects of so much more importance demand your attention: I mean no more than that you should not be ignorant of the nature of the many institutions that have taken place among men in latter ages: the knowledge of these things contributes not a little to let one into the temper of the times, and of those who presided over them.

The spirit which then animated mankind is perhaps more visible in those establishments, than in any of their other public proceedings. The political transactions

actions of one age differ little from those of another; war, peace, negociations, national triumphs or calamities, resemble each other in almost every circumstance, but those of time, place, and actors; but in the former instances we discover those peculiarities of character which distinguish the men of one period from those of another, and set, as it were, a mark on the humour and disposition prevailing among them, when they were at liberty to display it.

By the same rule, that in private life we see more of a man's native turn and inclination in those things which he performs from his own impulse, than when he submits to coercion or influence, so in public acts, the genius and bent of a people is much more completely exhibited in such undertakings as are spontaneous, and flow from a general willingness and desire to co-operate in them, than in those

Z   where

where the tide of superior power and compulsion hurries them along in spite of themselves.

LETTER XXXI.

AFTER surveying churches and their contents, and venturing some strictures on ecclesiastical matters, it will be proper to take a review of other buildings of note.

There are undoubtedly a much greater number of them in Paris than in London. The French often mention this by way of proving its superiority to our metropolis in magnificence and agreeableness. An impartial answer is, that if Paris surpasses London in these two respects, it does not however equal it in its numerous conveniencies, which in the scale of sound reasoning, are of much more consequence than the former.

The

LETTER XXXI.

The noblest monument of architecture in Paris, and in all France, is the Louvre. It truly deserves the name of a palace: the design is royal in all its parts, and wants nothing but to be carried into execution. It is surprising, that since the reign of Philip Augustus, who first projected this building, it should never have been brought to a final completion. Several monarchs have turned their attention to this object, but none have done it effectually: often has the resolution been taken to bring the work forward; it has frequently been resumed with great ardour, but as frequently discontinued. Had the reign of Henry the Fourth lasted sufficiently, it is probable the business would have been accomplished. Lewis the Fourteenth seemed for a while earnestly intent upon bringing it to perfection; but after expending considerable sums, he dropped it for the prosecution of other building schemes, none of which ever equalled the grandeur of that which he so unwisely neglected.

Thus from the days of Philip Auguſtus, unto the preſent epocha, a ſpace of ſix hundred years, has the plan of a royal reſidence, in their capital, been left unexecuted by twenty-ſix monarchs, including the preſent.

The completeſt palace in Paris is that known by the name of *Palais royal*. It was erected by Cardinal Richelieu, who bequeathed it to his maſter Lewis the Thirteenth. It has undergone various alterations ſince it was firſt built, and is by ſome connoiſſeurs eſteemed, in its actual ſtate, the moſt commodious and beſt contrived edifice of all the kingdom, though far from faultleſs in point of architecture.

Both the *Louvre* and *Palais royal* contain magnificent collections of pictures. You will find in them ſome of the principal maſter-pieces of the Italian and Flemiſh ſchool.

The ſame may be ſaid of the Luxemburg, which is reputed by good judges

the

the moſt elegant and perfect piece of architecture in its kind, and of its dimenſions, of any in Europe.

This beautiful palace was built by Mary of Medicis, the queen and widow of Henry the Fourth. No woman ever experienced more ſurpriſing viciſſitudes of fortune: after the death of that monarch, ſhe ruled France under the title of Regent during ſeveral years, but was at laſt, in conſequence of a variety of civil diſſentions, compelled to fly from that kingdom, and after undergoing ſuch difficulties and hardſhips, as one would naturally think her birth and ſtation in the world could not have failed to obviate, ſhe died at laſt an exile from the realm ſhe had governed, in the abſolute want of neceſſaries.

Of all the public buildings in France, erected for the ſupport and comfort of individuals in want, the nobleſt is that

ſtiled

stiled the *Hotel des Invalides*. It is incontestably the finest military hospital in the world, and does more honour to the memory of Lewis the Fourteenth, than any of those institutions which he either founded or patronised.

Nor should we forget on this occasion the person by whose advice and solicitation that monarch was induced to this truly munificent and generous undertaking. It was chiefly to the council, and to the care of Louvois, this useful and necessary foundation was due. While we therefore condemn his ambition, his arrogance, his unfeelingness in other instances, let us acknowledge that in this one he made some atonement for them; and that if other nations suffered from his evil qualities, still he deserves to be remembered with gratitude by the military classes in France.

As my plan does not aim at details, suffice it to say, that in this superb and

LETTER XXXI.

immense pile, food, rayment, and lodging, are provided for those multitudes who have spent their best days in the service of their country, or whom wounds and other accidents of war have rendered incapable of earning their bread.

The regulations made for the good government of this great number of men, are allowed to be framed with peculiar wisdom. They are said to be the joint production of the great Prince of Condé, and the famous Marshal of Luxemburg: two such names are sufficient to procure them universal esteem.

The church belonging to this foundation is particularly celebrated for its beautiful cupola, which is pronounced by the majority of connoisseurs, to be the most splendid and magnificent performance of this nature that is extant.

In the neighbourhood of the invalids stands an elegant and spacious edifice, destined for the education of five hundred young Gentlemen who are intended for the army. It was founded by the late King of France, Lewis the Fifteenth. The rules and statutes by which they are governed are said to have been mostly composed by the late Marshal Saxe.

At no great distance from these military foundations, you will find another of a more peaceable nature. This is the edifice so well known in Europe by the name of Observatory, and for the many curious and useful discoveries and improvements that have from time to time been made there in the science of astronomy.

This is one of those laudable institutions that are due to Lewis the Fourteenth. Happy could he have stinted his ambition to excel his cotemporaries in the encouragement and protection of literary genius, and of pacific arts and sciences.

LETTER XXXI.

This place deserves your particular attention from the ingenuity of its contrivance, and the remarkable apparatus it contains for the use of such as are employed in astronomical investigations.

While we are engaged in this subject, let me remind you to procure a list of all the considerable astronomers that France has produced, together with their respective discoveries. Were you to make out one of the astronomers of all nations, whose labours have been serviceable to the world, and to be at the pains of arranging it in a chronological order, it would prove both amusing and instructive. Nothing tends more to illuminate, as well as to satisfy the mind, than a review of the progress gradually made in the course of so many ages, in so grand and sublime a knowledge as that of the structure and order of this stupendous universe.

The squares and large openings in Paris are not so numerous as in London; but they

they are built with more exactness and regularity of architecture, and better decorated. There are only four that merit peculiar notice, the *Place Royale, Vendome, des Victoires,* and *de Louis Quinze.*

The first of these was built during the ministry of Cardinal Richelieu, under his countenance and encouragement. This great Minister was no less intent on works of this nature, than on the other objects that contribute to embellish a country and improve a nation.

This is a real square, remarkable only from its uniformity, and from being the model of that which our Inigo Jones erected in Convent-Garden much about the same time: but this latter is upon a far preferable scale; the piazzas are much larger and lighter; had the whole been finished according to his original design, it would have proved the most elegant square in all Europe.

The

LETTER XXXI.

The *Place Vendome* is a decagone of beautiful architecture, far superior to that of the *Place Royale*. It has two openings facing two stately porticos of churches, which add surprisingly to its appearance, and give it a peculiar air of grandeur.

The *Place des Victoires* is much in the form of the latter, though not so spacious nor striking.

The *Place de Louis Quinze* is the best situated of any, and in its present state is undoubtedly the finest area that can possibly be conceived. On the one side is a range of sumptuous edifices; facing to this the river Seine runs in a parallel line, and on its opposite bank are seen a row of palaces; on one of the two remaining sides stands the magnificent garden of the Tuilleries, and on the other the *Champs Elisees*. To build three other rows for the sake of conformity with the first, would at once destroy the whole merit of this

this beautiful spot; and yet I have heard individuals lament that it was not done.

In the midst of these four places you will find statues of those Kings of France in whose reigns they were erected. They are accompanied with fulsome inscriptions, such as never fail to decorate equally the images of the worst as well as the best Princes.

The *Place Royale* has the statue on horseback of Lewis the Thirteenth. It was set up at the expence of his prime Minister Cardinal Richelieu, a man who was no less odious than necessary to him; whom he hated for abilities the superior weight of which was oppressive to his pride, but whom he had sense enough to esteem on account of their utility to his interest.

In the *Place Vendome* is an equestrian statue of Lewis the Fourteenth, erected at the cost of the city of Paris with prodigious

gious solemnity at the commencement of this century. It was the last public compliment of the kind paid to the vanity of this ostentatious monarch. Shortly after that war commenced which proved so fatal a reverse of all his former triumphs, and brought him lower than his successes had ever exalted him.

In the *Place des Victoires* is a pedestrian statue of the same monarch, done at the private charge of one of his subjects, in order to testify his loyalty and gratitude for benefits and honours conferred upon him. Viewed in this light it does more honour to the erector than to him for whom it was erected. The person alluded to is the Marshal Feuillade, an intrepid warrior, an excellent officer, and one of the noblest minded men that France ever produced.

In the *Place de Louis Quinze* you will see the equestrian statue of the late King, put
up

up at the expence of the city of Paris, on the conclusion of the war wherein the arms of France were so successful in Flanders under the command of Marshal Saxe.

Forget not to read and to transcribe the inscriptions under these statues; though full of flattery, they are also full of elegance; they celebrate Kings for what they ought to have been, and give one a perfect idea of what long experience has taught men so seldom to expect, a great and good sovereign.

No people seem to harbour a greater prepossession in favour of their royal masters than the French. It is certainly a prejudice on the right side; men who see themselves well received and treated, will, one should think, endeavour to retain this good-will and kind usage by acting becomingly. But the French, like lovers whom no severity can cure of their attachment, continue in spite of harsh treatment

treatment to idolize those who trample upon them.

How far this forgetfulness of injuries may be laudable, is a question that will admit of some discussion: revenge often falls upon those who take it, even when they obtain it according to their most sanguine wishes; on the other hand, to bear oppression tamely is an invitation and encouragement to oppressors. It is therefore the duty of men to steer a middle course, neither to submit to tyranny by a passive acquiescence, nor yet to inflict upon it such a punishment as shall make the remedy worse than the disease.

An English gentleman who travels with a view of preserving and improving that character, will often meet with occasions of refreshing his memory with what he has read and heard of the relative duties subsisting between Kings and subjects, of the calamities which an infraction of them has
brought

brought upon mankind, of the neceſſity of allying firmneſs and reſiſtance with ſubmiſſion and obedience; he will from the ſight of undue praiſe and unmanly adulation, gather motives to refrain from ſuch meanneſs, and learn to beſtow his attachment, and to expreſs it, upon ſuch occaſions only as deſerve it.

A ſtatue which you will view with pleaſure on all accounts, is that of Henry the Fourth, juſtly the favourite monarch of the French, one whom they never mention without rapture, and propoſe with reaſon to their Kings as the brighteſt example they can follow.

This ſtatue ſtands on the Pontneuf; he is repreſented on horſe-back, armed according to the manner of his time; the figure perfectly reſembles the pictures that remain of him; his countenance is open, firm, and majeſtic, and he appears at once the King and the hero.

In the opinion of numbers of Connoisseurs this is the best equestrian statue in France, and inferior to none in Europe of modern performance: Bernini, it is said, used often to stop and admire it, and say the statue was worthy of such a King, no less than the King was worthy of such a statue.

Such applause from an artist who was the Phidias of his day, leaves nothing more to be added: this famous Italian sculptor often wished that the statue he had projected for Lewis the Fourteenth, might equal that of Henry the Fourth.

A Prince whose memory is still revered, and from whom the French had promised themselves much happiness, was remarkable for the attention he frequently paid to this representation of his royal ancestor. This was the Duke of Burgundy, grandson to Lewis the Fourteenth, and father to the late King of France.

Bred under the tuition of the illustrious Fenelon, he proved a disciple worthy of such a master. Allowing for some foibles which arose from an excess of religious fervour, he seemed born to render mankind happy. Many are the anecdotes recorded of the goodness of his heart, and the rectitude of his understanding.

Among others it is reported that he took particular delight in the History of Henry the Fourth, written by Perefixe, and that he would sometimes, after perusing it, take a walk to the Pontneuf, to look at this statue. It is plain from thence that he viewed it as Peter the Great did that of Cardinal Richelieu, not as a Connoisseur, but as a Prince, and that his admiration was directed not to the artist, but to the hero.

In this manner I sincerely wish you may principally attend to all objects of this kind. It has often excited my indignation

to

to hear gentlemen expatiating for hours on the various beauties owing to the pencil or the chiffel, without the addition of a fingle thought on the perfons reprefented.

The real truth is, I mention it with fhame, that they are often totally unacquainted with the characters of thefe perfonages: I have known men of fortune and confequence, vifit a gallery of pictures, and betray the groffeft ignorance in what related to thofe whom they reprefented.

I will conclude this article upon Henry the Fourth, with a reflection or rather an admonition, faid to have been given to his pupil by the Duke of Orleans, Regent of France in the minority of the late King. Croffing the Pontneuf one day in the fame coach, the Regent fixed his eyes very earneftly on the ftatue, then taking the young monarch by the hand, I wifh, faid he, you may be as great as Charlemain, and as good as Henry the Fourth.

This complimentary ejaculation reminds one of that, which it was cuſtomary to pay to the Roman Emperors, on their firſt going to the ſenate after their inauguration; this body always cloſed their congratulations with wiſhing them the felicity of Auguſtus, and the goodneſs of Trajan.

It is not unlikely that the Regent, who was a man of wit, as well as of reading, may have taken the hint from this paſſage; certain it is that he could not have produced a more applicable imitation.

I do not remember any other ſtatue of this great monarch worthy of note: there is one over the chief entrance into the *Hotel de Ville*, a place correſponding with our Guildhall, but it is far inferior to that of Lewis the Fourteenth, ſtanding in the court-yard of that building.

Notwithſtanding the indiſputable ſuperiority of Henry in all the qualifications neceſſary

necessary to forn a royal as well as an heroic character, such has been the adulation of the times, since the accession of Lewis to the throne, that where the former has one statue or bust, the latter has ten.

The last mentioned building is remarkable for several paintings in high esteem; it contains some very spacious halls in the taste of those that are seen in ancient Gothic castles; the reason of their spaciousness is that the King and his court are on great and remarkable occasions entertained there by the city of Paris.

The area facing this edifice is noted for two very different purposes, the execution of malefactors, and the public rejoicings on auspicious events': it is equally ill calculated for both, but continues to enjoy this prerogative for no other reason than because it has enjoyed it during some centuries. It is narrow, irregular, and hemmed

med in on every side by as paltry houses as any in all Paris.

The most elegant, airy, and agreeable opening in this city, is that before the *College Mazarin:* the front of this college is of a semicircular form, in the middle stands the portico of the church or chapel, which is a very noble structure; the area before it is terminated by the river Seine, on the opposite side of which stands the Louvre.

This college excepted, together with that of the *Sorbonne,* which is a grand edifice, there are none in Paris to be compared in point of architecture to those of Oxford and Cambridge, which are incontestably the most magnificent universities in the world in point of buildings and endowments, if not in every other respect.

You will observe however, that if our colleges exceed theirs in grandeur, they do not

LETTER XXXI.

not equal them in number: Paris alone has upwards of fifty, in ten of which are public schools open to all comers, and professors paid by the King, to teach gratuitously, not only his own subjects, but the natives of all countries.

This you must allow is truly generous and royal, and places the munificence of the French government in a very respectable point of view. There are indeed some severe observers of things, who imagine that much needless encouragement is hereby given to literature, which ought to be confined only to a certain portion of the community, and by no means to be made a common property of all.

Another impropriety in their opinion, is the chusing of the metropolis for a university: the seat of study and application should always, say they, be at a distance from that of idleness and dissipation.

There is some truth in both these allegations. The situation of our universities is more favourable to the advancement of students in their learning, nor is it indeed less conducive to the making a more considerable progress in all branches of knowledge, even in persons of maturer age, on account of the less frequent avocations arising from pastimes and diversions: these in capital cities are an insuperable hindrance to the close prosecution of study, in such individuals as possess the means of indulging in them; maturity of years is no security against the perpetual temptations with which men are invironed on every side.

To the remoteness of our universities from the contagious scenes of the metropolis, it is in a great measure owing that the list of profound scholars is not so considerable at Paris as at Oxford and Cambridge, in proportion to the respective number of students.

But

But the French have a ready anfwer to thefe objections. To thofe who difapprove of the facility with which individuals of all conditions may obtain a literary education, the reply is, that *didiciſſe feliciter artes, emollit mores, nec finit eſſe feros.* Liberal knowledge refines the underſtanding and poliſhes manners; that no man is compelled to proceed further in this career than fuits his fortune or his inclination; and, in ſhort, that the more learning is diffufed, the more there will be found of humanity and politeneſs among men.

To thofe who object againſt the eſtabliſhment of a univerſity at Paris, they anfwer that the intent of individuals in applying to learning, is not to facrifice every confideration to that alone; mankind is to be ſtudied as well as books, and even preferably to them, fince it is only with the view of being profitable to the community, and at the fame time of knowing
thoroughly

thoroughly human nature, that study can deserve any applause: to segregate one self from company, and to fly from the haunts of the gay part of the world, is therefore a very improper method of qualifying one self to live in it, with any satisfaction to one self any more than to others.

Both these replies have certainly their weight: a proof of it is that the French literati are in general much more conversant in the polite and fashionable circles than people of learning in our universities, and that the secondary classes in France are upon the whole less blunt and morose than their equals in England.

Another advantage accrues to literary individuals from residing at Paris; they contract acquaintances among the great, and retain them more easily than if they dwelt elsewhere: it is chiefly, if not only, in a metropolis that patrons are to be met with and effectually secured.

It

LETTER XXXI.

It is due to this fortunate circumstance that patronage is a thing much more common in France than in England: there is hardly in Paris any person above the level of vulgar abilities, who has not some friend of distinction, to whose company he is welcome, and who is ready to forward his interest upon all occasions.

Allow me also to add, what you will deem, I doubt not, another very solid advantage: by frequenting people engaged in the scenes of active life, an individual imbibes a principle of activity that inclines him to the like pursuits; he consequently will strive to make his studies subservient to this purpose, he will therefore not confine them to subjects merely of speculation; instead of burying himself as it were in the grave of antiquity, he will direct his attention equally at least to modern times and transactions; he will survey what has lately past and what actually passes on the stage of the world, and will

will qualify himself to be useful to the present, as well as to discourse learnedly of former generations.

The shameful ignorance of many individuals in modern affairs, while they are at the same time critically conversant in those of an ancient date, is often a subject of surprize to men of abilities employed in business of public importance. I remember to have heard an old gentleman, a French Refugee, mention that Count Bothmar, Minister at the court of Queen Anne, from George the First, while Elector of Hanover, used often to testify his astonishment at the little knowledge in modern history of some of the most sensible persons in this country, and express at the same time his determination to remedy this evil as soon as it was in his power: he kept his word; it was principally through his instigation, that Prince, after his accession to the crown of this realm, founded professorships of modern history in our universities.

Let

LETTER XXXI.

Let me advise you to be present at some of the public acts that annually take place in the principal colleges: the subjects of disputation will shew you at once the nature of the learning and philosophy that are taught in France, and enable you to draw comparisons between the doctrines of their universities and of ours: a few afternoons will suffice for this purpose.

Though, as already observed, there are no less than ten colleges possest of public schools and professors, yet, to the great honour of the university of Paris, they are constantly filled with teachers of prime eminence in their respective branches.—But what is much more laudable, these institutions are not sinecures, bestowed through family connections, or parliamentary interest. A professorship is a serious task, and obliges the incumbent to a close and laborious attendance during three parts in four of the year.

An excellent refult of this diverfity of schools, is that an emulation is produced between those who preside over them: the warmth and zeal with which it is exerted among the heads, soon is communicated to the members; challenges in the field of literature have occafionally happened between the refpective ftudents of thefe different schools: the efforts made in thefe reciprocal trials of skill, muft naturally awaken and fharpen the capacity of fuch as engage in them.

The number of perfons of extraordinary merit among thefe profeffors, has been at fome particular epochas truly remarkable. I have feen a lift of those who flourifhed in the days of Lewis the Fourteenth, and another of those in the middle of the fixteenth century: they both contained very celebrated names in the republic of letters: the latter mentioned a particularity well worth recording; in one college alone three men were at the fame time

time profeſſors, whoſe character yields to none for literary fame. Theſe were Turnebe, Muret, and Buchanan.

A piece of architecture that will ſtrike you is the *Ecole de Chirurgie*. Its conſtruction is of ſingular elegance, and is looked upon to be the firſt in Europe of the kind. But that which ought principally to fix your attention, is the prodigious multitudes that repair to it in order to learn ſurgery, and the uncommon diligence and care with which they are inſtructed in every department of this truly noble and neceſſary knowledge.

A witty foreigner, who came to Paris to improve himſelf in this art, during the reign of Lewis the Fourteenth, compoſed a poem on this ſubject, wherein he told that monarch, that in conſideration of the very great number of inhabitants of the countries bordering upon France, who were hurt and wounded in the perpetual wars

wars he made upon all his neighbours, he ought in conscience to establish a school of surgery for each of these nations, on their respective frontiers, wherein they should be taught it in their own language, and by professors of their own appointment, but maintained at his expence.

Another building of late erection is the *Ecole de Droit*. It is deserving of inspection on account of its beautiful simplicity. An occasional attendance on the lectures delivered here on civil jurisprudence, will be of utility in letting you into the general maxims of French legislation: you will not seldom be entertained with very ingenious dissertations.

There is a place in Paris which you must not neglect seeing, not for its architecture and magnificence, it has neither; but because it will convey a forcible impression of the immense disparity subsisting, in some very essential considerations, between

between the two capitals of England and France.

This place is the *Hospital des Enfans trouvés*. No foundling hospital in the world is burthened with such multitudes. The list of births at Paris for the year one thousand seven hundred and sixty-seven, amounts to near twenty thousand, that of foundlings to five thousand five hundred: nine years after, the former list amounted to much the same; but the latter came to six thousand three hundred: hence may we not infer, that either misery is encreased, or natural affection diminished, in that immense city? The last is perhaps too often the unfortunate consequence of the first.

I lay these two computations before you for two reasons; the one is to shew the constant continuance of the evil, which is indeed of long standing, the other to shew you its progress.

LETTER XXXI.

What a proportion of wretchedness among the generality of people must be found in a place where such a shocking one is acknowledged in so public a manner! Nothing surely but the most cruel extremity of want can excuse parents for consigning their offspring to the charity and care of the community: nothing therefore can prove more unanswerably the excessive poverty of the inhabitants of Paris, than this woeful abandonment of so many of their children, at that moment precisely when the feelings of nature are the most powerful, and when nothing but absolute inability can be supposed to prevent her calls from being obeyed.

You will on this occasion naturally turn your reflections home, and congratulate your country on the superior happiness of her circumstances. *Res est sacra miser,* is a maxim which generosity and humanity will jointly support: but though we should never exult over the distresses of our

LETTER XXXI.

our fellow-creatures, yet when forgetful of their situation, a people impertinently boast of advantages which they do not possess, it is not unfair to repress their vaunting, and to convict them of ill-founded pride. In this light, when the French attempt to set their condition on a parity of prosperousness with that of the English, there is no sort of inhumanity in reminding them of this dreadful dereliction of their infant progeny, which must effectually silence at once all those vain pretences to an equality of circumstances, which they are so apt to insist upon against all truth and evidence.

You will lament upon this occasion the causes of this general state of national indigence; and I hope you will not neglect to investigate them: a volume would hardly suffice to detail the many sources of vexation that abound in this country: every department of public administration is full of them; complaints are heard from every quarter; but the voice of the afflicted is in no country less attended to, and if lifted too high, sooner silenced.

When you have pondered at leisure upon these things, recollect England and its inhabitants, *fortunatos nimium sua si bona norint*.

LETTER XXXII.

IN the suburbs, and in the neighbourhood of Paris, you will meet with a variety of objects to excite your attention, and to furnish matter for reflection.

Near the river side, in a very pleasing situation, stands *l'Hospital general*, an immence edifice, designed for the reception and support of the female poor, and for the confinement and correction of women of ill fame.

The

LETTER XXXII.

The regulations obſerved in this houſe were framed by the illuſtrious Lamoignon, firſt preſident of the parliament at Paris, one of the wifeſt magiſtrates, and moſt eloquent men, that France ever produced.

This houſe was founded through his care, and is fitted in the moſt judicious manner, for the purpoſes it was intended to anſwer. It contains prodigious numbers who are kept in admirable order and neatneſs, and employed in the moſt uſeful and profitable manner: the rules are perfectly ſuited to thoſe for whom they were made: ſufficient indulgence and lenity are ſhewn, without relaxation of that neceſſary diſcipline, which is the only preſervative of decorum in ſuch places.

A foundation of this kind is much wanted among us. In caſe it ſhould ever take place, we cannot adopt a better ſyſtem than that which is eſtabliſhed here.

LETTER XXXII.

It has long been complained that the punishment inflicted upon the miserable objects of prostitution that swarm in our metropolis, only serves to harden them: it cannot be otherwise, when we consider into what brutal hands they are often committed. While severity alone is employed, and neither comfort nor instruction administered to them; while they are permitted an indiscriminate unregulated association with each other, the same disorderliness of disposition will of course remain; and this being the radical cause of an irregular and criminal life, we cannot, while it subsists, expect to retrieve them from the fatal habits which it has produced, and will continue to nourish in spite of repeated chastisement.

Far different from the methods practised in our places of correction are those that are followed in this. It is strictly in many respects on the same footing as our Magdalen-house: the principal difference is, that in this latter none enter through compulsion, whereas in the former force is used.

You will not, I hope, pass over slightly what has been said upon this subject, as it is incumbent upon every person of humanity to contribute to the alleviation of misfortunes, especially in the other sex. Gentlemen who travel should for that reason be extremely attentive to the police of the nations they visit in all things relating to womankind. An excellent collection of practical rules might be formed out of the various ordinances relating to them that prevail in Europe.

At no great distance from the hospital just described stands one still larger, called Bicetre. It is an ancient edifice of prodigious dimensions, a receptacle for characters of multifarious denominations, wild and disorderly young men, persons who can give no satisfactory account of themselves, or are guilty of mal-practices, defrauders,

frauders, cheats, pick-pockets, criminals condemned to imprisonment, convicts for petty larcenies, in short, the whole catalogue of such as have committed misdemeanours, for which labour and hard fare are appointed.

There are also multitudes of vagrants, idlers, mendicants, and others of that stamp, people out of work, and poor of divers sorts: for all these classes suitable employment is provided, and they are treated proportionably to their deserts.

Persons reduced through misfortunes and casualties to narrow circumstances, may for a moderate consideration find a maintenance here. This helps in no small measure to people it. Viewed in such a light, it is a very humane and useful institution, and with singular propriety situated near a metropolis where scantiness of means to support themselves is the fate of so many.

The

LETTER XXXII.

The last order of beings I shall mention are such unfortunate lunatics as are either deemed incurable, or have no friends to assist them.

The strictest regularity and discipline are observed in this place. The least mutiny or disobedience is punished with unrelenting severity. Such is the care taken at the same time of morals and behaviour, and so much of pains bestowed in admonishing and instructing those who are sent hither for that purpose, that many a youth of whom small hopes at first were entertained, has been restored to a right way of thinking and acting: the knowledge of this is a powerful inducement with parents who have unruly children, or guardians who are troubled with ungovernable wards, to consign them to the management of those who have the direction of this place.

From

From these various causes it is always full of inhabitants: their number is generally between five and six thousand.

One of the most curious characters that ever inhabited this place was an astrologer and fortune-teller. He had long pursued this business with sufficient success to raise a tolerable fortune; but aiming at a large increase of it, he hazarded all his worth in the famous Mississippi scheme, and lost it, as many others did all they had. This was a heavy disappointment, and reduced him to the necessity of resuming his former trade; in the prosecution of which he retrieved his affairs sufficiently to purchase an annuity, with which he retired from the world, and spent his latter days in this retreat.

Few men had experienced a stranger variety of vicissitudes. He was born of French parents at Aleppo, and travelled in the early part of his life in Arabia, Persia, and

LETTER XXXII.

and Indoſtan, of which countries he ſpoke the languages fluently. On his family's return to France, he accompanied them, and received a very genteel education at Paris. He was a man of excellent parts, and of a prodigious memory, but extremely addicted to pleaſures of all ſorts; this diſpoſition proved his ruin. On the demiſe of his parents, he launched into all manner of exceſſes, and in a few years diſſipated a very conſiderable inheritance: he then betook himſelf to commerce, and returned to the ſpot of his birth, where by his induſtry he accumulated a ſum of money ſufficient to enable him to re-viſit the countries he had ſeen in his youthful days; a project which aroſe from a rovingneſs of diſpoſition that accompanied him every where, and often prevented him from ſettling where it would have been highly to his advantage.

He remained however ſome time at Baſſora and Iſpahan, the latter city eſpecially.

cially. This being the capital of Persia, he might, had he pursued a commercial line, soon have enriched himself by it, considering his perfect skill in the language; but he availed himself of his knowledge in quite a different manner. Having an extraordinary versality of genius, he had among other studies bestowed much of his attention upon books of astrology: this made him appear a man of uncommon importance in a country where it is so highly prized, and where the superior stile in which he had been educated, could not fail to set him above the pretensions of the natives in that science: he soon eclipsed the most noted among them, and was consulted by the grandees of the court preferably to all others: he shortly acquired enough to return to France, where he bought an estate, on the income of which he subsisted a few years very comfortably; but the desire of travelling seized him again so irresistibly, that he sold it, and went to Constantinople as an agent for, and partner with, a houfe in trade at Marfeilles. When fettled in that metropolis of Turkey, he rendered himfelf by his addrefs and dexterity fo acceptable to feveral men in power, that through their means he was intrufted with fome tranfactions that were highly to his intereft. He left Turkey richer than ever, intending to fix his future refidence at Paris. Here he lived a long time in the midft of all enjoyments; but becoming acquainted with fome people of rank and fafhion, who delighted much in his company, and who were at the fame time addicted to play, both he and they fell into the hands of fharpers, who ftripped them of confiderable fums. His companions, who were men of large property, ftood the fhock; but he was totally ruined.

This was the moft fatal ftroke he ever met with. He was no longer young, and had befides indulged himfelf in fuch a manner for a long time paft, in the luxurious

rious ease that accompanies plenty, that he was not fit to encounter obstacles and hardships as formerly. His acquaintance did not forsake him in this calamity; but he had too much of the spirit of independence in him to subsist upon their bounty. He withdrew from them entirely, changed his name and appearance, assumed a Turkish dress, and maintained himself awhile by teaching Arabic and Persian; but this not answering his expectation so completely as he wished, he determined to associate the profession of an astrologer with that of a linguist: this scheme succeeded surprisingly; he was visited by people of various conditions, the fair sex especially, whose generosity enabled him to prosper, and to terminate his career in the manner that has been related.

France has often been the scene of astrological infatuation. In the reign of Charles the Fifth, surnamed the Wise, and who deserved the title in other respects,

spects, the belief in astrologers was so great, that matters of the highest importance were governed by their decisions. We read in the history of this Prince that he was at a considerable expence in prevailing upon a famous Italian astrologer to come and reside at his court. The fame of this man was such, that not only Charles, but another monarch, was equally desirous of his presence: the contest was very earnest between them, but the astrologer, doubtless for good reasons, decided it in favour of the former. On his repairing to the French court, he was received like a tutelar genius; a large pension was settled upon him; he was made a member of the King's privy council, and his advice followed in some occurrences of great consequence. This was the famous Pisano, who had already made a splendid figure in Italy, at Venice particularly, where he had been consulted on the affairs of that republic.

We

LETTER XXXII.

We find the same credulity prevailing at the court of France full two centuries after. Catherine of Medicis, Queen Consort to Henry the Second, notwithstanding her subtility and acuteness, was the slave of astrological absurdities. So powerful was their influence over her conduct in the minutest occasions, that it having been foretold, the persons and places bearing the name of Germain would be fatal to her, she retired from the Louvre by reason of its situation in the parish of St. Germain, and was at the expence of building elsewhere a palace for her residence.

The same prejudices infected the persons composing the court of France; the ladies especially did not dare to undertake any thing without having previously consulted their astrologers. This folly rose to such a height, that not only the church, but the state was at last obliged to interfere in order to prevent the evil consequences resulting

LETTER XXXII.

sulting from it, by prohibiting the sale of such Almanacks as contained predictions and prognostications that particularised persons and events too audaciously and circumstantially.

It was at this æra the great prophecier of modern ages flourished, Nostradamus, of whom no less than twelve centos of prophecies are extant, all of them together with their author in high request at his day: nor do they seem to be forgotten even at present; I have heard many of them cited by Frenchmen, warm and zealous for the honour and prosperity of their country. Among such a number of predictions, almost as obscure as riddles, it is easy to find some not totally inapplicable to events that have happened since his time. During a long course of years they were consulted among the French, like the oracles of the Sybils among the Romans.

Henry the Fourth of France, himself, was at a time hurried with the croud along

along the torrent of credulity: his bravest warriors were solicitous to be informed of their destiny, and at the birth of his son Lewis the Thirteenth, he commissioned his first physician, who was also an eminent astrologer, to cast the nativity of this young Prince.

It seems that some of the principal physicians of those times were almost equally renowned for their proficiency in astrology: the above-mentioned Nostradamus was a physician, and so were some of the most noted astrologers in Europe.

This infatuation continued even to the time of Cardinal Richelieu: during his ministry another physician made himself famous by his prophecies; he had even the boldness to foretel the death of Lewis the Thirteenth, and to fix it at the dog-days of the year one thousand six hundred and thirty-one; but the prediction was not verified, and the Prophet was sent to the galleys.

Nor

Nor were these ridiculous notions eradicated many years after. We have a remarkable instance of the belief in the influence of the stars, and other heavenly bodies, over human events, in the solicitude exprest by the friends and dependents of Cardinal Mazarin, at the appearance of a comet during his last illness, which happened thirty years after.

The same credulity prevailed in the Asiatic parts of the world. Bernier, the famous traveller, tells us in his account of the Grand Mogul's dominions, that the people of Asia are so prejudiced in favour of judicial astrology, that most enterprizes of importance are preceded by a careful consultation of astrologers.

Tavernier, another traveller into the east, relates much the same of the Persians, who, according to him, look upon astrologers as beings of a superior character, and hearken to them as oracles: their Emperor has

has constantly three or four of them near his person.

The Chinese do not differ from them in this particular. The descriptions of that country and people inform us, that public affairs are frequently determined by astronomical observations; the Emperor takes no resolution of great consequence without having consulted the constellation that presided over his nativity.

But without going out of Europe, or stepping back to the time past, the present will afford you some proofs of the propensity of men to have recourse to such as pretend to see into futurity, and to ascertain events by the study and contemplation of the stars.

Almost all the Almanacks in Europe are full of prognostications: they abstain indeed from details and particulars; but they abound

LETTER XXXII.

abound with wonderful events to take place in the courſe of the year.

Our anceſtors did not eſcape this contagion; the name of William Lilly ſuffices to remind us of their weakneſs. This celebrated aſtrologer ſurvived the reſtoration upwards of twenty years, during which ſpace he was not idle. But beſides his aſtrological lucubrations, other methods of foretelling futurity were in vogue, particularly that famous one ſtiled the *Sortes Virgilianæ:* Is it not ſurpriſing that ſuch men as Cowley and Lord Falkland, to mention no others, could ſuffer themſelves to pay attention to ſuch fooleries?

I have enlarged upon this ſubject, in order to excite your recollection, how lately it is ſince the reign of abſurdity and prepoſſeſſion has ended among ſome of the wiſeſt people, and how ready they ſtill are to reſume their authority, unleſs prevented by by a refolute and fearlefs profecution of truth.

You will, upon impartial examination, find the multitude every where inclined to efpoufe their caufe. But what is ftill worfe, you will find that when thofe who efteem themfelves above the vulgar, have once admitted the contamination, it is more difficult to eradicate it from their minds, than from thofe of the commonalty: thefe are impofed upon by others, but thofe are impofed upon by themfelves, which of all impofitions is the hardeft to remove.

LETTER XXXIII.

THE French of all people are the moft remarkable for fubjecting to regulations whatever is fufceptible of them.

You

LETTER XXXIII.

You will find this regulating spirit exercising itself in matters of little, as well as of great consequence. The fact is, that government is fond of meddling with every thing: one would imagine from this they were apprehensive the people at large were highly dissatisfied with their measures, and ready to seize any occasion to oppose them, as oppressive and contrary to the general good; but this is by no means the case; whatever the disposition of the French may have been at former periods, they are not in the least inclined at present to express discontent, unless manifestly ill-treated; and even then they always find out some obnoxious individuals on whom to cast the load of general odium, which at the worst of times seldom reaches higher than some of the ministry, and hardly ever approaches the throne, or any of the royal family.

This solicitude for the preservation of good order every where, is certainly attended-ed with a variety of beneficial consequences: the first and most essential is, that from the conviction how difficult it is to disturb the tranquillity of the public, one seldom sees disturbances of any kind; quarrels and fightings among the lower classes are instantly suppressed, and much more peaceableness prevails in the meetings of the populace than in England.

But without enquiring whether this watchfulness of the ruling powers may not sometimes be carried to an excess, equally odious and detrimental to the public, you will in many respects find it of much utility, especially in curbing that licentiousness of behaviour, and that audaciousness, to which the vulgar in all countries are addicted whenever they see no impediments.

It is principally in their markets and places of public resort for business, that this vigilance is exerted: in the midst of the concourse that is usual on such occasions,

LETTER XXXIII.

fions, perfons unknown to the reft are carefully ftationed, whofe duty it is to prevent confufion and diforderlinefs, and to feize immediately all offenders.

Among other markets, the French have one at Paris for horfes, which is the beft regulated of any in Europe: the bufinefs is tranfacted in a fair open manner, and no improper advantages given to dealers in that commodity: the buyer and the feller are both under the ftricteft controul of others, to whom it intirely belongs to fee that juftice is done to each of the parties concerned: there is an office in this market, where fuch as chufe it may depofit the purchafe money; eight days are allowed them for trial and examination of the horfe; if at the expiration of that term any faults are difcovered and properly verified, the bargain is cancelled and the money returned.

This market is remarkably convenient for its cheapnefs, and for the conveniency

of

of finding at once horses for draft or saddle, or any purpose whatever: by thus collecting them into one place, and regulating the manner of sale, frauds are obviated, as well as the trouble of running to a great number of stables and repositories in quest of what is wanted. I have heard several English gentlemen wish for an establishment of the same kind in London.

There is at Charenton, a village two or three miles out of Paris, an institution called *Ecole Veterinaire*. It is a school of anatomy and surgery for the cure of diseases incident to horses, and of instruction how to use and manage them for the preservation of their health and strength.

Such as are desirous of acquiring a perfect knowledge of all that relates to this useful creature, cannot go to a better place; it is open to all comers; and lessons are publicly given four days in the week

week gratuitously, it being a royal foundation.

There is also in this place an hospital for sick horses on the same liberal footing; it is of great utility to the poor and to the inexpert; attendance, food, and medicines being provided for the animal till his recovery.

In the proximity of the horse-market afore-mentioned, stands the most beautiful manufactory in Europe for tapestry work: it is a large building situated on a rivulet called *Gobelins*, from whence it derives its name; the King is proprietor.

I have heard that during the calamities that accompanied the latter years of Lewis the Fourteenth, this beautiful manufactory was so neglected, that some of the workmen abandoned it, and would, had they met with suitable encouragement, have brought their art over to England: it is

rather

rather surprising, that in the midst of so many improvements, this very ingenious business should have hitherto remained in the hands of strangers; and it is much to be lamented that the attempt to introduce it here, made some years ago at Fulham, should have so speedily failed.

You will see at Chaillot, a pleasant village on the banks of the Seine near Paris, a noted manufactory of carpets in imitation of the Turkish and Persian: it has been carried to great perfection; but does not, in the opinion of such as understand these matters, exceed, if equal, the goodness and duration of our Wiltons, though it must be allowed the patterns and designs are uncommonly beautiful.

The glass manufactory in the *Fauxbourg St. Antoine* is particularly worthy of your inspection: it is esteemed a great curiosity by connoisseurs, and is thought to surpass any thing of the kind.

LETTER XXXIII.

The glafs manufactory is one of thofe in which we preceded the French. So long ago as the reign of James the Firft, an affociation of perfons of wealth and diftinction was formed, who profecuted it a while to great advantage: the troubles that followed in the fubfequent reign were probably the caufe of its being difcontinued.

There are in France feveral manufactories of china; but the principal one is at *Seve*, a village between Paris and Verfailles: it produces moft exquifite performances, fuperior in tafte and richnefs to thofe of any other country, not only in the eftimation of the French, but of many others.

To what this fuperiority is owing, on a fuppofition of its exiftence, is certainly worth an enquiry among thofe whom it concerns to bring this manufactory to an equal degree of perfection.

Certain

Certain it is that for taste and delicacy of design and workmanship nothing of the sort can claim the preference: no cost is spared to give them all the perfection possible; the whole business is carried on at the expence of the King, to whom the manufactory belongs; no other but a royal purse could defray the charges attending it.

After viewing these magnificent manufactories, it must, I imagine, naturally occur to you, that England is a country where establishments of a similar kind might, and ought therefore, one would think, long ago to have taken place: the general opulence of individuals is far beyond what is known in France; much more effectual encouragement might therefore be expected by those who would engage in such undertakings: why then are they not attempted? This is a question which has often been propounded, and

LETTER XXXIII.

to which very different answers have been given.

That which is most frequent in the mouth of foreigners, places our ingenuity in no advantageous light: they ascribe our neglect of the two most beautiful of those manufactories, tapestry and china, to a want of genius for the invention of models and designs, and of discernment in the generality of our people, sufficient to relish beauties of such a nature.

But is it not more likely that this neglect may originate in causes of quite another kind. May we not ascribe it to the greater cheapness and facility with which we are able to procure each of those articles from abroad, than we could do such as might be manufactured at home? In a commercial nation the spirit of calculation presides over all proceedings, and influences even those who are not engaged in commerce; to make the most of one's money is a maxim that pervades all degrees:

grees: when they perceive therefore, upon due examination, that a much higher price would probably be exacted by our artists than is done by those who manufacture these commodities abroad, they prefer an importation to an encouragement of them at home, and employ those sums that would be necessary for this latter purpose, in branches of business productive of greater and more certain profit.

That neither taste nor capacity are wanting in the natives of this country, is sufficiently evident from the constant success they have met with in every enterprize which they have been earnest about, and have prosecuted with alacrity and vigour: it is not only in commercial undertakings they have displayed extraordinary talents and activity, they have equally manifested both in the cultivation of the polite arts: no people surpass them in solid knowledge; sciences of every denomination are incontestably on as brilliant a footing in England

land as in any part of Europe; works of wit and literature abound in our language, and of late years an emulation has arisen among our artists, that promises in time to place them on a parity with the most eminent and famous of modern days.

It is not therefore to a deficiency of genius, but merely to an exclusive application to a variety of other more essential objects, that we must attribute the lesser attention hitherto paid by the English to ornamental arts: in those of general utility they rival, if they do not exceed the most ingenious nations. It may of course be justly presumed, that whenever they turn their thoughts to those branches wherein others have unto this time excelled them, they will with equal care, diligence, and encouragement, be able to make an equal figure.

LETTER XXXIV.

THERE are two large hills, or rather, mountains, near Paris, of which the situation is extremely agreeable. The one is contiguous to this city, there being a continuation of houses to the village that is built upon its principal summit.

I have often been surprised, that considering the beauty and extent of the prospect one enjoys in this place, it is so thin of houses and inhabitants: the first are old and mean, and the second consist of poor working people. The few good houses one meets with, shew the advantages of this situation, and make one regret that they are not accompanied by a larger number.

The name of this mountain is *Mont-matre*; it received this appellation from

the

LETTER XXXIV.

the martyrdom of some saints on this spot in the days of Yore: a small church has been erected here in honour of them, on the porch of which you will observe a statue, if I am not mistaken, of St. Denis, the principal of these martyrs, whom the French have chosen for the patron of the kingdom.

He is represented holding his head in his hands, in commemoration, I suppose, of his having, according to a vulgar tradition, carried it in this manner from the place where he was executed, to that where now stands the famous abbey which bears his name, a distance of about three miles.

Should you lodge in the neighbourhood of this hill, you will find an early morning walk to its summit equally agreeable and beneficial. There is a house of entertainment, from the windows of which you will enjoy a delightful view, and

where

where you may breakfaſt either in the French or Engliſh manner.

Caſting your eyes to the South, you have a full and comprehenſive proſpect of the whole extent of Paris: it lies before you in a ſpacious valley, and exhibits, in a clear day, a very diſtinct perception of all the large edifices and remarkable objects it contains. It is altogether as curious and magnificent a ſight as you can well imagine.

Looking towards the North, on the oppoſite ſide of this mountain, you diſcover an immenſe extent of country, richly cultivated, and full of villages pleaſantly ſituated, and of large appearance to the eye: this is owing to the materials of which they are built, which are a very white ſtone, dug out of the quarries, with which this hill abounds, or a chalky ſubſtance that ſoon acquires a hardneſs and conſiſtence almoſt equal to ſtone: ſeen

at

at a distance, especially in a sunny day, they loom large, to use the sailor's phrase, and seem to cover much more ground than they do in reality.

In the vast plain, at the bottom of this side of the hill, a battle was fought during the civil wars on the score of religion, in the sixteenth century, and won by the famous Ann Montmorency, constable of France. I mention this fact on account of some particularities relating to this celebrated man, very well worth your recording. He was near eighty years old, and yet had strength of body and mind sufficient, after receiving eight mortal wounds, to unhorse him that gave him the last. It is of him the story says, that a friar exhorting him to death in his last moments, think you, said he, that I have lived so long without learning how to die.

He was in some respects an epitome of the times he lived in; magnanimous yet artful, haughty and proud yet supple and condescending, bold yet wary, vigilant yet quick and impetuous, brave to an excess, yet humble and submissive when courage was unavailing; uniting, like most of his cotemporaries, intrepidity and fearlessness with bigotry and superstition; and while ridiculously devout on the one hand, sanguinary and cruel on the other.

It is reported of him, that he would often, during a march, employ himself in telling his beads, and while taken up with this method of praying, would coolly give orders for the burning of a village, the cutting off a party, or the massacring of a garrison.

Characters of this kind claim your particular attention: no occasion should be missed of bringing them to notice and recollection; they teach us what to think of human nature better than any formal dissertations; and it is principally to study and learn that through practice and observation,

vation, it behoves you to be diligent and inquisitive both at home and abroad.

I was acquainted at Paris with a surgeon who was a person of great knowledge and experience in his profession: he had projected an association of some of the faculty, for the building of a large mansion upon one of the sides of this hill, for the reception of sickly persons and valetudinarians. The declivities every way are gentle, and have an easy slope; they are interspersed with pleasant levels, most agreeably situated, and upon which spacious and airy houses might be constructed, accompanied with sufficient room for kitchen and pleasure gardens. But he complained at the same time, of the difficulty to persuade people to make this their place of abode, notwithstanding they could assign no just reason for their repugnance.

The other mountain that is mentioned in the beginning of this letter, lies three miles

miles diftant from Paris. It is the moft pleafant walk in the environs of this metropolis: the afcent is fteeper than that of the former; but when you have gained the top, an enchanting profpect offers itfelf on every fide: the appearance of Paris is truly grand and ftriking, and to connoiffeurs in the picturefque, is preferred to that from Montmatre, though not fo difcernible in the detail of particular objects.

Forget not, when you are upon this fpot, to vifit a convent of hermits, who dwell here in a neat folitude, far removed from the noife and buftle of the world: they who founded it, could not have chofen a more healthful nor a more retired fituation; it is both in the completeft degree; the river Seine flows at the bottom of the hill, which is furrounded with orchards, gardens, and pafture grounds; and the tranquillity of thofe who refide on the fummit is feldom interrupted by vifitors.

LETTER XXXIV.

You will often have occasion to observe, that the curiosity of the people of France is much less than that of other nations, especially of the English. I ought however to explain what I mean by curiosity: of that which relates to anecdotes, characters, and the knowledge of men and transactions, no people have more, if so much; but they are not so active and alert as the English in their enquiries after those curiosities that gratify the sight: hence the environs of Paris are not so much frequented by the Parisians, as those of London are by its inhabitants; short and easy walks are much more the taste of the former than of the latter: for this reason numbers of agreeable spots in the proximity of Paris are hardly known to multitudes in that city: the pleasurable excursions of the lower sort are chiefly to houses of refreshment in the suburbs, or very little further: such as can afford to pay for a carriage, if they go to a greater distance, are usually more intent on the procuring

of

of good cheer and social festivity, than on the inspection of what may be worth going to see.

You will be much pleased with the little church belonging to this delightful hermitage; it is truly *simplex munditiis*, plainness and cleanliness in perfection, and conveys a just idea of those for whom it is designed.

They are usually persons of middle, and often of inferior stations in society, who chuse to devote themselves to a stricter system of life than is practicable in the world.

Unaffected piety and primitive simplicity are the principal virtues that adorn this humble retreat: they who inhabit it have entirely bid adieu to all those pursuits that bring men into public notice: study and learning are quite out of their sphere; religious exercises and devout books

LETTER XXXIV.

books excepted, their time is taken up in manual induſtry of various kinds.

This is not merely for the ſake of being employed, and kept out of idleneſs; it is in order to maintain and ſupport themſelves by the labour of their hands, as the ancient hermits were wont to do in the primitive ages of Chriſtianity, when they fled from perſecution, or through motives of ſanctity withdrew to deſerts. Here they could not have ſubſiſted, unleſs they had betaken themſelves to the cultivation of the ground, or occupied themſelves with ſuch work, as either through ſale or exchange procured them food and raiment.

In imitation of this precedent, the reſidents in this hermitage apply themſelves to ſeveral uſeful occupations for the common benefit of their fraternity: they principally excel in knit work: ſtockings, waiſtcoats, caps, and other wear of this ſort, are made here in great perfection, and

diſ-

disposed of very advantageously on account of their superior goodness.

Such is the life that is led by the members of this pious and industrious community: their number is about four or five and twenty. Small as it is, one may venture to assert it contributes more to the real edification of the public, than many a convent, of which the inhabitants are much more numerous, and think far more highly of their importance.

In the intercourse which you will occasionally have with the constituents of the various orders that abound in France, you will very soon perceive an amazing attachment to that of which they make part, and a prepossession in favour of its super-eminence over all the others, that betrays itself in spite of affected modesty: it corresponds precisely with what in the French army they very pertinently call *l'Esprit du Corps*, and is no less productive of warmth

LETTER XXXIV.

warmth and altercations, with this sole difference, that while the military decide their disputes with the sword, the others decide them with their pens.

Were I inclined, or were it worth while to take up your attention with such matters, I could soon make you sensible of the uncommon zeal with which these classes maintain the rank and dignity to which they think themselves entitled, and how unwilling they are to part with any worldly advantages of which they are in possession.

The spirit of the present age does not militate in their favour; but there was a time when the world thought much otherwise; gifts and presents of every denomination were showered upon them: they have not forgot this time, nor is it fit the world itself should, for a multiplicity of reasons, forget the profusion of generosity and distinctions with which they were treated: among other inftances let it be recorded that a Francifcan friar compofed twenty volumes in folio on the privileges belonging to his order.

Far different will you find the difpofitions of the good hermits on this mountain: they harbour no views beyond a bare maintenance to be earned by their daily occupations, and not beftowed upon them gratuitoufly.

Some years ago a very remarkable perfonage dwelt occafionally in this place. He was by birth a Fleming; he had fpent the youthful part of his life in the army, and had been prefent at more than fixty battles, fieges, engagements, and fkirmifhes, without ever receiving a wound: a moderate patrimony falling to him, he fettled at Paris, where his oeconomy enabled him to live many years in a very decent genteel manner: having originally been defigned for the church, he had received a fuitable

edu-

LETTER XXXIV.

education, and being a man of excellent parts, he had improved it in a manner that seldom is adopted by gentlemen of the military profession: but he was in all respects an exception to the common track and habits of life. On the demise of a relation who had patronised him during his studies, he found himself without a friend: in this situation, much more through necessity than choice, he entered into a monastery, intending to devote his life to study and contemplation; but the warmth of his temper, and the activity of his disposition, would not permit him to persevere any longer than the year of his noviciate; at the expiration of which, it becoming necessary he should make an option between a convent and the world, he preferred the latter: his circumstances however were not better on his leaving the former, than they had been on his reception there; but having taken his determination to renounce a monastic life, any thing seemed better to him, as he often
used

used to say, than such a state of servility, equally unworthy of a manly disposition, and inconsistent with the natural exercise of human liberty. Such were his thoughts of monastic institutions.

In the mean time he had no resources but his education, assisted by a vigorous constitution, a good person, and a great share of courage; these soon inclined him to try his fortune in the military line: he entered into the French army, the latter years of the reign of Lewis the Fourteenth. As he was a complete master of figures, he was employed at first in adjusting regimental accounts; he acquitted himself of this task with so much dexterity, that an old officer who had the principal direction in this department, took him into favour; through his interest he obtained a preferment in the corps of engineers, where he remained till the demise of the foresaid monarch.

LETTER XXXIV.

France being at that time at peace with her neighbours, his active disposition would not suffer him to remain in tranquillity while any prospect appeared of gratifying his inclination to see service: to this intent, he went to Vienna on the breaking out of a war between the Turks and the Emperor: he was present in this war from its commencement to its termination; and was also promoted in the imperial army.

He became acquainted about this time with a Flemish woman of pleasure, who made a very splendid figure at Vienna; she was handsome, witty, and generous: she had been kept by a person of very high rank; but on his being slain at the battle of Belgrade, she resolved to return to her country with the acquisitions she had made in the profession she had followed, which were very considerable: she determined at the same time to abandon it,

and

and to enter into wedlock with the first man of good character on whom she could place her affections. As notwithstanding the freedoms of her former life, she had always conducted herself with honour and discretion in other respects, and had always been considered as a person above the vulgar, she met with many offers, but none that suited her inclinations: it was precisely at this period, that our Fleming formed an acquaintance with her: fortune was more propitious to him than to her other wooers; she received graciously his addresses, and consented to accept of his hand; but while preparations were making for this union, the footing of friendship and intimacy subsisting between the two lovers, occasioning them to conceal no secrets, and to embosom themselves freely to each other, it came out at length, in consequence of these mutual confessions, that they were brother and sister.

Such

Such a difcovery, you may imagine, put inftantly an end to all matrimonial purfuits on either fide: but they had conceived fo tender a regard for each other, that they refolved never to feparate, and never to marry. They returned together to the place of their nativity, which was in the neighbourhood of Lifle: here they lived feveral years in great harmony and happinefs; but going one day to fee a review there, an officer of diftinction who was prefent, on perceiving her, immediately accofted her, and defired fhe would favour him with a few minutes converfation. She directly recollected he was the man who firft had the poffeffion of her heart, and of her perfon: fhe was at that time waiting woman to a lady of great quality, in whofe good graces fhe ftood high, and from whom fhe entertained very flattering expectations; but this adventure, the confequences of which became too vifible for concealment, obliged her to quit her patronefs. Her lover, after doing as much for her

LETTER XXXIV.

her as his circumstances, which were then very moderate, would permit, was obliged to leave her in order to attend his duty. Neceſſity compelled her to hearken to the addreſſes of a man of high rank, and great opulence, with whom ſhe lived ſome time in much ſplendour, till involving himſelf in ſome of thoſe intrigues that were formed againſt the French government, during the regency of the Duke of Orleans, he was arreſted and ſent to the Baſtille. This broke off their connection; but her beauty and charms were ſuch, that it was in her power to chuſe whom ſhe pleaſed.

Among her many admirers was a young gentleman of a very amiable character and agreeable perſon. He was ſon to a farmer general, who in order to give him every accompliſhment that could adorn an immenſe fortune, had determined he ſhould make the tour of Europe. He was preparing to ſet out for the court of Vienna, when our young lady was deprived of her

LETTER XXXIV.

her friend in the manner that has been mentioned.

He had long nourished a violent passion for her: on hearing of this accident, he waited upon and made her a tender of his purse and person; they were accepted, and it was concerted between them, that she should accompany him in his travels disguised in mens cloaths.

Arriving at Vienna he paid his respects to the French Ambassador, to whom he had letters of recommendation: as he was frequently at that Minister's house, he contracted an intimacy with his principal Secretary, a handsome young gentleman of polite address and uncommon abilities: being often together, this latter had many opportunities of seeing his friend's companion; it happened that he very well knew her first lover, and was privy to their connection.

LETTER XXXIV.

Looking at her ftedfaftly one day, he took the liberty to tell her, that fhe was the very picture of a lady with whom he had formerly been acquainted: the emotion fhe felt, and her blufhes, convinced him fhe was that very perfon; fhe was fo overcome, that fhe confeft it, intreating him however to be filent: as no third perfon was prefent, the matter remained concealed for a time; but the affiduity of his vifits excited the fufpicion of her friend: he became by degrees fo jealous as to tax her with infidelity: her fpirit could not brook fuch an accufation; fhe took a formal oath of her innocence, and inftantly left him, with a proteftation never to admit of his company.

This affair brought on a very ferious expoftulation between the two gentlemen. A duel infued, wherein the farmer general's fon received a very dangerous wound, which though not mortal, confined him a long time, and proved very difficult to cure.

LETTER XXXIV.

cure. On his recovery, he was obliged to return home in compliance with his father's injunctions.

Mean while the Ambassador's Secretary acted a very generous part with the lady: friendship soon ripened into love, and she lived some time with him in much union; till being dispatched to the French court on business of great secrecy and importance, he was kept there much longer than he had expected.

His income being too narrow for the subsistence of both at such a distance, indigence obliged her to submit to the importunities of a Bohemian Baron, whom she attended to his seat: at the expiration of no long time he died, not however without leaving her a considerable legacy.

Her next friend was a nobleman of the same country, who left her shortly after, on his marrying a lady of great fortune and uncommon generosity: she insisted, on her marriage, that her husband should bestow a very considerable sum of money on his mistress.

She now returned to Vienna in very prosperous circumstances, intending henceforth to live regularly. But a relation of her lately married friend followed her to that city. He was a widower, and possest of an ample fortune, in the prime of his age, agreeable in his person, and highly engaging in his manners: she avoided him at first, in order to oblige her last lover, who had besought her to give him no encouragement; but his attachment to her was so strong, that she could not resist it; he promised in case of issue by her, to settle all he was personally worth on herself and progeny; such an offer she could not refuse.

They did not however live long together: going a volunteer in the imperial army,

LETTER XXXIV.

army, he loſt his life, to the great grief of his miſtreſs, whoſe affection he had won, and well deſerved, by the nobleneſs of his behaviour,

It was after this event that preparing to leave Vienna, ſhe was accidently diſcovered by her brother in the manner that has been related,

Such had been her adventures when her firſt lover recognized her after many years abſence. He told her that his affection had never cooled, that he had on that account refuſed a variety of advantageous matches, reſolving, if ever he ſhould meet her again, to make her an offer of his hand.

Such an affectionate declaration was anſwered on her part by an ingenuous acknowledgement of what had befallen her ſince their ſeparation: but he generouſly confeſt himſelf the original cauſe of all her frailties,

frailties, and that it was his duty to make her all the reparation in his power, for the injuries she had suffered upon his account.

A first passion, it is said, seldom is totally extinguished: she felt its revival so forcibly, that she could not give him a denial. On consulting with her brother, he did not hesitate to give his consent, and they were in a few days married.

Some time after the war broke out between France and the Emperor on account of the succession to the crown of Poland: through her husband's interest her brother had a commission in the French army, and served during the whole war, at the end of which he obtained a pension.

In the ensuing hostilities against the late Empress Queen, he served in Germany and Flanders under Marshal Saxe.

About this time he became heir to an uncle, who, like himself, had experienced

a variety

a variety of adventures; but had lately been concerned in some successful privateers out of Dunkirk. This inheritance, though not very large, was abundantly sufficient to enable him to live independent. He retired from the service, and settled at Paris with an intent to spend there the remainder of his days.

His system of living was to deny himself no reasonable pleasures; but to dedicate most of his time to reading and to the company of the learned and ingenious: he was peculiarly fond of solitary walks, and often would pass whole days alone in wandering about the fields and rural places adjacent to Paris. It was in one of these excursions that being on this mountain, and falling into conversation with one of the hermits of this place, he conceived the design of making it occasionally a place of retreat from the croud and busy scenes of life.

In

In this design he was by no means governed by any fit of devotion; his religion was manly, and tinctured with no sort of bigotry; but he delighted in variety, and his retirement being voluntary, and lasting no longer than he pleased, it was a mere pastime to him, who had gone through so many diversities in life, to conform for a few days to the rules enjoined to such as chuse to dwell with the good people of this hermitage.

His intention was, on his demise to be interred in the burying-ground of this convent, with this inscription on his gravestone, *hic jacet Umbra, Cinis, nihil.* This epitaph it seems was formerly made for himself, by Cardinal Barberini, brother to Pope Urban the Eighth. This Cardinal was raised to that dignity much against his will, by the express command of his brother, a man of great wisdom, wit, and learning, who conferred this exaltation upon him, in reward of his extraordinary
humility;

LETTER XXXIV.

humility: but this good man would not relinquish the humble manner of living of his former condition, which was that of a Capuchin Friar; he continued it to the last, and ordered the above words, and no others, to be ingraved on his tomb-stone.

Our Fleming would sometimes jokingly say, that having on several occasions been bountiful to the Capuchins, he thought himself intitled to borrow an epitaph from one of their order.

I will not advise you to follow the example of this gentleman, any farther than to take as many walks to this charming spot as you can make it convenient; you will find it equally conducive to health and to pleasure.

I make no doubt that both those motives co-operate in the inducing even of pious people to retire sometimes to the convent of this solitude: add to this that the

the price is very reasonable; at the rate of about two shillings a day you are provided with decent board and lodging, for as long a term as you please; but not shorter than a week.

I have heard that a citizen of Marseilles engaged in commerce, and intending that his only son, then at Paris with a relation, should follow the same occupation, placed him, during some time, among the brethren, as they are called, of this fraternity, that he might be thoroughly instructed in the art of knitting, which, as before observed, they practise in perfection: his motive for doing this, was that in case his son should, in his future voyages to the Levant, happen to fall into the hands of the corsairs of Barbary, he should be able either to maintain himself, or to work for his master, without being condemned to drudgery and hard labour.

This reminds one of a custom that formerly prevailed in many parts of Europe,

LETTER XXXIV.

and is not yet totally difused in Germany and Hungary. As exorbitant ransoms were exacted for persons of distinction taken in battle, it became customary to teach them in their youth some mechanical business, the better to conceal their rank, and lessen the demands of those into whose hands the chance of war had thrown them.

To this day there are Hungarian gentlemen sufficiently expert in handicrafts to pass themselves off for persons of low degree: they find this, it seems, of no small service when prisoners among their neighbours the Turks, either in procuring their liberty at an easy rate, or in working for their subsistence.

Besides the church and convent of Hermits, there are upon this mountain a number of little chapels dedicated to the commemoration of the passion and death of Christ. From this circumstance the mountain has received the name of Mount Calvary;

Calvary; it is known also by that of *Mont Valerien*.

In each of these chapels is represented, in wooden sculpture, some particulars of that event; the figures are coloured, and large as life.

It is not unusual in Passion-Week, and especially on Good-Friday, for numbers of devout people to visit these chapels, and to pray before them on their knees with much humility and fervour. Some, I think to have heard, perform these devotions bare-foot.

This custom of kneeling at prayer, is one of the most inconvenient that were ever introduced by way of mortifying the human frame; the hours that are spent in this incommodious posture are many in convents, seminaries, and even in some colleges.

LETTER XXXIV.

It does not appear upon cool consideration, that devotion is either excited or assisted by placing the body in a disagreeable position; we can only therefore attribute this practice to the absurd excesses in devotional practices, to which men of more zeal than sense and discretion have in all ages been more or less addicted.

In religion, as well as in other matters, the wisest do not always dictate: forms in worship, like fashions in dress, are often the result of private caprice; with this difference, that when established they last longer, and acquire weight and reverence in proportion to the length of their duration.

People of discernment must know that climate, constitution, and the various incidents of human life, should be consulted in all those *exteriorities* of religion that are indifferent in their nature.

Among these is evidently the posture observed in praying. The Jews of old prayed standing as they do at present; the primitive Christians kneeled much less than at this day; on Sundays and great festivals it was positively forbidden them to kneel at all; whence we may reasonably infer that it was not enjoined them to kneel much at any time: the travellers who have written accounts of Abyssinia, tell us that according to the forms of Christianity established there, which are known to be of great antiquity, people stand during divine service: in Russia, kneeling is little in use; it is even by many held in detestation, as imitating the soldiers of Pilate when they derided Christ.

All these particulars concur in proving the impropriety of continuing so needless, and at the same time so irksome a practice: but prescription authorises it, and the imbecility of mankind in submitting to still more

more abfurd ufages, has long been proverbially notorious.

Formerly the warmth, or rather the violence with which people purfued the ftudy of bodily mortification, was much more diffufed and general than at this day. Ecclefiaftical writers of the fifth century mention a fect that went by the name of *Nudipedales*, from their going barefooted.

This abfurd method of doing pennance has frequently been imitated, and is not intirely difufed. The progrefs of enthufiafm is rapid, but that of reafon flow, and it often requires the wifdom of ages, to deftroy the effects and overcome the influence of a few years of folly.

LETTER XXXV.

IN the proximity of the mountain which was the subject of my last, stands, not far from the borders of the Seine, a very ancient house, wherein I have been told that a lady resided, whose history is so remarkable, that I will venture to make it the subject of this letter.

This lady was of the illustrious house of Foix, and was at a very early period of life married to the Count of Chateau Briand, a man of a morose and jealous disposition. In order to secure the fidelity of his wife, he kept her confined in a remote part of Britanny, far from the public sight and enjoyments of the world.

His friends often represented to him, that he took a very wrong method to obtain

tain the end he proposed, and that unless he could gain possession of her heart, the imprisonment of her body was no effectual security.

But the austerity of his manners and the obstinacy of his mind acted in concert against all remonstrances: he continued to debar his young wife from the amusements in which her rank and fortune claimed an indulgence, and watched all her motions with a solicitude that rendered her situation extremely painful and mortifying.

Thus, instead of a husband, he assumed the part of a jailor, and laid himself open to the malevolence and reproaches not only of his wife's relations, but of his own, who scrupled not to tell him, that soon or late he would meet with that punishment for the ill treatment of his wife, which he studied principally to avoid.

In the mean time her beauty and her sufferings were in every body's mouth; the first was a theme upon which the world expatiated without end, and the second was a subject of universal indignation.

She lived at an æra when a turn to intrigue began to characterise the court of France: the prince who wore that crown was in the flower of his age, of a gay temper, and a most amorous disposition.

Before his reign the ladies had been used to a solitary and retired life, and were never seen at court, unless upon very solemn occasions: but the pleasures and diversions which he delighted in were of such a nature as necessarily to put an end to this strictness of conduct: festivals and pastimes were introduced of a more elegant form and contrivance than had hitherto been known; dancing and music were their incessant concomitants, and had lately

LETTER XXXV.

lately been polished and improved in a manner that rendered them far more desirable objects of cultivation than heretofore: the graces and attractions of social intercourse had received no less an addition through the spirit of politeness arising from a more extensive increase of genteel and liberal education.

This revolution in the manners of the French, was chiefly brought about by the character of their king, Francis the First. Had he been only remarkable for a turn to pleasure, perhaps his example would not have been so powerful; but possessing a number of great qualities, whatever he did commanded attention; and precedents, which in princes of inferior talents would have had little influence, in him were striking and persuasive.

Such were the times wherein this lady was destined to make her appearance, and to act a part which has made her memory remarkably conspicuous.

She could not remain so perfectly concealed as not occasionally to be seen and admired. In process of time the fame of her beauty did not fail to reach the court, together with the hard fate which it occasioned. At a magnificent festival given by the king, while he was employed in viewing the ladies assembled on that occasion, an officious courtier told him, there was an object in his dominions much more worthy of his admiration than any one in that assembly; he then informed him of every thing relating to the countess, and represented her in such a light, as excited in the king the strongest impatience to see her.

But this was not an easy matter to compass: besides that the kings of France were not then so absolute and omnipotent as now, nor the courtiers so pliant and acquiescing, he did not chuse to have recourse to such methods as might alarm and offend the pride of his nobility. He
there-

therefore endeavoured to entice the husband to bring his wife to court by the most flattering and specious invitations; but the count, who saw his master's drift, alledged various pretexts for keeping her at a distance: he described the countess as a haughty and imperious beauty, full of arrogance and disdain for all other women, and her humour so unconciliating, that she would be apt to disoblige by her behaviour the ladies with whom she must of course associate. He alledged at the same time, that she was a woman of very rigid morals, who led an uncommonly strict and regular life, and entirely disapproved of the innovations introduced at court; that she never would therefore be prevailed upon to resort to such a place, much less to reside there.

But the king paid little regard to these representations, of which he rightly conjectured the real cause. He insisted, in a polite engaging manner, that the count
should

should not refuse to grace his court with one of the most brilliant ornaments his kingdom could boast; that it would be ungenerous and unjust to debar his wife from so agreeable and innocent a gratification, as that of seeing the splendour and magnificence which accompany royalty.

The count, who did not dare to disoblige his sovereign by a positive refusal, feigned a persuasion of the justness of what he had urged, and assured him of a compliance with his request on the first opportunity; but resolving at the same time never to perform his promise, and foreseeing also that he could never appear in the royal presence without fulfilling it, he determined to banish himself totally from court, as the only means of preserving untouched that treasure, which he perceived the king coveted with so much ardour.

But he was by unforeseen circumstances compelled to alter this determination: his presence

presence at court became absolutely requisite, and no pretence was left him for denial.

It now remained to frame a plausible excuse for the absence of his wife. He was summoned by the king to fulfil his promise, and censured by the courtiers for refusing, in conformity to their example, to bring his wife to court, were it only in compliance with the request of so gracious a master. But the exhortations of the king, and the censures of his courtiers, were equally fruitless; he still continued immoveable in his resolution.

He had, previous to his setting out for Paris, contrived to place his wife in the hands of a relation, who was abbess of a female monastery. The pretext was a vow he had made in a fit of illness, to dedicate a certain portion of time to prayer and retirement, in case of recovery.

A great

A great variety and long continuance of business had prevented him from performing his vow; but though he had not found leisure to do it, yet, as he thought it incumbent upon him to avoid remissness in so serious a matter, he had charged his wife to act upon this occasion in his stead, and to dwell in a pious retreat during the same space which he had himself intended.

This excuse was by no means relished at court, where by this time his excessive jealousy had rendered him an object of particular notice. As courtiers usually delight in tormenting such characters, knowing that in this instance they would correspond with the intentions of their master, they vied with each other in devising methods how to perplex the count, and defeat the measures he had taken to insure and to justify the absence of his lady.

After

LETTER XXXV.

After employing a variety of means to no purpose, an accident happened, which supplied them with what proved a sufficient motive to authorise her immediately repairing to Paris.

The king had given a splendid entertainment: one of the diversions consisted in running at the ring, which was very fashionable in those days, as conducing much to render horsemen expert in hitting their mark. The count, who partook of it in company with others, had the misfortune to fall from his horse: the hurt he received was not considerable; but as it disabled him from continuing the sport, and obliged him to withdraw, an idea suggested itself to one of those busy promoters of mischief that always abound in courts, which appeared quite apposite to the design of bringing his wife out of her retreat.

This officious courtier had a sister in the convent where this lady resided: he wrote her directly word that the count had been thrown from his horse and lay in a very dangerous condition. On receiving this intelligence, the countess thought it incumbent upon her to set out immediately for Paris, in order to attend him in his illness.

The king, who had been apprised of the whole stratagem, did not let slip so favourable an opportunity of gratifying the wishes he had so ardently formed. He carefully visited the count every day, and testified much concern on account of the accident that had befallen him.

It was during one of those visits that happened the arrival of the countess. It was announced by a servant, whom she had dispatched a little way before her, in order to apprise her husband, and to prevent

vent his spirits from being discompofed by
a fudden appearance.

The fervant had not long delivered his meffage, when the countefs and her attendants entered the court-yard of the houfe. As the count was too lame to quit his couch, the king told him in the friendlieft terms, that he would upon this occafion wait upon her in his ftead.

He accordingly received her in his arms on her alighting from her horfe, and conducted her very refpectfully to her hufband, whofe aftonifhment at all that he faw may be better conceived than expreft.

From the motives which fhe alledged for this unexpected journey, it clearly appeared that fhe had been impofed upon; but it was too late to remedy this impofition: the count would willingly have remanded her to confinement; but the king, who was ftruck with the moft violent

lent paffion for her, had already obviated all defigns of this nature, by pre-engaging both at a magnificent feftival.

The count hefitated in what manner he fhould proceed in this critical conjuncture. He was confcious that he held his wife by no tie of affection: this being the only fecurity againft the temptations that would affail her in a court fo full of gallantry, he foon concluded that fhe would yield to them.

Had the rival whom he dreaded been any other than a royal one, he would readily have extricated himfelf from his apprehenfions; but there lay the difficulty; he faw it was infurmountable, and that coercive meafures could no longer be adopted.

He now for the firft time had recourfe to lenity, and endeavoured by gentle infinuations to make his wife fenfible of the peril

LETTER XXXV.

peril her virtue stood in, while exposed to the allurements of such a court, and that to quit it instantly was the only sure means of preserving her reputation.

But this was a language to which she was not in the least disposed to hearken. She had seen enough to wish to see more, and to feel resentment at his having so long precluded her from seeing any thing. To the fervour with which he exprest his wishes that she would not delay her departure, she opposed a sullen silence and a countenance full of displeasure and indignation.

Mean while she was surrounded by crouds of female courtiers, impatient to behold one, of whom they had heard so much, and of whom they expected to hear so much more.

The king's frequent entreaties of her husband to bring her to court, and the
latter's

latter's reluctance to comply, together with the contrivance used for the effecting of this purpose, were become things of notoriety..

Francis was known at the same time to be a man not easily repulsed in his intrigues, and who would leave no methods untried to succeed with any female whom he thought proper to attempt.

The countess was therefore viewed in the light of a future favourite. The homage paid her in consequence of this general expectation, could not fail proving highly acceptable to a young and beautiful woman, sensible of the superiority of her charms, of the power which they procured her, and of the slavery from which they would obtain her a release.

Full of these flattering ideas, she saw with scorn the humble endeavours of the count to persuade her to put herself again
into

into his possession. Regarding him as a tyrant, from whose fetters she could not too soon be relieved, her whole behaviour indicated that she rejoiced in the thoughts of parting with him, and that whatever might be her future destiny, it could not be worse than he had made it.

In the full conviction of the inutility of all his efforts to obtain her concurrence with his desires, and entertaining no doubt of her compliance with those of her royal lover, he took the resolution, as he could not prevent the disgrace awaiting him, not however to give it the least countenance by consenting to remain any longer at court.

Having taken this determination, he departed abruptly, and returned to his country seat in Britanny, leaving his wife in the enjoyment of that liberty he had so long denied her, and free to dispose of herself as she might think proper.

His departure, though expected and not lamented by the countess, still placed her in a situation equally novel and critical.

She was strongly advised by a relation of the count, to follow him without a moment's hesitation, this being the only means to secure his good will and opinion, which otherwise she must be conscious would inevitably be forfeited; that however flattering the prospect of being a royal mistress might seem, such an elevation, if it was one, must be purchased with the loss of her character; and was at best but precarious, especially with a prince of so voluptuous a disposition as Francis was known to be: that should he cool in his attachment, a case by no means unlikely, she would then experience the double mortification of not only losing the possession of that prize, but of being constrained at the same time to renounce the world, and pass the remainder of her days in repentance and obscurity.

Had

LETTER XXXV.

Had the count retained any place in her affections, these arguments might have had some weight; but her dislike of him was so deeply rooted, that they were totally ineffectual.

Among the acquaintances she had formed since her arrival at Paris, was a young widow in the bloom of life and beauty like herself, and who had also experienced the miseries of being married to a jealous and ill-tempered husband. The similitude of their destinies had produced a reciprocal sympathy between them, which had speedily ripened into great friendship and confidence.

To this lady she unbosomed herself without reserve on the difficulty of her situation. But far different was the advice of this last from that which had been given her by the former.

This young widow was near of an age with the countess; but having since the demise of her husband, which had happened about two years before this period, lived at large, and enjoyed unconfined liberty, she was much more experimentally conversant with the world.

She advised the countess never to admit the idea of returning to her husband, with whom she could hope for nothing but imprisonment, and a renewal of all the horrors she had suffered, together with an infallible addition of still more, to revenge himself for the disquietude and vexation he had undergone from the journey she had taken to Paris, and her appearance at court without his previous knowledge and consent.

As to the royal predilection, which was represented to her in such alarming colours, she sincerely congratulated her upon

upon so auspicious an event, which, whether of long or of short duration, a woman of sense and spirit would always be able to convert to her advantage. It was a post at which numbers of females of high rank aspired in private with much fervour, whatever repugnance they might affect in public: were she fond of her husband, or had any reason for being attached to him, she would be the last woman to hold such a discourse; but as their characters were wholly incompatible, it were folly to seek for happiness where it could not possibly be found.

She added, that she had herself been lately solicited upon honourable terms by some men of very high distinction; but that the dread of making an unfortunate choice had kept her from listening to their addresses; that apprehensions of this kind would, she believed, long, if not ever, operate against a matrimonial connection, upon the indissolubleness of which she could

could not look without fear and trembling.

Her counsel was therefore to bid an everlasting adieu to all notions of re-union with the count, and to exert all her powers in order to captivate the heart of her royal lover, from whose well-known generosity and nobleness of mind she had every thing to expect.

Such a Prince was not to be confounded with others in the same station: exclusive of his rank and power, he had an innate dignity of disposition, which rendered him amiable for his own sake; she frankly acknowledged, that were he to offer himself as a lover, she would accept of him with open arms; but that not being the case, she exhorted her, as a sincere well-wisher, to act as she would do herself, were it in her option, and not to suffer herself to be deterred from a connection with that monarch, by the interested or groundless representa-

LETTER XXXV.

representations of false friends, or weak-minded people.

Whether this young widow spoke her genuine sentiments, or was secretly deputed to use these arguments, certain it is they made an impression upon the countess: she threw off the timidity which had hitherto accompanied her, and assumed that air of freedom and gaiety which characterised the court of her lover.

In the mean time his passion for her daily gained ground. She was unquestionably one of the most charming women of that age; her person was enchanting, her humour affable and obliging; she was sensible and sprightly, and her manners were soft and engaging: all these were invincible attractions to a Prince in the flower of his age, and of a most amorous constitution.

But

But independent of the propensity, common to all men, to admire handsome women, Francis had a delicacy far above the usual level: beauty alone was not sufficient to subdue him; he looked for something beyond what met his eye; where internal merit was wanting, internal charms lost their effect; his admiration was that of a man of genius and discernment, and he was never known to bestow his attachment upon a meer outside.

The countess was precisely such an object as his wishes coveted: the more he saw her, the more cause he found to be enamoured; her native modesty gave unaffected lustre to the liveliness which she gradually acquired by her transplantation into the gayer scenes of life: he attentively observed her conduct in a situation so new to her perceptions and feelings, and constantly discovered in every part of her behaviour a cautiousness and discretion, that convinced

convinced him she was a woman of exquisite sensibility and refinement, as well as of the most lovely frame.

He now determined to make her the object of his particular assiduities. He laid himself out to obtain her good graces with all that polite earnestness which is so pleasing to the sex, as it convinces them that they are no less respected than beloved.

Far from presuming on the exaltedness of his station, he behaved with as much courtesy and gentleness, as if he had been a private individual, suing with many others for the happiness of her smiles and favour.

Such a lover as this was not formed for a repulse; he soon perceived what he ardently desired, that her partiality for him was equal to his predilection for her, and that he should enjoy what he was wont to
stile

stile the greatest of all mortal felicities, the pleasure of being loved for his own sake.

It was not, however, till after some time that she yielded to his courtship. The merit of her concession was enhanced by the unfeigned difficulty with which she prevailed upon herself to make it. Her struggles with the strictness and regularity of her former life were accompanied with a gracefulness that shewed they were void of all affectation.

Francis was now in possession of the jewel he had so long and so diligently sought. He exprest a satisfaction in having acquired it, that did the highest honour to his taste: not only the monarch, but his whole court were of opinion that he could not have chosen a more amiable partner of his softer moments.

She became in a short time the absolute mistress of his heart, not so much by exercising

ercising those blandishments with which nature has so powerfully adorned the sex, as by displaying a dignity of sentiments, and a propriety of behaviour, that captivated her royal lover's mind, and excited his esteem no less than the others invited his attachment.

What equally delighted Francis, and conciliated all his court, were the gentleness of her deportment, and the moderation she displayed in her conduct: people of all degrees met with the kindest treatment from her, and she behaved so courteously upon all occasions, that it was evident she was solicitous in the highest degree to give no causes of offence.

This meekness and condescension were the more laudable, as the king grew continually more fervent in his affection, and testified such a consideration for her, that it was plain she had only to ask to be gratified.

But

But she made no improper use of her credit; her family was already so respectable, that it could disgrace no honours that might be conferred upon it. She had three brothers, as brave men as any in France. The king promoted them to high commands, in which they greatly signalized their valour and capacity.

In the mean time the count, her husband, was not absent from her remembrance. Notwithstanding his ill usage of her, she thought it incumbent upon her, to soften as much as lay in her power the mortification of having slighted him for another. As she possessed an absolute power over the king, she prevailed upon him to make the most advantageous offers to the count, by way of atonement: the highest posts in the realm were laid before him; but he rejected them with scorn, and forbad any mention of the countess in his presence.

He lived at a time when a sense of honour was supremely prevalent over all other considerations. Though proud and aspiring, he was not of a temper to sacrifice his character to any views of ambition: " The higher the king means to raise me, said he, the more notorious will be my degradation, were I to accept of his offers."

So resolute a refusal highly chagrined the countess. She had written him a supplicatory letter, intreating him to reflect like a man of sense on the impropriety of the connection that had once subsisted between them, so much to the uneasiness and the unhappiness of both; that a separation therefore was what each party ought reasonably to desire; that a reconciliation being now impracticable, it were the wisest thing they could do, to forget each other; that nevertheless it was her earnest wish to contribute to his welfare to her very utmost; conformably to this intent,

tent, she had induced the King to shew the value and respect he entertained for him, by conferring upon him the most honourable and most important employments in the realm.

But the resentment of the count was proof against this and all the subsequent sollicitations that came from her: they were frequent and pressing; the countess, who was a woman of equal understanding and feeling, laboured with all her might to convince him, that what had happened was best for both: but her endeavours were lost upon a man who, though he acknowledged his love was extinguished, yet as violently asserted that his resentment would always subsist.

In the mean time the affection of Francis continued with unabated warmth; she was the principal object of his cares and pleasures, and the sum of his happiness was centered in her.

LETTER XXXV.

Such was the situation of the countess, when Francis left her to put himself at the head of his army in Italy. No expedition ever proved more unfortunate; he was defeated, wounded, and taken prisoner at the battle of Pavia, and carried to Spain, where he was kept in close confinement by his rival and bitter enemy, the Emperor Charles the Fifth.

The news of this misfortune was near proving fatal to the countess. Her attachment to Francis rendered her inconsolable, and she gave herself up to grief and lamentation.

But what made her condition truly deplorable, was the power that was now devolved into the hands of some persons who envied her ascendency over the mind of Francis, and resolved to avail themselves of this opportunity of wreaking their revenge, on account of some disappointments their ambition had met with from her superior credit.

Among these was the Duchess of Angouleme, mother of Francis, an ambitious and haughty woman, who had long borne with secret indignation the influence of the countess, and had strove by indirect means to lessen it.

This unhappy lady was intirely abandoned through fear of the duchess, now become regent of the kingdom in the King's absence and imprisonment. Seeing herself exposed to her insults and ill-treatment, without any prospect of protection, she withdrew from the public world, and retired to a country mansion, in order to consider at leisure, what measures were most adviseable to adopt.

But so distressful was her situation, that no one dared to express any commiseration for

for it, or seem inclinable to administer any assistance to her.

In this doleful state she was visited by a religious old lady, who had often, during her prosperity, waited upon her with warm exhortations to forsake the court, and retire to penance and solitude.

This good old lady renewed her sollicitations with much earnestness, and prevailed upon her to shut herself up in a nunnery, with an intent to remain there for life: but an alarming decline of her health, together with the exhortations of those who presided there, soon altered her determination. The Abbess was a well-meaning woman, ignorant of the world and of human nature; the confessor of the convent was a rigid moralist, unacquainted with mankind, and wholly taken up with exercises of devotion. In a fit of illness which seized the unhappy countess, they assailed her weakened faculties with such terrifying descriptions of the enormity of the sin she had committed, in forsaking her husband, that as soon as she was sufficiently recovered, she resolved to go and throw herself at his feet and crave his forgiveness.

Some friends, who had more experience and discretion, endeavoured to dissuade her from trusting herself into the hands of an enraged man, who had often vowed the severest vengeance against her, and who was known to be of a violent and vindictive disposition; but the resolution she had taken, was too firmly fixed to be shaken by all the arguments that could be used: Life, she said, was become a burden, of which she cared not how soon she was ridden; if her husband did not think her fit to live, she was willing to die.

In these penitential sentiments she set out for the seat of her husband, careless of the consequences of so hazardous a step.

LETTER XXXV.

He received her with a sternness and silence that foreboded no happy issue to her undertaking. She was conducted to a remote part of his mansion, and lodged in a dark room, of which the hangings and all the furniture were black.

In this gloomy retirement she was waited upon by persons who had orders to hold no conversation with her. She was supplied with books that treated of death and a future state, and bid to read them with particular attention, and prepare herself for another world.

She was kept in the dreadful expectation, in what manner all this would end, during the space of six months. At the expiration of that time, the count came one evening and informed her that on the following day she was to die. Next morning accordingly he entered the room, accompanied by eight men with masks on, and two of whom were surgeons: they seized the unfortunate lady, tied her to the bed, opened the veins of her arms and legs, and left her in that condition to expire.

Such was the revenge of this inhuman wretch upon a lovely woman, whom his cruel treatment alone compelled to hate and forsake him, and who neverthelefs, touched with repentance, had committed herself to his mercy.

It is not meant that he should have received her again to his arms; but that indifference and neglect would have been a sufficient punishment to a woman of her character, and would have afforded ample fatisfaction to his resentment.

This horrid murder did not long remain concealed. The perpetrator was obliged to fly his country and live many years in exile, in order to avoid the wrath of his wife's lover, from whom he had no mercy to expect.. Francis, on hearing of the

the tragical end of his beloved countess, vowed the most signal vengeance on the guilty, and dispatched instantly some resolute men to carry it into immediate execution wherever they could find them: but they were too well concealed; researches were vain, and he had not the pleasure of making this just sacrifice to her memory.

LETTER XXXVI.

AT the distance of about three miles from Paris, in a pleasing situation on the banks of the Seine, stands the palace of Conflans, belonging to the archbishops of Paris.

The purity of the air, and beautifulness of the country in its neighbourhood, induced the late archbishop to make it his residence during great part of the year. It was here that he enjoyed him-

himself with those friends and intimates that adhered to his ways of thinking; it was here that he held those consultations with them, the result of which brought him more than once into difficulties; and it was here that persons who had favours to ask, always found him in the most accessible and complying humour.

The apartments of this palace are uncommonly neat and elegant; though grand and becoming the rank of the possessor, you will observe a decent dignity throughout them, that will please you the more on reflecting that you are in the house of an ecclesiastic, in whom exterior greatness ought peculiarly to be tempered with moderation.

This agreeable place lying so near Paris, I would advise you frequently to make it an object of your walks: you are always sure of an entrance into the gardens, which are laid out in a very noble and
judi-

LETTER XXXVI.

judicious taste, and are for that reason much resorted to and admired by connoisseurs.

You will find here another place equally easy of access to individuals of decent appearance: it is a large and spacious gallery, adorned with a prodigious number of portraits of the most eminent personages in modern times.

A very considerable proportion of them are unquestionably originals, and give an exact resemblance of the persons represented; but from an injudicious desire to extend the catalogue of these representations, they have exhibited a regular series of the kings of France, ever since the foundation of that monarchy.

This you will readily conceive is in a great measure the work of fancy, and just as much to be depended on, as the

cuts

cuts and images that are so commonly found in books of history.

It is difficult to ascertain the date from whence performances of this kind begin to claim authenticity; but I believe that portrait painting was very little in vogue before the middle of the fifteenth century.

Since that epocha people of eminence have been transmitted to posterity in pictures and in prints; you may therefore rely with tolerable certainty on those you will find in that gallery, that were done for such as have lived since that time.

I knew a young gentleman who had a remarkable talent at catching a resemblance. He had been at the pains of copying every picture in this gallery, the truth of which he looked upon as probable. His intention was to imitate what Cornelius Nepos reports of the famous
At-

Atticus, to write a summary account under every picture of the person whom it represented, in the same manner that Roman had done under the images adorning his hall.

This young gentleman was a native of Poland: his family seat was in the neighbourhood of Cracovia: his design was to enrich it with the copies he had drawn: it was, he said, an edifice of moderate dimensions, but good architecture, built upon a plan sketched by a very ingenious artist, formerly employed by the great king Sobieski, and whose papers had been purchased by his father, who found this plan among them.

Of all the travellers I ever met with, this was the most diligent in his examination of all that was worth notice, and the most laborious in transcribing whatever deserved it. Being at the same time an excellent draftsman, nothing escaped him in the whole circle of architecture, painting, and sculpture. He had a collection, entirely the work of his own hands, of all that he had seen remarkable in these branches, accompanied with critical notes and observations: those which I saw were very pertinent and judicious: French was the language he used; he wrote and spoke it in great perfection, having indeed learned it from his cradle.

But he was far from being a mere virtuoso. Among other compilations, he had written memoirs and anecdotes of every person of note whom he had seen or heard of in his travels. This he valued beyond all his other performances, as it contained characters actually existing, and with some of whom he expected, in process of time, and in the course of affairs, to form more or less either a personal acquaintance or a correspondence.

Were

LETTER XXXVI.

Were I to propose a model for your imitation, I could not chuse a more happy one than this young gentleman, one whose failings were so few, and whose good qualities were so many.

He excelled particularly in the distribution of his time, and in the rare art of losing no opportunity of improving. I have known him return from what to others would have proved a bare party of pleasure, with a stock of information gathered from every quarter whence it could possibly arise on such an occasion. He would on setting out look as it were into every one that composed it, and settle his plan of examination accordingly: the scholar, the soldier, the priest, the lawyer, the merchant, the man of business, every profession, in short, afforded him materials of speculation and knowledge. In order to be never out of the way of improvement, he made it a rule always to travel in a public vehicle, where he might have a chance a chance of converſing with a diverſity of characters, and where I have often heard him ſay more inſtruction was to be obtained than by any other method.

I am convinced by my own experience that he ſpoke truth. People that meet on a travelling party, being uſually total ſtrangers to each other, and meeting together for the firſt and laſt time, are not fettered by any apprehenſions of what may happen from the diſcourſe that paſſes among them: they indulge themſelves therefore without any reſtraint, and ſpeak of men and things with a latitude and freedom, which they would not dare to uſe elſewhere.

Excluſive of French and Latin, of which this young gentleman was complete maſter, he was thoroughly converſant in German and Italian: but he frequently complained of the loſs of time he had incurred in the perfecting himſelf in languages, which he called the neceſſary evil of a good education, lamenting that the polite nations did not agree in ſelecting one only for univerſal uſe, diſcarding every other, and confining it to its own country.

How far he was juſtifiable in this idea would bear too long a diſcuſſion; but nothing is more certain than that as it is much better to be acquainted with things than with words; abſolute neceſſity ſhould alone induce us to aim at the reputation of a linguiſt.

Pleaſures being the requiſites of youth, our young gentleman was no enemy to them. In truth he was formed to give as well as to enjoy almoſt every kind of liberal entertainment. He had a fine taſte for muſic; he ſung well, and played ſkilfully on the harpſichord; he danced moſt gracefully, was an admirable horſeman, and uncommonly expert at fencing.

I men-

I mention these various accomplishments by way of proof that indolence alone stands in the way of their acquisition. With a temper that led him to the pursuit of a variety of diversions, which necessarily consumed much time, he yet found means to repair that loss, by employing the remainder with an activity and judiciousness that made ample amends for all juvenilities. Have I not a right after this to say, *abi tu et fac similiter*, go thou and do likewise.

In the frequent retrospects which all men are wont to take of their youthful days, there are perhaps none that afford us more delight than those that present to our remembrance a brilliant and amiable character. Such was that which I have been describing; and such, I hope, yours will prove in the memory of those who may hereafter have occasion to remember you.

LETTER XXXVII.

AMONG those objects of curiosity that employ antiquaries, may be counted the famous abbey of St. Denis, situated about four or five miles from Paris.

The monastery itself is a new building, very noble and spacious. Nothing remains of the old but a gate-way, the upper part of which is said to have been the residence of the celebrated Suger, Abbot of St. Denis, and principal minister of state under Lewis the Sixth, and his son Lewis the Seventh. He was by this last, during his absence on a crusade, appointed regent of the kingdom, and died about the middle of the twelfth century, with the reputation of being one of the most upright statesmen, and profound politicians, that ever held the reins of government in any country. Posterity has confirmed this opinion; the French writers unanimously agree in speaking of him in terms of the highest praise. Forget not to visit the apartment of this extraordinary man; it will give you an idea of his own modesty, and of the simplicity of the times he lived in. Some letters of his remain upon state matters, a perusal of which will afford you just notions of the spirit of that age.

The church of this abbey is a magnificent monument of Gothic architecture. It is kept in excellent order. In it are the tombs of many of the kings of France; but such as are anterior to the beginning of the fourteenth century, are to be considered only as cenotaphs, or empty monuments erected to their memory.

You will observe a striking disparity between the personages interred in this church, and those that lie buried in West‑
minster

minster abbey. The French would hold it a profanation, to mix the ashes of their kings with those of any others but of the royal family, unless their merit were of so eminent and sublime a nature, as in a manner to command so signal a mark of distinction.

Kings and princes of the blood excepted, you will find only two men of the rank of subjects buried in this church. The one is Bertrand du Guesclin, constable of France in the reign of Charles the Fifth, at whose feet he lies interred.

No man could have a juster claim to this honour; until he was placed at the head of the French armies, those of England had proved invincible. It was he that retrieved the military honour of France, and recovered that monarchy from the fatal degree of humiliation, to which it had been reduced by the victorious arms of our third Edward, and his son the Black Prince.

The other is the still more celebrated Turenne, Marshal General of the armies of France; a title with which none but he and the late Count Saxe were ever decorated.

The character of Turenne was truly great. His mind was elevated above every consideration that occupies the generality of mankind; his ideas, his discourse, his manners, displayed an innate grandeur of soul, that inspired esteem and respect. His talents in the field were not superior to those he manifested in council; he was equally sagacious in pointing out wise measures to ministers, and in directing military operations. It was fortunate for Lewis the Fourteenth, that he had such a general to support his cause in the civil wars that arose during his minority.

Let us not forget the words spoken by the great Montecuculi on hearing of his death, *Il faisoit honneur a l'homme*, He was an honour to man. This was a concise but pathetic elogium of a rival, whom he alone was thought able to oppose, and of whose worth no man was a better judge.

It has been said, that had Marshal Saxe not profest the Protestant religion, he also would have had the honour of being interred at St. Denis. Certain it is that his services to France were rendered at a very critical time, and that if he had been unsuccessful at Fontenoy, it would in all likelihood have proved a most fatal day to that monarchy.

There is not that profusion of tombs in the church of St. Denis as in Westminster abbey; but those in the former seem in better preservation. They will afford you a full morning's amusement.

The treasury of this abbey is one of the greatest curiosities of its kind in all Europe. It does not enter into my plan to specify the rarities and antiquities with which it is replenished; I shall only say that, allowing for a few fabulous or doubtful objects, it is altogether a very entertaining sight.

It once had the honour of being under the care of one of the most learned men of his age, the celebrated Mabillon, who was a conventual of this abbey, and entrusted with the business of shewing this treasury: but growing weary of mixing truth with falsehood, as he exprest himself, he petitioned to be released from this employment.

Of all the royal houses in the proximity of Paris, there is none to compare in point of situation to St. Germain. It is an ancient venerable building, not unlike the castle of Windsor: the apartments are grand

LETTER XXXVII.

grand and roomy, and quite worthy of a royal gueſt. Several of them are ſtill inhabited by deſcendants of ſome of thoſe families that followed the fortunes of our James the Second.

The gardens of this fine old palace exhibit a beautiful model of the taſte of the laſt century. They are a curious mixture of the French and Engliſh manner of laying out gardens at that time: the bowling-green ſtill ſubſiſts, that was made for our dethroned monarch, who, like his brother Charles, took particular delight in that amuſement; it retains its original name, being called *le Boulingrin* to this day.

But what will pleaſe you beyond all the reſt, is a terraſs highly elevated, and of ſingular conſtruction, from whence there is a proſpect of twenty miles extent, richly variegated by every object which the nobleſt landſkip can offer to the eye.

LETTER XXXVII.

It is observed by the French that no place in the neighbourhood of Paris, is so much relished as this by the English. This does not arise from any desire of communication with the descendants of their countrymen who fled from England at the time of the revolution, or those who have since left it from similar motives: with fugitives from this island on political principles the English are not in the least fond of associating: it arises from the ruralness of the situation, the beautiful aspect of the country around, and the remembrance it inspires of some delightful spots in our own island, not far from our metropolis, by the resemblance it bears to them.

I have heard that James used to say, that his brother of France not being able to restore him to the possession of his kingdoms, had, however, by way of comfort, bestowed upon him the beautifullest spot of his own dominions to dwell in.

LETTER XXXVII.

If at any time you should be inclined to spend a few days in a country recess, you cannot chuse one at once more elegant and rural. It is in the vicinity of a forest cut into a variety of walks and avenues, which all terminate in some agreeable object.

In this forest, I have been informed, Lewis and James used frequently, in the latter days of this monarch, to enjoy the close of a Summer's afternoon in walking together. Though the first was incontestibly much superior in abilities to the last, yet their characters corresponded in many essential respects: they were attached with equal bigotry to the religion they profest, and equally averse to all others; they were no less under the influence of a persecuting spirit, abhorrent of toleration, and ready to propagate their belief by violent and coercive means: nor were they dissimilar in their notions of government; they were both immeasurably fond of unlimited

ed power, and impatient of the least controul: in the private concerns of life they were far from unlike; James in his younger days was noted for having his mistresses as well as Lewis: they agreed also in some meritorious respects; they were kind husbands, and fond parents; they were gentle masters, and good-natured men within their domestic circle. These qualifications were a sufficient ground for mutual liking and confidence, especially when we consider how much they were personally interested in each other's prosperity.

LETTER XXXVIII.

YOU will undoubtedly pay more than one visit to Versailles, Marli, and the other royal houses in the vicinity of Paris.

A description of them does not belong to the subject I have in view, which is to make

make them subservient to reflections of more importance to a thinking man, than the mere sight of buildings, and of the curiosities which they contain.

Pursuant to this intention, I would wish you to consider, while you view this immense palace, that it was erected against the advice of all impartial judges, on a spot where nature was forced, where the elements were unfavourable, and in the defiance and contempt as it were of far preferable situations, at a little distance and almost in sight, inviting him, in a manner, to forsake the worthless favourite of which he was so fond, as one of his wittiest courtiers would often take the liberty of stiling this costly palace.

The sums expended to render this place habitable, would have defrayed the charges of building half a dozen on more advantageous ground.

But

But such was the temper of that Prince; he delighted in carrying difficult projects into execution: could he have repressed this disposition, the good which he did might have been doubled, and the mischief lessened by half.

It cannot be denied that he rendered Versailles the most sumptuous and magnificent palace in the world: you will find in it a profusion of grandeur and magnificence, which you must not expect to meet any where else: its gardens and other appurtenances are in the same stile, and display a richness of fancy and design, which, though not in the taste of the present age, never fail to excite the admiration of such as favour it most.

A sensible foreigner of distinction, who visited France at the time that Lewis the Fourteenth was constructing this palace, and laying out the gardens, told some of his courtiers, that though their master was

king

LETTER XXXVIII. 493

king of the earth on which he built, yet he would be an exile from it for want of water, alluding to its scarcity at Verfailles: this obfervation fuggefted the thought of bringing it from the Seine near Marli, which is at three miles diftance, by means of the ftupendous machine that bears the name of this place.

When you have fatisfied your curiofity in thefe and the various houfes erected by that monarch, recollect the luxurious and expenfive life which he led in them, while his fubjects were oppreffed with all kind of mifery; recollect the ruinous pomp he affected about his perfon, and that his houfehold troops alone amounted to an army, no lefs than ten thoufand men, a number greater by three thoufand than that of England after the peace of Ryfwick. But at this you will not be furprifed, when you have been told, the lift of his domeftic attendants at Verfailles, including all ranks

and

and capacities, consisted of twenty thousand individuals.

Such a multitude, for the most part of useless people, maintained for the sake of ostentation, accounts at once for the distresses of many others. This was a waste of treasure unpardonable in a prince, who was perpetually wanting money to supply the numerous channels of private and public expence in which he was constantly engaged. It showed that, notwithstanding the wisdom with which he is said to have presided over his affairs, he was essentially deficient in one of the most important branches of government, the administration and œconomy of his finances.

No King of France, nor of any other country, has been so highly praised and exalted by his people as Lewis the Fourteenth: he doubtless deserved greatly both of them and of mankind in general in a
variety

LETTER XXXVIII.

variety of respects; but does the good, or the mischief he did, preponderate?

I was acquainted with a French abbé of great reading, observation, and sagacity, who seemed to have ballanced this account with much faithfulness and impartiality. Every page of his manuscript was divided into three columns; at the head of the first was written the word useful, of the second, useless, and of the third, pernicious. This was manifestly a fair and judicious arrangement. He had perused a multiplicity of books and manuscripts, and consulted many persons well versed in arts and businesses, in order to form his account upon just grounds, and to venture on no decision without good and sufficient authority. I will add to this, that he was in a situation fully adequate to an attempt of this nature. He was a man of good family, possest of a decent patrimony, and a genteel sinecure benefice, which enabled him to enjoy life in a very comfortable manner.

He

He was no bigot: though very difcreet and guarded in his converfation, it was eafy to perceive that he was no flave to any fect. He frequented all companies, and took notes of all that he had heard remarkable: he fhewed me two thick quartos of what he had felected from them. He underftood Englifh perfectly, and had read almoft every good writer in our language. He ufed often to fay, that an Englifhman grafted upon a Frenchman, or a Frenchman upon an Englifhman, was the beft compound in nature. He was a mortal foe to nationality of every fort, and a warm friend to merit whoever had it: this led him to affociate freely with ftrangers, and to rebuke with great earneftnefs thofe among his countrymen who undervalued other nations.

Such a character you will allow to have been peculiarly adapted to the tafk I have mentioned. He was turned of fifty when I knew him, and had commenced it more than

than ten years before; but he did it quite at his leisure: he was hurried by no pressures; he indulged himself in a diversity of pastimes, and finally did not intend it should come forth while he was living: he meant it as a legacy to the world, by way of proof that he had not existed to no purpose; such were his words.

It is many years since I lost sight of him. The work was in forwardness, but not near finished: he had only completed the first part, which went no further than the peace of Nimeguen; a period at which, had Lewis died, he would, in the abbé's opinion, have left a name unsullied by errors and imprudences.

This gentleman is now dead; but no performance of a tendency similar to that he was writing, has appeared either in France or elsewhere. From thence I conclude, that either he thought proper from prudential motives to discontinue, or perhaps deftroy it, or that fuch as had the revifal of his papers, took upon them to fupprefs it; a thing not unufual in France, efpecially when religion or government are in queftion.

You will frequently have occafion to obferve, that moft Frenchmen, as well as moft foreigners, are more pleafed with Marli, Choify, or Bellevue, than with Verfailles: the fuperiority of the latter in riches and magnificence is inconteftible; but all this refults from art; whereas the beauties of the other places, though affifted by art, have more of nature; they are fituated near the Seine, and poffefs thofe rural decorations of landfkips and profpects, the abfence of which no artificial grandeur can fupply.

Profufion pleafes in no fhape: poffibly the very fuperbnefs of Verfailles renders it much more an object of admiration than pleafure. The mind is fatigued with fo much

much contemplation of the surprising and marvellous, and seeks for rest by the same rule that it is needed by the body after a long walk, which, however fine the road may be, is always wearisome at last.

Mediocrity in the proportion of ornaments is always found to make the most agreeable impression; for this reason the taste in architecture and in gardening which admits of the fewest, and approaches nearest to simplicity, is by judges allowed to be the best, and is indeed upon experience the most relished by the majority; which is a substantial proof of its merit.

Nature chiefly delights us when only cultivated to a certain degree: we are much more amused, while travelling, by casting our eyes around on a country in a high state of agriculture and fertility, than by examining walks and gardens trimmed and arranged with the nicest care; the plainer

plainer these are laid out, the less they are apt to tire one's attention.

Lewis himself, however he might exult in the pomp and grandeur that invironed him at Versailles, often forsook it to enjoy himself with ease and freedom in some other place, as he frankly acknowledged. Fontainebleau and Marli were his favourite abodes; in the latter, especially, he would chearfully divest himself of all state: here, it is reported, he was wont jokingly to say, that he was Lewis of Bourbon, but that at Versailles he was King of France.

LETTER XXXIX.

THE most essential advantage that Paris enjoys over London, is the number of gardens and walks designed for the use of the public.

Without

LETTER XXXIX.

Without being at the pains of going out of town, valetudinarians, persons of sedentary occupations, or immersed in too much business to quit Paris, may at any time of the day repair in a few minutes to a place elegantly accommodated for recreation and exercise.

Paris is surrounded on every side by a magnificent walk, consisting of four ranges of trees, making three beautiful alleys; the middlemost is very large, being intended for carriages, the others are also very spacious: here on Sundays, and on the afternoon of Thursdays, in fair weather, multitudes of people and of carriages are seen. This, however, is only to be understood of that part of the circle which incloses Paris on the northern side: that on the south has been made and planted with trees, only within a few years; but when these are come to their full growth, this semicircle will unquestionably be the pleasantest walk of the two; the prospects from it open far into a fine country, to which you are invited by a number of noble avenues of stately trees, that cast an extensive shade in the Summer season.

The sight in the north walk is obstructed on one side by Montmartre and Montfaucon, both which have in many places a rocky and dreary appearance; but on turning yourself towards Paris, the eye is instantly relieved by the vast variety of fine houses and gardens which border the whole length of that walk.

As this side of Paris is inhabited by the fashionable classes, in a much larger proportion than the other, the walks belonging to it, will, from their proximity, long maintain their prerogative against those on the other side.

This circular range of trees round Paris goes by the denomination of Boulevards, from being seated on the spot where bulwarks

warks formerly stood in the time of their civil wars.

In no place in or near Paris will you meet with such diversity of every kind: the crouds that pass and repass on foot consist of all that are not persons of rank; these never or very seldom quit their coaches in this place; on the contrary, it is precisely here they parade in state: all people indeed who can keep or hire carriages, are fond of exhibiting themselves in this manner upon the Boulevards.

A prying observer will find here a variety of objects to employ him; it is here you will be chiefly able to discriminate between the appearance at large of the inhabitants of Paris, and those of London.

A sensible Englishman who was settled at Paris, but whose business occasionally required his presence at London, was wont to amuse himself with counting the number of silk gowns that met his eye in this place on a Sunday afternoon, and those that he saw in St. James's Park and Constitution-hill on the same day, within an equal space of time. His computation was incomparably in favour of our people, the general superiority of whose circumstances struck him, he confest, the oftener he visited his own country.

The testimony of this person is the more to be relied upon, as he was an inveterate foe both to the religion and government of his country, and noted for his attachment to France, and malevolence to England.

A few afternoons examination of such individuals and objects as will occur to you on this spot, will induce you to coincide with his sentiments.

Whenever you are inclined to cast a cursory glance on the greatest farrago of

amuse-

amusements the world can afford, you will certainly find it here: jugglers, fire eaters, tumblers, rope and wire dancers, puppet shews and buffooneries; all those exhibitions, in short, that serve to entertain the vulgar, are in a manner concentered here.

There are also some attempts at elegant pastimes, such as rooms with vocal and instrumental music; but the performers tell you at first sight by their appearance, that they are none of the primest, and their execution soon confirms your suspicions.

It is said the police of Paris is at the expence of providing these last, for the entertainment of the multitudes that croud the Boulevards on summer evenings: if this be true, it shews the general poverty of individuals in a very striking light: none of these methods of keeping people in good humour are wanted among us; every man that frequents a place of pleasurable resort, is supposed to have
where-

wherewith to pay for his share of the enjoyment.

This very indulgence of the superintending powers, proves how well they are apprised of the deficiency of means prevailing among the inferior classes: in a country where the natives are so fond of pleasure, it is altogether a strong argument how little the commonalty is able to procure it.

It is principally in such instances as these, that you will be satisfactorily convinced of the much greater prosperity attending the situation of the similar ranks in England: Vauxhall has nightly a considerable proportion of them; so formerly had Marybone: the other amusive haunts that swarm about our metropolis, are in a great measure supported by them.

Reflections of this nature will, if you are as attentive as you ought to be, accompany

company you, not only on the Boulevards, but in many other public places of the French metropolis.

Adjoining to the *Place Louis quinze*, is one of the noblest walks in Paris, called *Le Cours La Reine*. It lies on the borders of the river Seine, opposite to the invalides; which ever way you turn yourself it offers either agreeable or magnificent prospects.

There is a tradition that La Fontaine, the famous fabulist, took such peculiar delight in this spot, and another which is contiguous to it, the *Champs Elisées*, that when engaged in any composition of length, he would sometimes spend the whole day there in rumination and study.

These Elysian fields are environed by a variety of fine objects: houses, gardens, and avenues, form a grand and pleasing mixture, in the midst of which are fields and

and meadows that give an air of novelty to the scene by their ruralness and verdure.

Here, if you are either inclined to ride or to walk, you may take your choice; the area is of vast extent, and is completely situated for either of these exercises: you are sheltered from the northern and eastern blasts by rising grounds covered with houses, and to the west and south you command a spacious level, intersected with rows and groups of trees.

This in my opinion is one of the most pleasing and healthful spots about Paris; if you should dwell at any convenient distance, I would advise you to make it a frequent object of your early morning excursions: the ascent from it towards Montmartre, is a gentle slope all the way, and will procure you an excellent stomach for breakfast, if you rise in proper time to take such a previous circuit.

I re-

LETTER XXXIX.

I remember an old officer, grown grey in the French service, who lived in this neighbourhood, and took almost every day, weather permitting, the walk I have been recommending: he was a hale strong man, middle sized, and full of activity. He attributed the duration and vigour of his health to the bodily exercise to which he had been accustomed from his youth.

He was upon the whole an extraordinary personage. Smitten with the reputation of the famous Charles of Sweden, and with the desire of seeing foreign countries, he left France in his younger days, and went to Constantinople, in company with a relation who belonged to the French ambassador. There, by means of this latter, he was introduced to some Swedish officers, whom he accompanied to Bender, at the time their monarch was endeavouring to arm the Ottoman empire against Russia: being then a handsome, sprightly, and active youth, he was much noticed by Charles; to ingratiate

gratiate himself with whom, he applied with uncommon diligence to the study of the Swedish language, in which he perfectly succeeded. He was serviceable to that prince, and to some of his principal officers, in several transactions of importance, after he had been seized and confined in consequence of his rash attempt to resist an army with a handful of attendants. On the return of Charles to Sweden, he followed him, and had a commission in his army at the time he was slain at the siege of Fredericshall: he then quitted the Swedish service, and came back to France, where he obtained a preferment in the army.

He was a man of amazing memory, and indefatigable observation. He was a sort of a Folard, studying the art of war upon the same plan, and continually occupied in making comments on all he had seen in the various scenes of his military life. He had, among other performances, written a treatise on the respective merits

of

of all the European nations in martial affairs; the English were mentioned in it with particular distinction. The two greatest objects of his admiration were Hannibal and Marlborough, whom he scrupled not to place at the head of the whole list of ancient and modern warriours: he knew not which of the two was the first; but in this he was positive, that none ever surpassed them in the judiciousness of their plans, the steadiness of their execution, the celerity with which they obviated or encountered difficulties, and that none equalled them in the astonishing capacity with which they held together and governed armies composed of various nations independent and often jealous of each other, whose different tempers they had to consult, and interests to reconcile.

This gentleman's moderation was of an original cast. Contrary to that ardour which prompts men to signalize themselves

for

for the sake of rising, he never coveted any promotion higher than that of captain; content to give his advice when asked, and indifferent about every thing but the pleasure of speculating upon the events in war of which he had been witness.

The truth was, that he did this with a freedom and boldness, which, though they might gain him many admirers, procured him at the same time as many enemies: these probably had interest enough to prevent his rise; but having a genteel income beside his commission, and being of a philosophical turn, he resolutely persisted in the exercise of his criticisms, careless what the consequences might prove.

LETTER XL.

THE most pleasant, though not the most frequented garden in Paris, is *Le Jardin du Roi*. It lies at a distance from the fashionable world, in a remote and obscure quarter, and remains therefore unnoticed and neglected by the majority, whose principal view in resorting to such places, is rather to see and be seen, than to enjoy the recreation arising from exercise and pleasantness of situation.

It is open, airy, and spacious. In it is a rising ground, on the summit of which an artificial mount has been raised, that commands an enchanting prospect far into the beautiful country that lies on the southern banks of the Seine.

This agreeable garden owes its being to Cardinal Richelieu. He founded it for the reception and cultivation of exotic and medicinal plants, of which large quantities are kept and reared with great care and induſtry: they form all together a very noble collection of natural curioſities, which is open twice a week for public inſpection.

A large hall belongs to this garden, wherein lectures on botany and pharmacy are delivered gratis to all comers of decent appearance: two profeſſorſhips have been inſtituted for this purpoſe.

I have been told that one of the moſt learned naturaliſts in Paris was once a poor lad employed in ſweeping the hall after the company was departed. His native propenſity to hear and to improve was ſuch, that a ſurgeon who attended the lectures took notice of it, and befriended

LETTER XL.

friended him so effectually, that from one step to another, he rose to great knowledge in the branches taught here, as well as in the profession of his patron, whose daughter he married, and whose fortune he inherited.

From the borders of the Seine to the Bastille, runs a long and elegant garden belonging to the arsenal or storehouse of war, resembling our armoury in the tower.

The principal reason that induces me to mention this place, is to remind you of the able and upright statesman who presided over that department with so much splendour and success, during the reign of Henry the Fourth, the famous Duke of Sully. It was here he laid the foundation of that excellent work which has already been recommended to your perusal, and which cannot be too much prized.

Over the gate-way of this arsenal are the two Latin verses that follow:

Ætna haec Henrico vulcania tela ministrat,
Tela giganteos debellatura furores.

They are highly esteemed in France, and were written at the request of Henry the Fourth himself, who desired his namesake, Bourbon was the author's name, to comprize in two verses the description of what that building was intended for.

This Bourbon was one of the best Latin poets that France has produced. It is said the above lines struck the celebrated Santeuil with that emulation which rendered him so great in the poetic world. He held them in such admiration, as to declare he would give half his works to have composed them.

A garden which the majority of connoisseurs prefer to all the others in Paris, is that which belongs to the palace of Luxembourg. It is of great extent, of an elegant simplicity, well shaded and verdured, and stands in the wholesomest air of Paris, which alone is a sufficient motive for its being much frequented.

As it lies in the neighbourhood of the colleges and other buildings constituting the university, it has by scholars been dignified with the title of *Honos Regionis Latinæ*, in allusion to the name of *Païs Latin*, which the Parisians have bestowed on this quarter of the metropolis.

In consequence of this situation, it is much resorted to by students and collegians of all denominations: a French wit stiles it somewhere *La Revue des Habits noirs*, the review of black coats, of which indeed there is sometimes a prodigious number, oftentimes a great plurality.

There was some years since a remarkable character appertaining, if one may so say, to this place; he wore the dress of an Abbé, but was suspected to be a person of quite another class: those who saw him in this garden, all agreed in acknowledging they had never seen him elsewhere. He was a comely man, well made, and had all the appearance of an individual of rank; his voice was uncommonly harmonious, and his articulation the most clear and distinct that ever I heard; he had an easy politeness about him, which prepossessed every one in his favour: such was the respect, or rather predilection, shewn him, that one would have thought all present had received some particular marks of his friendship.

It was observable that he never made his appearance until the dusk of the evening, and never came accompanied. Sunday night was his usual time of exhibiting;

biting; wherever he found the moſt numerous company ſeated, he would join them with that chearful and familiar civility which is uſual in France in ſuch places. Whatever the converſation might be, it would immediately, on his partaking of it, aſſume a gaiety and ſprightlineſs, of which one would have hardly thought it ſuſceptible: every body ſeemed inſpired by his preſence; ſtories, bon mots, and repartees, flew from all ſides; one might have compared him to the ſun in the centre of the world, ſhedding light and warmth on all the ſurrounding planets.

A particularity that eſcaped no one was, that he never mentioned the leaſt circumſtance, by which one might be led to gueſs at his rank or profeſſion; he never indeed introduced himſelf into any tale, much leſs made himſelf the hero of it: notwithſtanding the jocoſeneſs of his talk, and the infinite fund of entertainment his wit and vivacity afforded, there was a something of superiority attending his manner and behaviour, that precluded all those questions which arise from familiarity.

Many were the conjectures formed concerning him. Some thought him an actor, who disguised himself in order to learn the notions and ideas of the various classes of society, and to mix into company with less danger of discovery. Others imagined he was an author, who delighted in this manner of studying mankind, and furnishing himself with a multiplicity of characters for the portraits he drew in his writings. No few were of opinion he was a lawyer, who took this method of using himself to speak before an audience, strangers to him as much as he to them. As many adjudged him to be a man employed by people in authority, to feel the pulse of the generality on the public transactions of the times. Some again pronounced him the hanger-on of some personage

sonage of high rank, for whose amusement he collected all the private anecdotes of a diverting nature which he could procure. Others concluded him to be a humourist, who indulged himself in this vein of merriment from natural impulse, and with no other intent than to pass his time agreeably.

Whatever his reality might be, his appearance and manners were so acceptable, that every one concurred in declaring they had never met with so entertaining a person. He grew at last so popular in this place, and the circles wherever he was found became so crowded, that probably disliking such multitudes, and being averse to a manifestation of himself, he relinquished this garden, and was never known to have re-appeared in any other.

A gentleman once ventured to beg the favour of his acquaintance; it was on the breaking up of the company at the customary

mary hour of shutting the gates; but the answer he received, though polite, was very laconic and decisive, Sir, you do me much honour, but you must excuse me.

The garden of the *Palais Royal* is, in proportion to its dimensions; which are not extensive, the most frequented of any in Paris. As it stands in the center of the fashionable parts of this metropolis, it is the rendezvous of the beau monde. Here you will meet with ladies and gentlemen of the haut ton in greater number than any where.

Some people have qualified this place with the appellation of *rus in urbe*; but this is more than it deserves: were it not for the company that is to be seen there, I fancy it would be very much neglected. Exclusive of a large alley, where the company sits, walks, or assembles in groups, the rest of the garden is quite solitary, and has nothing to recommend it: you are

surrounded

LETTER XL. 523

furrounded by the back parts of indifferent houfes, that clofe in, as it were, upon you, and leave no fpace between the garden and their very walls.

While we are in a place that made part of the refidence of Cardinal Richelieu, it may not be amifs to apprize you of an anecdote, which, if true, difplays a fund of ambition and thirft of fame, of an equally infatiable and fingular nature.

It is reported that lying on his death bed, and having with great magnanimity taken leave of his friends and intimates, he directed, in order the better to recall him to their remembrance, whenever they entered a houfe where they had been fo well treated, and received fo many favours from him, that on the inftant of his giving up the breath, the public clock of his palace fhould be ftopt for ever, and the needle left pointing to the minute when he expired.

LETTER XL.

Notwithstanding the character of a *petit maitre* is by no means commendable, yet as many of them are young men of real merit in various respects, and as this garden and the adjoining coffee-houses abound with them, you must occasionally frequent these places, if you intend to acquire a knowledge of the younger sort of French gentlemen. Here you will see them in their genuine colours, free, open, airy, chearful, and what will atone for many defects, extremely sociable and well-bred. In such company you cannot fail to spend your time agreeably. Perfection is not the portion of either young or old; but it will be your own fault intirely, if you should not contract some valuable acquaintance in these places among those of your own age. Hardly any of them are free from that levity and intemperance of behaviour and manners, which are too justly imputed to the juvenile part of the French nation: but you must take people as you find them; put up complaisantly with their

their failings, and they will make you ample amends by their fprightlinefs, their gaiety, their readinefs to oblige, and by what you muft allow one of the moft ufeful qualifications in fociety, their willingnefs to overlook your own deficiencies.

Youth, in the words of Gay, is the feafon made for joy: it is no lefs the feafon for contracting pleafant and lafting friendfhips, and you are in a country which of all others produces that character in perfection, of which Horace fays, *nil ego prætulerim jucundo fanus amico*.

LETTER XLI.

YOU will find the Tuilleries inconteftably the moft magnificent garden in Paris; and, what will doubtlefs induce you to give it a preference to all the others,

others; it is most of any frequented by the young and gay of all denominations: that of the Palais Royal is chiefly used for a place of appointment; but it is in this they chiefly delight to walk.

An elderly French gentleman, of great good sense and long observation, was wont to say, that the Tuilleries was *le jardin de la jeunesse*, the garden of youth, and the Luxembourg *la jardin de l'age mur*, the garden of mature age.

There was certainly much of truth in his observation. The splendour and brilliancy of every object that offers itself to view in the first of these, accords perfectly with the warmth and vivacity inherent to youthful minds. In the same manner, the unadorned beauty of the second, resulting from simple nature, is more acceptable to people arrived at a more thinking period of life.

Add

Add to this, that from the Tuilleries the fight is entertained with perpetual scenes of activity: the noble key just under the terrafs, is all hurry and motion; it is one of the chief outlets of Paris, and is the high road to Verfailles, which is faying enough. The river is continually covered with boats, going to, or coming from the principal villages and refidences in the neighbourhood of Paris; it is the chief channel of trade between that city and the rich, fruitful, and populous province of Normandy. All this affords a conftant fund of that variety of which youth is particularly fond.

Nothing of this appears in the Luxembourg. Tranquility reigns every where: the palace is accompanied by two or three fine houfes fronting the garden; but even this palace pleafes more by its elegance than grandeur. The garden itfelf is quite in a rural tafte; the only profpect from it is into fome other gardens, efpecially

cially that of the Carthusians, neat, plain, and solitary.

All these concomitances render this place an excellent spot for meditation, or sober and serious discourse; it is accordingly the favourite resort of sedate and thoughtful people, such as the generality of mankind become at the middle ages of life.

In all these gardens there is a convenience in use no where else in Europe; beside the benches on which one may sit gratis, chairs may be hired by the year, month, week, day, or single sitting.

Another convenience peculiar to the Tuilleries is that you may breakfast, dine, sup, in short have any refreshments you please, at the divers entrances into it on every side.

One

LETTER XLI.

One of the chief advantages of this garden, is that it communicates with the moſt beautiful parts of Paris, and of its environs; go out which way you will, you meet with noble edifices, or fine proſpects.

The entrance into theſe gardens is free to perſons decently clad; but rigorouſly interdicted to domeſtics in livery, or women of ſervile appearance. Whoever they may be that are admitted, they muſt not ſeem of the low claſſes.

Before we quit the chapter of gardens, let us not forget that belonging to the Prince of Soubize. Two reaſons will render it worthy of your notice; the firſt is the politeneſs of the owner in dedicating it to the uſe of the public; the ſecond, his generoſity in granting a free acceſs to his elegant and numerous library, to all perſons of character. I have heard that he has the moſt conſiderable collection of Italian

Italian books of any person in France, amounting to near twenty thousand.

It is happy for the inhabitants of Paris, that they have such a multiplicity of gardens to range in at pleasure. They do not seem so gifted with that disposition to active recreation as the people of London; and were it not for these accommodations, would possibly want the little exercise, which these places invite them in a manner to take.

On the other hand, I have heard it asserted that these gardens hinder them from exerting more activity in their pastimes, and are an incitement to indolence: that were no such places in existence, they would be obliged to bestir themselves in quest of fresh air, and would of course extend their walks to a much greater distance.

Whatever

LETTER XLI.

Whatever the truth may be, these numerous and spacious openings contribute to purify the atmosphere of Paris in a very necessary degree, when we consider that it is situated in a bottom, and hemmed in on the north by two large hills or mountains, that greatly intercept the winds that blow from between the north-east to the north-western points. The excessive narrowness of the streets, and closeness of the houses, call no less for such a help, as well as the height of them, and the crouds they contain.

These gardens are also very friendly to the constitution of such as can spare an hour in the morning to the embibing of fresh air, and bracing their limbs with exercise: were these advantages to be only had at a distance, they would either interfere with the time allotted for business, or, what is more probable, would be totally neglected.

In London, where numbers of people are well able to give such a portion of their time to relaxation, the length of the walk they must take, ere they arrive at the desired spot, would absorb the whole hour intended for this purpose. The consequence is, that they remain at home, or adjourn perhaps to a coffee-house, where most certainly their constitution cannot receive any benefit.

Wherever you chuse to reside in Paris, as you will always be in the vicinity of such a place, you cannot render your body a better service, than by visiting it before or after breakfast. An hour spent in this manner, will give you spirits for the whole day, if it should be requisite to remain within doors during the remaining part. I speak from experience.

During the Summer and mild seasons of the year, let me advise you to follow a method

method of improving both your health and underſtanding, which I ſaw practiſed by a French young nobleman of great rank. He dwelt near the Luxembourg, and whenever the weather was fine, would employ a conſiderable part of the morning in what may very juſtly be ſtiled a peripatetic ſtudy of languages. His birth and fortune intitling him to high expectations, and his friends intending to accompliſh him ſo completely as to fit him for any poſt, he was taught the principal languages of Europe. The manner he learned them was chiefly by converſation: a ſubject was choſen, upon which as much was ſaid as both the teacher and the learner could ſuggeſt: the ideas were firſt expreſt in French words by both parties, and then tranſlated into the words of the language to be learned.

The progreſs he had made was very conſiderable. He had not purſued this plan above two years, and was able to converse fluently in Spanish and Italian, and tolerably in German and English. This, considering his other studies and occupations, was doing a great deal.

I have mentioned this particular as a precedent for your imitation, and am convinced you cannot adopt a better for the speedy acquisition of French, or any modern language.

LETTER XLII.

TO a young gentleman at your time of life, Paris will in some respects prove a more agreeable abode than London.

You will in particular meet with a much more frequent recurrence of sights and shews to amuse you. Here, if we except our lord mayor's day, and the king's going to parliament, there are none of those
ceremonial

ceremonial exhibitions that occasion a great concourse of people.

One of the most curious sights at Paris, is the vast variety of processions on that holy day which goes by the name of *Fete Dieu*, the festival of God. This extraordinary name was given to it, by way of signifying that on that day, the Deity enjoyed a sort of personal and visible triumph upon earth, in the honours paid to the body of Christ. This you know the Roman Catholics believe to be contained in the host, that is carried about on this occasion with the most pompous solemnity.

This is incomparably the most magnificent festival in the Roman church. It was instituted in one of the Gothic ages, I believe the eleventh, in opposition to the opinion of those who denied the doctrine of transubstantiation.

The most brilliant and costly of these processions in Paris, is that of St. Sulpice. I will not anticipate your curiosity by a description of it here: suffice it to say, that what with music, rich vestments, number of attendants, and diversity of ornamental concomitances, it is one of the grandest and most sumptuous parades of religion throughout Christendom.

It will be worth your while to rise early on the morning of this day, to view the number of beautiful pieces of tapestry, that are hung up in those streets through which the processions are to pass. Forget not especially to see those of the Gobelins, and of the Louvre, both belonging to the crown. The splendor with which the churches are decorated during this festival, which lasts a whole week, will, I doubt not, prove an incentive to visit them, particularly when you consider it is the best opportunity of gaining a proper insight

LETTER XLII.

infight into the genius and fpirit of the Romifh religion.

There are two folemn occafions, on which you will have a view of the parliament, and of the corporation of the city of Paris in all their grandeur, and refpective formalities. Thefe are the commemoration of that city's returning to the allegiance of the crown in the perfon of Henry the Fourth, and the renewal of the vow made by Lewis the Thirteenth, when he placed his family and kingdom under the protection of the Virgin Mary. Both thefe ceremonies are very fplendid, and merit your attention. The firft takes place in March, the fecond in Auguft.

One of the moft curious entertainments in Paris is the *Foire St. Germain*. This fair lafts from the beginning of February till within a few days of Eafter. It is an epitome of all the bufinefs, as well as of all the diverfions in Paris.

Notwithstanding the crowds that frequent it all day and part of the night, it is attended with an orderliness and regularity, the more admirable, as it is the continual and well-known rendezvous of all the sharpers and ladies of pleasure in Paris.

What adds to the vivacity of this pastime, it falls within the duration of the carnaval, an amusement for which the French seem peculiarly calculated. Omit not, upon the three days preceding Ash-Wednesday, to see the humours of the multitudes that go about the streets in masquerade; wit, laughter, and merriment seem to have taken possession of every body: unless a man is overwhelmed with misfortunes, or afflicted with illness, it is an enjoyment which poor and rich, high and low must equally relish, from the odd figures, and risible fancies displayed on every side.

The whims and jocularities of these three days, are succeeded by a sudden conversion to the extremes of sobriety and seriousness, which is no less worthy of your notice: on the morning of Ash-Wednesday, the churches swarm with penitents of all ranks and sorts, who kneel down with great seeming contrition before the altars, and whose foreheads a priest crosses with a pinch of consecrated ashes.

This ceremony, which is customary in all Roman Catholic countries, has, together with the extravagances and vagaries that precede it, and to which it puts a period for a while, been very happily described, by applying to them the two following lines out of Virgil's Poem on the Bees:

*Ili motus animorum atque hæc certamina tanta
Pulveris exigui jactu compressa quiescent.*

One

LETTER XLII.

One of the most elegant sights in Paris is that which is seen at the end of Lent, in Passion-Week, in case the weather happens to be fair.

On the banks of the Seine, after traversing the Bois de Boulogne, stands the nunnery of Longchamp. It is celebrated for the musical pieces performed there during this season. All the fashionable people at Paris repair thither to hear them; some in coaches, others on horse-back; both carriages and horses are on this occasion set off with all the taste and magnificence possible, and form one of the most superb cavalcades that can be conceived: the distance from Paris to this place is about three miles, and if the day be fine and sunny, the whole length of the way is crowded. The coup d'oeil of this brilliant assemblage is highly worth your curiosity.

Another

LETTER XLII.

Another opportunity of employing it, is that which recurs annually some time in May. The king, accompanied by his whole court, in all its state and grandeur, reviews the military of his houshold, which compose a numerous and splendid body of men.

One of the greatest curiosities in France are the fine water-works at St. Cloud, a delightful village lying on the Seine at a small distance from Paris: the walk to it is extremely pleasant, and accompanied by a variety of beautiful and amusing objects. These waters play on the first Sunday of every month regularly.

The Duke of Orleans has a palace here, the situation of which is enchanting. The gardens are laid out on a gentle ascent, and adorned with terraces rising successively over each other, in which are contained those water-works: the prospect from thence extends to Paris and all the adjacent

cent country. You cannot, in a mild and clear day, treat yourself with a more delicious party of pleasure on foot, or in an open boat, with a philosophic friend or two. The banks of the Seine are quite rural, fields, meadows, country houses, and gardens.

A gentleman of a solid and yet a very gay disposition, always recommended this method to those with whom he went a pleasuring. A vehicle, he said, obstructed the two most agreeable ends in view, which were conversation and prospects: the noise and motion of a carriage deranged both thoughts and words, and only permitted a desultory intercourse; for this reason, in short excursions, he always preferred walking, or going down a stream.

During the latter days of the year, on the last especially, be sure to repair to the *Palais Marchand*; you will there find a world of those things which the philosopher

pher of old congratulated himself for not wanting. But that philosopher did not live at Paris, nor probably much in the female circle: if he had, it is highly probable, that however he might have affected to slight these things on his own account, he would quickly have found them useful in obtaining and preserving the good graces of his fair acquaintance.

Let no man who wishes to be favoured with the smiles of the Parisian ladies, suffer this day to pass without bringing them, from this agreeable magazine of fancies, some token of his remembrance.

This *Palais Marchand* is truly a *mundus muliebris*, a repertory of all those ornaments and decorations, that constitute so capital a part of the wants and desires of womankind.

These are, on the afore-mentioned day, displayed with an art and ingenuity that catch

catch the eyes of all spectators. New years gifts of all denominations, and of all prices, offer themselves to your sight: fail not therefore to imitate the numberless examples that will be set before you, in presenting to those among the sex, with whom you are on a friendly footing, some genteel proof of your attention to their civilities.

LETTER XLIII.

I HAVE heard observant travellers remark, that the greatest curiosity at Amsterdam and at London, is the prodigious number of people who frequent their respective changes. This at the same time they unanimously allow to be a convincing argument of the multiplicity of business carried on in both places, as well as of the industry of the inhabitants.

By

By the same rule, the thinness or desertion of a Change, prove the narrowness of circumstances in such a place; witness the once rich and commercial city of Antwerp, where grass grows on the Change, and where nothing remains but the skeleton of its ancient grandeur.

The Change of Paris, situated in the Rue Vivienne, exhibits no great symptoms of prosperity. It is but indifferently frequented, when we reflect on the extent and populousness of Paris; the middle part is hardly ever trod, and the piazzas never crouded.

In the management of their lotteries you will no less discover an inferiority of means in those upon whose exertions and contributions they depend; the price of the tickets and the worth of the prizes not approaching to ours.

There are no less than three lotteries in Paris; the royal one, that in favour of the foundlings, and another of a charitable kind. The first is drawn twice, the others once a month.

It is not certainly in money matters the French can pretend to make a figure equal to that of the English; we are comparatively a much wealthier people. It will prove one of the most profitable and instructive employments of your studious hours, to enquire into the various causes why the kingdom of France, which is equal at least in natural fertility and goodness of soil to England, is not, in proportion to its dimensions, either so populous, or so rich and plentiful in its productions.

Among the places of curious resort in Paris, one may class the conveniencies for bathing near the *Palais Bourbon*. Every thing that is necessary and commodious for this purpose, has been contrived with the utmost care and propriety: there are two separate buildings, one for men the other

other for women; this latter is guarded by regular centries, and attended only by women. All is conducted with remarkable neatness and dispatch. These baths are accessible at all hours both of day and night; every one has a bath to himself, which is heated or cooled at his option. Books and newspapers are taken in for the use of such as chuse to read and rest themselves after bathing; there is nothing in short wanting to render this a place of no less agreeableness than utility.

The amusements at Paris have by some fretful peevish people been represented of insufficient variety to please the different taste of those numerous travellers that croud hither from all parts of Europe.

It is difficult to tell upon what ground this complaint is founded. The theatres are open all the year, and there is no day in the whole twelvemonth, which does not afford some pastime or shew, either temporal or spiritual, if one may use such an expression.

I have already taken notice of their standing theatres, which are three in number, the opera, and the French and Italian play-houses. Others are opened at particular seasons, such as those of the Foire St. Germain in February, and of the Foire St. Laurent in August.

In the article of pleasure and recreations, you will observe a material difference between the police of Paris and that of London. Here the observance of the Sabbath, as it is called, is enforced with a strictness unknown any where, excepting Scotland and New England, where indeed it is much more rigorous than in England itself. But in Paris the ruling powers have been more indulgent to human nature: aware that numbers of people have, and can have no other day of relaxation from their business or labour, they

they have endeavoured to make it pass agreeably to all conditions of men.

It is precisely on the Sunday that diversions of all kind abound; not only plays, but balls and masquerades are tolerated.

The only exception is in Passion and Easter week, and upon very solemn days: but even then, there is a public pastime allowed. It is indeed of a spiritual nature, and something in the manner of our sacred oratorios. It is called *le Concert Spirituel*, and is a very genteel and elegant amusement, where you will always find the best of company.

A famous lieutenant of the police, in support of the necessity of allowing great latitude in sports and diversions of a public nature, declared that in the *Quinzaine de Paques*, as Passion and Easter week are called in France, more disturbances happened, and more mischief was done, than in in any other fortnight throughout the year. This he attributed to the shutting up of the theatres, and other houses of like entertainment.

In order to help out the *Concert Spirituel*, another place of public amusement has been permitted on high festivals. You will be rather surprised, when I have told you that this place is a bear-garden, where dogs, bulls, lions, tygers, bears, and other beasts are baited and worried to death.

This savage pastime is as much frequented as any at Paris, and is exhibited in winter as well as in the mild seasons; which is the more remarkable, as this scene of blood and carnage passes in an open area, surrounded by seats which, though covered over head, leave one otherwise exposed to all the inclemencies of weather.

LETTER XLIII.

Thinking people have often exprest their astonishment, that so ferocious a pastime should have been substituted in lieu of certainly the more gentle and humane entertainments of the stage. Manners must clearly receive more detriment by indulging in such barbarous sights, than by all the fun and laughter, which the jocosest comedy, farce, or pantomime, can possibly occasion.

You will, I doubt not, rejoice that so vulgar and base a diversion is now in England abandoned to the meanest of the populace, and is not as in France licensed by public authority.

Should you hear the epithets of rude and rough bestowed on the character of your countrymen by the French, which many of them too readily do, I think you cannot answer them better than by informing them, it is not in their power to reproach us with the above barbarities, which have long ago been exploded from the lift of our paftimes.

The French of late have, in imitation of our Vauxhall and Ranelagh, fet up two places of amufement fomewhat on the fame plan. The firft goes actually by the name of Vauxhall, the other is called the Colifée. They are both, the latter efpecially, contrived with much tafte and elegance.

The firft is fituated upon the Boulevards. It confifts of a variety of rooms, all laid out and decorated in a different and very pleafing manner; fome of thefe are defigned for dancing, others for walking or fitting. The profpect on one fide of this place opens into the country afcending towards Montmartre, on the other you have the view of the company upon the Boulevards: there are alfo little fhops or ftalls, very artfully difpofed, full of toys, trinkets, and jewels for fale: the
illu-

illuminations at night are very numerous and beautiful.

The *Colisée* is far superior in magnificence, and is much more frequented by the better sort. It stands near the *champs Elisées*, which makes it of easy and convenient resort to the company that have been walking in the Tuilleries. The appearance and decorations of the Rotunda are very fine, and the walks very grand and spacious: it contains a large piece of water, on which justs in boats, and fireworks, are occasionally exhibited.

But notwithstanding the pains that have been taken to render this place complete, it was reported, when I was last at Paris, that it did not answer the expence, and that the undertakers were apprehensive they should be obliged to drop the design. If true, this corroborates what has been said concerning the pecuniary deficiencies in France, and shews there is a better diffusion

fusion of opulence among us than the French. Renelagh is far from being confined to the superior ranks: it is as much indebted for its support to the middling and decent classes.

LETTER XLIV.

AFTER laying my thoughts before you, on that variety of objects which present themselves to the eyes and observation of a traveller, it is time to recall your attention to that principal object of all, the motive and end of your going to Paris.

Your intentions were to instruct yourself in the ways, notions, and knowledge of the French, to compare their progress in laudable attainments with those made by the English, to imitate them in those things wherein they deserve to be proposed

LETTER XLIV.

posed as examples, to avoid the failings and errors you may discover among them, and finally to render all you see subservient to the public good of your country, as well as conducive to your private interest.

In order to compass these purposes the more effectually, I have been particularly attentive to awaken in your mind, upon all occasions, such reflections as might lead you to extract a solid and permanent utility from what is too often considered in no other light than that of a curious pastime.

It is the unhappiness of most travellers to exercise their eyes a great deal, and their understanding very little; but without the exertion of both, they would have done better to have staid at home.

We are sent abroad not only to see, but to reflect: the first of these is the threshold to the second. It is an agreeable invitation

tion which the external senses give to the mind, purposedly to induce it to summon its faculties to work, and to employ them in a useful investigation of objects.

These are in many respects but surfaces: if we mean to derive from them the whole benefit they are able to produce, we must be at the pains of diving deeper than our ocular researches can go.

A meer connoisseur and virtuoso is a character by no means to be coveted by a gentleman. They who aim at no more, misunderstand the only justifiable purpose for which men of rank, education, and fortune, ought to travel; which is to adorn their minds with proper ideas of men and things, and not to learn the trade of a collector of curiosities.

It is of such individuals the poet rightly says, *cælum non animum mutant qui transmare currunt*, their voyages are attended with

with no other change than that of air, and they return from beyond sea, as unimproved in essentials as at their setting out.

The œconomy of time is the capital maxim you must never lose the sight of. It is the polar star of a traveller, and will enable him to make a long and prosperous voyage in a short space.

For this reason, though you cannot be too diligent in your enquiries and examinations, let them not be needlessly extensive. There are numbers of individuals, as well as of other objects, with whom gentlemen who are on their travels ought to be acquainted; but intimacy is too precious a gift to bestow where the returns of utility are but small.

Stint yourself therefore to few intimates: you will find no difficulty in selecting them; persons of liberal knowledge and sentiments, and of sociable dispositions are soon discernible.

In the company of such you will acquire, without much labour, all that information, which without them no labour will ever procure.

Divide your researches equally between these and your books: experience will quickly teach you that neither of them can be neglected with impunity.

Remember the proverb you was taught at school, *Aurora musis amica.* In a traveller the remembrance ought to be more practical than in any other man: he has much to see, much to hear, and much to do: he has but a limited time for all this; which, if lost, is irreparable, as opportunities of this sort occur but once in our lives.

Our travelling days are like the seed-time of the year: if we sow abundantly, we shall reap in proportion; but if our tillage is scanty, so we must expect will prove our harvest.

Now

LETTER XLIV.

Now is the time to lay in an ample stock of all that is fit to be treasured up in your memory. It is the grand season of observation, especially from the continual diversity of objects and events that afford such ground-work for a reflecting mind.

To obtain so desirable an end, you must obey the injunction of the apostle, *omnia probate, quod bonum est tenete*; go into all companies, converse with people of all characters, hearken to all opinions, and form your judgment with carefulness and deliberation.

A multiplicity of acquaintance is not so great an evil in your present case, as a narrow circle would prove. We can always find means to shake off the supernumerary; but without a competent number, we shall want that variety of tempers, tastes, and dispositions, which are necessary fary to obtain an adequate knowledge of human nature in the countries we visit.

After devoting one half of your time to the improvement of your mind by study and reading, you have not only a right, but you are bound, by the laws of reason and propriety, to devote the rest to conversation, company, and pleasure.

Among the modes of conversing I will venture to class epistolary correspondence. This I earnestly recommend as the surest method of not only acquiring the use of the French language, but of gaining a complete insight into the genius, turn, and spirit of the people themselves.

To this intent, let me advise you to follow a precedent which I quote with the more willingness, as I was witness of the success attending it.

A young

LETTER XLIV.

A young gentleman of good family at Dresden, was sent by his parents to Paris, in the company of a relation who was extremely fond of him, and who being rich and without children, had adopted him his heir. This young gentleman had not only an excellent capacity, but was equally remarkable for his diligence and application. His relation, who was a man of sound judgment, directed him with great care and discernment in all his occupations and studies.

Being at the same time a person of distinction as well as fortune, he introduced him among people of the highest rank, whose favour his young friend had the happiness to secure by his conciliating behaviour, and to whose house and company he was admitted with great kindness and civility.

As he was a keen and circumspectful youth, ever intent upon making the best use of every opportunity, he found means to ingratiate himself with a lady, and a gentleman, both of them persons of distinguished wit, whom he had the dexterity to induce to favour him with an intercourse of letters, and who, luckily for him, had leisure and inclination to answer his wishes.

This was the best school he could have chosen for his improvement. As he possessed an unusual fund of vivacity, and had been excellently educated, he was no less agreeable to them in the light of a correspondent, than they to him: add to this, that nature had given him a comely person, and that fortune had befriended him with very brilliant expectations; both of them, the latter especially, powerful inducements in the preserving, as well as the procuring, of so advantageous a connection.

In imitation of this auspicious precedent, lay yourself out to obtain the good will of some persons of consideration of both

both sexes: a little docility and engagingness of manners will soon procure it; you have all the requisites to succeed; youth, sprightliness, a prepossessing form, and a competency of means to produce yourself in the best companies.

With all these advantages, you alone will be to blame, if you do not connect yourself in the same manner as the young gentleman did, whose example I have proposed for your imitation.

Allow me to warn you to be particularly cautious in the objects of your selection: chuse if possible neither youth nor age; the middle stages of life are the fittest for your purpose: it is among them we find wit without flashiness, and reason without austerity; speculation is then ripened into practice, and activity gives life to precept. Mere experience of transactions past long ago, and of which you can only hear the narration, is not to be set in competition with the vivid profpect of things actually paffing under your eye, and of which, though you fhould not be perfonally concerned in them, thofe who are, may have the power of rendering you no indifferent fpectator.

Vivacity on the other hand, while inexperienced, is always prefuming; it foars on the dangerous wings of hope and expectation; and confides too much in the future, to judge rightly of the prefent. Avoid therefore if you can both the extremities of life; when young we are too precipitate, when old too frigid.

After you have chofen an epiftolary acquaintance to your mind, let the fubjects of your letters never interfere with the affairs of your correfpondents: if, relying on your difcretion, they fhould unbofom themfelves on perfonal or family matters, remain wholly paffive; add no thoughts of your own to thofe they may think proper

per to communicate, and act the part of a simple auditor. If practicable, hear all and answer nothing.

By neglecting this rule, and making yourself a party, you will possibly be involved in difficulties, from which more inconveniencies may arise than you are aware of. Remember the old saying, *vox audita perit littera scripta manet*. It is better to hazard the speaking of a dozen things, than the writing of one.

While you keep this maxim constantly in view, you may indulge your fancy in whatever flights you please: you cannot appear too chearful and jocose; it is the taste of the nation at large; they carry it into every subject; the more you chime in with this humour, the more you will become acceptable.

Of the two correspondents I have recommended, let the fair one be the principal;

cipal; endeavour by all proper assiduity to engage her to be copious and frequent in her epistles: the benefit you will derive from it is more than I can here describe. Women of education are in all countries the most pleasing correspondents; there is a vein of ease and politeness in their manner of writing, which baffles all the study and preparation that usually direct the pens of men of learning: these are too much under the controul of art; but those are more under the guidance of nature; they write with less labour, and with a quicker effusion of thought; the facility of their stile is genuine and unaffected, and is accompanied by those graces, which, whether on paper, or in their behaviour, women alone are mistresses of, and which carry more strength and conviction than all arguments.

Such a correspondence will necessarily refine your ideas and polish your stile: you will imperceptibly slide, as it were,

into

into their manner, and catch that soft insinuating air which gives them such an ascendancy, and makes the expressions that flow from their pens, almost as irresistible as those that fall from their lips.

If the French ladies are worthy of being courted in the light of correspondents, they deserve no less to be sought as companions. The liveliness of their tempers inspires them with a variety of ways to make the time pass pleasurably, without having recourse to that foe to wit and merriment, card-playing.

You will always find them disposed to hold the chearfullest converse, and to enter into every project tending to good humour and pleasantry: they have to that intent invented a variety of ingenious amusements, wherein thought is exercised without fatigue, and the mind improved, while agreeably employed.

A detail of thefe amufements is not neceffary here. An indication is fufficient to awaken your curiofity and defire to partake of them. Experience will foon convince you of their utility in furthering your progrefs in the French language, in giving your manners a turn to eafy and familiar gaiety, and in thereby enabling you to render yourfelf agreeable in all companies and to all characters.

But be mindful at the fame time, that it is not enough for a judicious traveller, to fhine in the brilliant accomplifhments of fafhionable fociety. Another tafk remains to be performed, the neglecting of which will defeat the main purpofe of feeing foreign parts,

This effential and ultimate intent of your prefent voyage, has been fufficiently explained and enforced in the courfe of thefe letters, and recapitulated at the beginning of this laft and concluding one.

The

The parting advice, I shall now give you, is to keep it frequently in view; let no occasions of improvement pass without recollecting it in a proper and efficacious manner.

There is a nation of which the travelling individuals have sometimes laid themselves open to the criticism and cavils of wits, for too scrupulous an attention to minute objects and occurrences. This nation is the German: but allowing the gentlemen of this country to be unnecessarily curious and inquisitive, it is certainly a fault on the right side; and considering that it is easier to retrench than to add, they are not perhaps to blame for swelling their observations to a larger bulk than is done by the travellers of other countries.

It may be that this very reflection engages them to neglect the remembrance of nothing that is thought worthy of being

ing shewn to them: as the future utility of their present remarks can only be determined by experience, they think it wisdom to preserve all the information they can acquire. Should some, or even much of it, prove useless to themselves, it may be of benefit to others: in this light the notes they have taken, however numerous and seemingly uninteresting, may in cases unforeseen become highly serviceable. But supposing such an emergency never to happen, still it is a satisfaction of no small degree to all men, at a certain period of life, to review the passages and transactions of their younger days. This is a pastime in which the gravest have a right to indulge, and wherein the wisest have always taken particular delight; it is in some shape a renovation of youth; it refreshes and enlivens the mind by the pleasing recollections which it excites; imagination is amused by the pictures which memory draws, and judgment

ment itself is not above bestowing on them a smile.

What is it that chiefly renders persons in years not unacceptable to the young, but this power of entertaining them with a recital of the adventures of their former lives, and of the various things they have seen? The more they can remember, the greater diversity they can give to their narrations, and the ampler pastime to their auditors. Whether we view this in the light of instruction or of entertainment, it is a good reason why we should lay up in our youth a sufficient fund from whence to derive pleasure and profit both to ourselves and others.

An apology for such travellers as I have been describing, is a recommendation of their example to your imitation. Let not therefore the groundless strictures of the thoughtless and the negligent, discourage you from pursuing a plan of strict observation

tion and enquiry. Let your paper and pencil claim a constant place in your pocket; and be not ashamed to produce them whenever it is requisite. How many gentlemen that have made the tour of Europe, are at this hour repenting the neglect of these useful companions.

Remember that you are now engaged in a business, which, if ill performed, can never be mended. It is better you should over than under do it: you can hardly be too attentive, too diligent, too curious, in matters of real importance. The more you act up to these epithets, the less reason you will have hereafter to be dissatisfied with yourself. It is by these qualities the nation I have been speaking of, is particularly fitted for travelling.

The most knowing and intelligent travellers that I have met with, were usually Germans. What they wanted in brilliancy,

LETTER XLIV.

liancy, they amply made up in folid utility. I have been often furprifed at the extenfivenefs of their refearches, and at the patience and care which they muft have exercifed in order to obtain the knowledge they poffeft.

They did not, however, feem on this account to have denied themfelves the gratifications arifing from paftimes of a gayer complexion; they were men of the world, had frequented the beft company, and contracted acquaintances that fhewed they were perfons of merit and addrefs.

But it is not the love of gaiety that obftructs improvement; a man may fhine at balls and affemblies without difqualifying himfelf for the moft ferious and moft arduous occupations.

It is indolence that ftands chiefly in the way of knowledge and acquirements of every fort: this is the moft dangerous foe
you

you will have to encounter; conquer him; and you will easily master every other difficulty.

By indolence, I do not mean that inactivity of body, which prevents the due exertion of its faculties; but that carelessness and inattention of the mind, which holds its powers in a state of suspense, and deprives them of the vigour requisite for the prosecution of necessary duties.

It often happens that a man's person is continually on the wing, and his thoughts as perpetually rambling, and never fixed upon a precise object for any constancy, or with any determinate view. This is the worst species of indolence, as it conceals itself under the appearance of activity.

Too many of our young travellers betray the symptoms of this disease. The precipitation with which they hurry from place to place, the shortness of their stay where

LETTER XLIV.

where it ought to be of some duration, and its length where no reasons can justify it; their little notice of things deserving much consideration, and their extraordinary attention to matters of small moment; their neglect of useful or agreeable knowledge and information, and their shameful preference of uninteresting and trivial subjects; these and other instances of gross misconduct, have long contributed to render travelling a business of great charge and little profit.

I flatter myself that your conduct will clear you of these imputations. They are the disgrace of numbers of our countrymen, who seem to consider themselves as authorised by their opulence to act without any regard to rule and method in their proceedings, and to riot in the waste of time, as if it were as much at their command as money.

With persons of this character be no further connected than good manners and necessity

cessity require; their society is peculiarly contagious; in no case will evil communication produce its usual effects with more speed and certainty: many a young gentleman has left England with the fairest expectations of improving by travel, who has been arrested in the most hopeful career, by falling unluckily into such company.

THE END.

www.ingramcontent.com/pod-product-compliance
Lightning Source LLC
Chambersburg PA
CBHW031934290426
44108CB00011B/551